MW01590737

From An Outlaw
to the Cross

Robert Travelbee

Copyright © 2008 by Robert Travelbee

From An Outlaw to the Cross
by Robert Travelbee

Printed in the United States of America

ISBN 978-1-60647-419-8

All rights reserved solely by the author. The author guarantees all contents are original and do not infringe upon the legal rights of any other person or work. No part of this book may be reproduced in any form without the permission of the author. The views expressed in this book are not necessarily those of the publisher.

Unless otherwise indicated, Bible quotations are taken from The King James Version. Copyright © 1992 by Word Resources Group.

Cover illustration by Rodney Travelbee

www.xulonpress.com

april 9, 2011

Allen,

May you find a smile
and a blessing in these
pages,

God Bless

Bob

Preface

I did not want to write this book, as I did not want to brag on my past. My brother Randy and my Wife Cora (Sis) kept after me and it wasn't until I realized that to tell where you are you have to tell where you have been. However, the hurt I caused people by the breaking of Gods commandments will not be in this book. This book is for everyone. You will laugh, maybe shed a tear but most important you will see your situation is not as hopeless as you may think or maybe not as good as you may think. To see where I ended up will be a blessing to all and it will be, to anyone seeking something and like myself and didn't know what it was until I found it. Christians and non-Christians alike will see that there is one who cares about every person. And to my wife Cora, who spent so many nights alone and still encouraged me to write the book. She said, "When you are gone no one will know how to find a tree with that beautiful figure in the wood or the ways to make a black powder gun shoot a playing card in half edge ways, or even know how things used to be before you gave your life to the Lord. Don't take all that knowledge to a place where no one can use it." Many times I would say to her, the book is almost done and she would say, "I don't think so." And I would spend another night writing, sometimes until 4:00 in the morning. My sincere hope is that some who are where I used to be can see their way ahead sooner than I did. I was that daring man who was thought of as a guy that everybody wanted to be like, but the risk was not worth the penalty. You will see you made the right decision. But that you can still be endowed with power is possible. Yes, I am talking about the Lord Jesus Christ and Father God who loved the world so much He gave His son that whosoever believed on Him would have everlasting life. So to Cora, Randy and everyone else that helped me along with this testimony I say, "Thank You, and God Bless."

Table of Contents

Chapter 1

Son of an Outlaw

This is a story of a man and his struggle in the world. Taught from a young age by his Father to be an outlaw, not a gun-blazing outlaw but one of Fishing, Hunting and Trapping. Its there and its yours, take it anyway you can. In the process see what you can get away with. Those around you will know who you are. And I always wondered why people went hungry with all the game around.

I am going to change names around to protect the guilty. Duane was his name though no one called him by it, except his Mother when she was mad and would yell at him.

" Duane! You are going to end up like your Dad! " Lets call him Bob, we did call him several others names too, I won't mention them. But this is his story. As it would be told by him.

I don't remember when I was real young but heard stories. I was the first child to come along of my Mother and her two sisters, and of course I had to be spoiled. They tell me all I had to do was point and make a noise like Annnah! and it was mine. They broke their necks to get it for me. I do remember when I was young, Mom and my Aunt Myrna taking me to an ice cream parlor. We had just come from a shopping trip and they had bought me a sheriff's kit, badge, gun& holster, and a pair of handcuffs. Mom ordered a small dish of ice cream for me and they ordered a large one for themselves. I wanted to play with my new toys so I eat my ice cream real fast and the waitress took away my dish. I messed around with the handcuffs and got them on my hands and there I sat, hands on the table, cuffed! And Mom and my Aunt were eating their ice cream people would walk by and give them a strange look. They could not figure out what the deal was, they looked over at me, handcuffed, no ice cream and they were eating ice cream. What could I have done to deserve this!

I remember when I was 5-6 yrs old Dad would Trap and the muskrats would be piled in the kitchen like cord wood waiting to be skinned and stretched. I had no fear of them and would carry one in each arm around the house, even put a few under the Christmas tree. However, shake a dried rat at me and I took off screaming thru the house.

A word about my Dad. He lived to Fish, Hunt and Trap. To this end. When I was small there were no jobs. We ended up in Ohio where a friend got my Dad a job in the spring. The weather turned off cool in the fall and triggered something in Dad. He told my Mother, " I'm headed back to Michigan. Trapping season's coming", quit his job and back we came. I have to tell you, my Dad was good at Trapping, in fact, anything that had to do with the out of doors.

Mink, my Dad could catch more of them than anyone I ever knew. He caught 9 of them in an old gas tank one day, someone had thrown in the river, every time one would stick it's head out he would club it. Mink have a funny thing happen to them ever now and then, one would be what they call a "Cotton ". Their hair would be like cotton instead of fur, they were worthless on the fur market, that is unless they were my Dads, he would take a flash-light battery, tear it apart and take the black carbon rod out. Then he would take the carbon rod, scrape it into cotton and comb it out until it looked as good as any regular mink. You have to remember that back in those days mink were worth $32.00. And we always had a nice Christmas.

I was his first-born and he taught me everything but taught me in a way I would learn and remember. He would not show me how to trap. He set the trap for me and I would go put it in the lake. I remember about the age of 8 I took one his traps in the house and he set it for me. Away I went swinging the trap in a circle over my head, It landed on my head and caught my stocking cap and my hair.

I will never forget how I hated to go back to house and have him remove it. He got quite a laugh but set it again and away I went. And then when I bought my first traps He had me go set them and then in a couple days, would go with me and show me the right way and another way. He said this is how you can do better but it's against the law, however do thus and thus and you will be ok. So it started, I got the law book and studied it If it was against the law it had to good or else it would not be in there.

I believe Dad made all his kids feel one was as important as the next, like me, He had trouble showing how he felt. In his later years he seemed to be angry at the world and anyone around him caught the blunt of it. Yes, he made people laugh with his stories and in outward appearances seemed happy. You have to remember that Dad was in bondage to cigarettes and beer. Unlike me, Dad could not make a good deal no matter how hard he tried. And to see his children prosper beyond where he had been made him both proud and more angry. A deadly combination, for saying things he did not mean.

When I was young around 8–10, I was small and a target of kids at school, I always wore a hat and kids would grab it from my head and tease me by throwing it from one person to the other. This only happened a couple of times. The next kid who grabbed my hat was rewarded with long shank bullhead hooks in his hand. The hat had a bunch of them in it. That ended that!

I had 3-4 friends who would have give all if their Dad was like mine. I trapped and fished with all of them later in life. But without the teaching of my Dad, it was just frustrating to them.

I had four brothers and a sister. We grew up eating Muskrat, Raccoon, Deer and Fish. At the time we eat better than most. I remember one time the law locked up Dad for shooting a rifle next to lake. They were looking for a reason to lock him up. They told him if would give them the names of people he sold fish to they would let him go. Fat Chance. My Dads word was everything. He always said, "If a man don't have his word he has nothing." Passed that on to all us kids. When I was 11 I used to ride my bike down to river at night to fish for Bullheads, course in those days we used casting rods and level wind reels. I would get home and dress out the bullheads and like Dad had a lot of people who liked fish and would pay for them. I would deliver them in the canvas bag I had on my bike that I delivered newspapers with, just a kid delivering papers. When I got older I read that trot lines were against the law, Hmmm, must be a good way for a guy who sells fish to get a lot of them. It was my friend Corb that helped me. It was easier for one guy to row the boat and the other guy to set lines. We did real well. One time we seen a guy messing with our lines. That night we got his rowboat, dragged it to the middle of the lake and filled it with holes, I guess it's still at the bottom of the lake.

Dad and I would catch minnows for the bait shop, we designed boxes that would keep them alive, and were tied to our belt and would float ahead of us as we waded down the creeks catching minnows. They were the large ones for pike fishing, about 7-10 inches long, we would take the barbs off our hooks so the hook didn't tear them up. Dad had an old freezer box in the pickup, it had a heater motor from a car with a rod with fins and would put oxygen in the water and we would haul the minnows to the bait dealer. We got 9 cents apiece for them, always got a couple hundred. One day while we were counting them out, a guy came into the shop and said " I need a dozen of the largest minnows you have." Fred was the guy who had the bait shop, he put a dozen in the pail the guy had, when Fred came back he said " That guy had me put them in a pail with very little water, they will all die, Oh well he paid for them." when we were done counting we looked out the back and there was the guy cleaning the minnows. We asked what he was doing, He said "I been up north trout fishing and was busy with other things, I have to take some fish home, Wife don't know one from the other."

My Dad knew 100s of stories and of course I inherited them. When I was quite a bit older I was the tall tales champ of Michigan. And of course the man with the minnows became one of them. A guy who worked with Dad for 17 years came to Dad's funeral, he had the same days off as Dad and other than vacations and sick days they worked together, name was Ernie, he told me at the funeral, "Your Dad told me a different story everyday for 17 years!"

One I always liked was the time I was in Texas walking along the river, had a 7-foot walking stick. I felt something hit the stick, when I looked down there was a 6 Foot rattlesnake with his fangs stuck in the stick. I cut off his head and left the head stuck in the stick. I went home and threw the stick against the barn, when I came out in the morning the stick was a log, seems the poison made the stick swell up. Well being one not to pass up a good thing I sawed the log into planks and put up a small hen house, put in 8 hens, Only thing was it rained that night, washed the poison out of the wood and squashed the hens.

Speaking of chickens, my friend Bill talked me into going into business with him. He had found a way to raise chickens with four legs, 2 extra drum sticks, sounds good to me. Course we went bust, ever try to catch a chicken with 4 legs?

These stories go on thru this whole story. When a subject comes up one will be told, No matter what you said to Bob, he would always say " I know a story about that," he did too!. Bob loved to make people laugh, But get this, He knew a lot of the stories from the Bible too. When he went to a country school there was a Minister who would come to the school once a week. He really made an impression on Bob and it seemed like a lot of the stuff he taught, Bob had some kind of knowledge about. Bobs friends called him "Preacher" whenever he related a story from the Bible. He said. "I should have known the Lord was on my side. Later in life, He said, "one day I went down to the basement, at the foot of the stairs was a freezer we were not using and as I walked by it a little voice said, " open it up!" anyway I listened to the voice and opened it up and there was my Sister locked inside. I don't know how long she had been in there but she just smiled at me and went on her way," guess you know we fixed it so it could not be shut.

There was the time I was coming home from school, we always cut through the cemetery as it cut about a half mile off the walk to and from school. Anywho, I was coming home from school by myself and I passed by a new grave that the grass was just starting to come up in, and as I walked by there were footprints walking beside in the new grass, after the footsteps came up there would be no depression in the grass, as though no one had stepped on it. Here's the strange part, I was not alarmed at this, I guess I knew this was a sign that an angel was with me.

I regret that you will not see much about my Sister in this book. She was still a youngster when I went into the Navy and of course when I got out I was out in the world. I did come to her aid a couple of times but in later years we became closer.

I asked my Dad for shotgun to hunt with when I was old enough, 12 years old, for whatever reason he said no. Never have figured that out. However I had saved up the money for the gun so I took it and bought a new Bow and some Arrows. Don't know what I thought I was going to do with that. My friend Rich had guns at his house and would let me use one when we went hunting for rabbits, a double barrel 410 with hammers. Not knowing about guns I would load it and cock both hammers and walk with it that way. Dad found out and said I could have my own shotgun and showed me how to use it. He had me keep it in their bedroom so the kids would not get it. Whenever I went to get it Dad was in bed sleeping as he worked nights. If I just walked in it was fine but if I tried to sneak in he always woke up. Speaking of shotguns, the one I had shot so far I had to put salt in the shell to keep the game until I got up to it.

Chapter 2

U S Navy

Three of us decide to go into the Navy. There was Trenton, Jim and myself. The reason I wanted to go was to get an education, more about this later. We enlisted at Jackson, and within 3 weeks we were on our way. I had never been in such a structured environment, at home I eat when I was hungry, slept when I was tired, and basically done what I wanted when I wanted. Here there was someone telling when to do everything. Boot camp was something else, (by the by, Trenton and Jim had been sent somewhere else, we went in on the buddy system, I would not see Trenton until 15 yrs later.) while boot camp was strict it was easy if you played the game. I built a model airplane while in boot camp. I had a rough time in service week. Service week is where one company does the work, with this method everybody got a chance to work, and everything gets done. Without having to hire anybody. I was assigned to the mess hall; we served meals, cleaned up after. Once I had to mop the galley, and the person in charge said, "Get some of that soap in the 5 gal can and put it in the mop bucket." And walked away, I did, just took my hands and scooped up some and put it in the mop pail, here come the charge person back with a scoop and said, "Use this to put the soap in the mop bucket." I said, "I already did," He said, "How." I said "I scooped it out with my hands." He Said, "Come here quick and wash your hands with this stuff!" Too late, the lye soap had burnt my hands, bad. He rushed me to sickbay and they smeared some stuff on my hands and sent me back to the barracks. I didn't even know what lye soap was. The pain was like sticking your hands in a fire. My hands hurt so bad that I tied cords around my wrist's to stop the pain. The Duty Officer seen that and took me back to sickbay and had them give me a shot to sleep. Here's the bad part, I could not get paid for a month as the lye soap burnt off my finger prints off and you had to put your print on the slip to get paid. And here I am making 23 cents an hour, course that was 23 cents 24 hours a day.

They would wake us up at 4:00 am, put me in mind of the guy who went into the service and the sergeant came around and woke him up at 4:00 am, the guy says, "Sarge, you better get some sleep we have to get up early tomorrow morning!"

Here's a smile, we had to go into a building where they had 2 inch pipes set into the floor then an elbow set horizontal. You would stand behind them and they gave each man a piece of line (rope) and they were going to teach us to tie knots on to the pipe. Needless to say the first time went like a Chinese fire drill and when we marched out I looked back and there was a guy trussed up the pipe. Probably some of those guys from New York, they were a crazy bunch.

I took a lot of tests to see what my interest was, course I had always been crazy about airplanes and went into the Air force part of the Navy, They sent me to Oklahoma City, Oklahoma to aircraft recognition school. That was a rush! They would flash a picture of an aircraft then ask who knew what plane that was. After I identified about 15 the instructor told me to be quiet and let someone else guess. After a couple weeks there I was tested and they asked if I would like to go to aircraft maintenance school, I said sure, they then transferred me to Memphis, Tenn. I was to be here 2 ½ months. I really liked the school. I ended up an Aviation Structural Mechanic. What I worked on was the Structure, Tires, Brakes, Painting, Hydraulics, Tail Hook and the Plastics, like the Canopy. This education would cost $ 20,000 at that time was a fortune. From there I was transferred to Corpus Christi, Texas and started to work on aircraft. For you airplane buffs, I worked on Douglas Skyraiders, and T-28 Trainers. This was a base where they taught Pilots to land on aircraft carriers. The aircraft carrier deck was painted on the runway. This was really easy duty. Two guys I went thru school at Memphis were also transferred to Corpus Christi. They invited me to go fishing with them in the gulf; we were fishing for salt-water trout and this was a rush. On your line you put a cork, about the size of a thermos jug cork, behind that 3 foot of line with a small treble hook with a shrimp on it. You would throw out your line and pop the cork and the trout would strike, they fought like crazy, when I got my first one in they said, "be careful of their fangs!" I thought they were ribbing me. But sure enough, right out of the roof of their mouth they had 2 big teeth. Plus they had other teeth as well. They were sure good eating.

While stationed in Texas, two other guys and myself went down to a river. It was called the Neucses River, this was a big river, and as we walked along the bank we found the remains of large fish. One of the guys that was from the area said they were Alligator Gar, the remains we found were 12 to 16 ft long. These things had a head like an alligator and the rest of the body looked like a huge pike. He also said this river was fresh water but that it ran into the gulf which is salt-water. And the Gar would go from fresh to salt and back again. They would go into the gulf to nest. One had made a nest at the bottom of an oilrig, when the diver went down for maintenance check it attacked him and he had 160 stitches down the side of him. They went down and killed it and it was 14 ½ foot long. The remains we were finding along the bank were from guys that had caught them on hook and line, I can only imagine.

One time they had an AD (Skyraider) with a fuel leak at the bottom of the fuel cell, these cells had a plate on the bottom with about 20 bolts to hold it on and they were safety wired tight, safety wiring is where the head of the bolt has a hole cross ways in it, after they were tight they would put a wire thru the head of the bolt and twist it until they came to the next bolt. This was to keep the bolts tight, with all the vibration of the aircraft. Here is the problem. One of wires was broke and the fuel cell was leaking, this over 100 octane gas, and could not be drained. What had to happen was someone was going to have to cut the wires off, tighten the bolts up and safety wire them again. All this had to happen with out making a spark and blowing everything up. Sure I volunteered, the person who done this would get 3 days off. And I like this kind of thing. So here is what they did. They emptied one of the hangars out, put the plane in the middle and that was where I was going to work on, this way a blast would be contained. I was a little nervous but got it done. Another time they had a F3H Demon (fighter-bomber) with a fuel problem and here they come to me, seems the bottom of the cell had a problem that could only be fixed from inside the cell, This plane was a monster, with the after burner on it would burn 1600 pounds of fuel in 15 minutes. This one they put clear at the end of the runway. I pulled off the turtle back, pulled off the safety wired plate about 30 bolts, and went inside and repaired it, bolted it back on, safety wired it and put the turtle back on. And it was done. Time? 3 hours, got a week off for that one. This all started in boot camp in fire control school. The instructor asked if anyone knew how to use the big fire extinguisher, it was about 3 foot high with a big horn to spray CO_2 with. Of course I said, "I do", he said OK pick it up and go stand on the yellow X, I did and he threw down a match and I was surrounded in circle of fire, 3 foot high. Good thing I knew how to use it, you pull the pin, hold the horn down in front of you and pull the trigger and dust back and forth in front of you and walk thru.

I was a Petty Officer 3rd Class in charge of 11 airplanes. They were F9F Panthers, this one had landed with the wing fuel cell full of gas. Pilot said he was unable to dump the fuel. Here is how this is supposed to work. When the plane got back from a flight the pilot would pull a lever that would open a tube running thru the wing tip and it would suck the fuel out It was not a good idea to land with fuel in the wing. If you touched down too hard the wing would break off and then a fire. Anyway, I called for an airbowser, this was an air compressor on a tow dolly and what I was going to do was blow some air thru the tube and blow out what ever was blocking it. Problem was, it was blocked at the back, now jet fuel is kerosene with igniter called JP-5. When I put the air to it the air built up in the fuel cell, backed up and dowsed me with fuel. I had a driver take me to sickbay; I went up to a corpsman and told him I was soaked in JP-5, he took off running away from me. I hadn't noticed he was smoking a cigarette, closest I ever came to being a torch. One of my plane captains's reported a hydraulic leak on one of the F9s. I went out to take a look, the plane captain is a recruit who watches over the plane when the pilot is not in it, and reports anything that wrong.

When I got out there I see the MIL-5606 on the ground (hydraulic fluid), here the problem with this plane there was no way to get hydraulic pressure with out the planes engine running. The plane captain knew how to start and run the engine. I had to crawl into the jets intake with a flash light find the problem and fix it. This plane had the intake on the wing stub next to fuselage. I told him to start it and I would crawl into the intake and find the problem and then throw a wrench out and he should shut the engine off. To build the hydraulic pressure I needed the plane captain could run the engine at 20%, he started it, I went in found a hydraulic line split, threw a wrench out and he shut it down. I took the line off and went back to hangar and built a new line. Went back to plane and told the plane captain I would put the line on, throw out a wrench out and he should then start the engine and I would make sure the new line was ok, there was an officer around the plane and he climbed up to watch the plane captain start up, I told the plane captain not to let him touch anything. Went in, put on the line, threw out a wrench and the engine started, I was watching the line and my shirt was dragged off me, I could not breathe, the engine was being turned up too high. Then it shut down. I came out of there with fire in my eyes; here this stupid officer had told the plane captain he would start the engine. The dummy thought the engine had to be at 80%, that's almost take off power. Had the tie downs broke, the plane would have run 30 feet into another plane that would have trapped me inside while it burnt. I guess you know that officer was written up.

Had a deal at the base one time, there was a change that had to be made in the cowling of the Ads. All it was is a hole had to drilled in the cowling in case it got a crack in the cowling the hole would stop the crack. Not a major deal, however they had a kid just out of boot camp drill the hole. They gave him a pattern to lay on the cowling and just drill where it was marked. Some where down the line they forgot to tell him the cowling had to be removed when the hole was drilled, he drilled the cowlings with the cowl on the plane. Later that day I heard the sirens go to blasting and went out to look at the runway, usually the siren meant that a plane was in trouble and they would lay down foam on the run way to keep the fires from breaking out. Looked into the air and there was 8 ADs with their landing gear half way down. Hydraulic problem! Sure was, the kid drilled though the cowling and hit a hydraulic line, when the planes took off the hydraulic oil started to leak. Hydraulic pressure on these planes is 2000 PSI (pounds per square inch) after being airborne for a while it had all blew out, and here they come in for landing with the wheels half way down, my crew chief sat there with a pencil and pad and was writing down the parts for each plane as it skidded in. Funny thing I never did hear about anybody in trouble over this, just what had happened.

As a Petty officer and because I had the schooling, I would teach pilots how to use the ejection seat. When you sat in the aircraft, right above your head was a handle with two hand grips. If you needed out you reached up, pulled the handle down over your face, this blew the canopy off, pull it to your chest and you were shot out of the plane at 400 feet per second. (I saw an article on TV where it is now 600 feet per second as the planes are so much faster.) There was a tube on the seat that slid over this huge shell that fired you out, about 3-inch diameter shell. The pilot usually got two black eyes from the force of the wind hitting him in the face when he went out. To teach these pilots I would meet them at the main base about 50 miles away, this by the by is where the Blue Angels called home. At the main base there was a tower with tracks on it, it stood 75 ft in the air, at the bottom was the same seat as in the air craft, and the pilot would sit in it and pull the ejection lever and it would shoot him in the air on the track and then it would slowly descend back down. Quite the deal and the pilots loved the ride. One time in the hangar a pilot was messing with ejection seat and fired it, he was in the girders in less than a second, and he won't try that again. DOA!

Ahhhhhhhh, the Blue Angels, what a group! These guys drive their cars the same way they fly the jets, I would see them around while I was over to the main base, but one time they came over to our small base. The guy in the control tower didn't know what to do, they came across our runway from all four directions and the guy in the tower heard them before we saw them. You have to get permission to cross any runway, all in one voice they said, " request permission to cross Cabniss field runway, 1,2,3,4, all four came across at the same time from four different directions about 50 feet apart.

Then they called the tower again and said, "requesting permission to land at Cabniss field," 1,2,3,4, and they all landed at the same time again about 50 feet apart. Taxied up and parked with their wing tips 1 foot to 18 inches apart. Two of them got out and put some tape on the wing tips of the other two, tape from no 1 wing tip to no 2 wing tip, this was that glass tape, quite strong, then the tower heard, "requesting permission to take off, 1,2, and away they went. Got airborne and done all sorts of maneuvers and the called the tower, "requesting permission to land, 1,2, and land they did. The piece of tape between the two wing tips was not broken!! I know what they said as I was friends of the tower control officer, he said they would request what they wanted to do then do it without his OK! Every pilot has to ask permission and the wait for the control tower to give them permission, not these guys. Their cars had been brought over to our field, Thunderbirds of course, each pilot had one and they drove to our mess hall for lunch. We got to talk to them before they drove back to their planes, quite an experience. Poor control officer almost had a break down over this deal.

I had to go over to the main base to show some pilots how to use the ejection seat. I called for a carryall (like an SUV) to take me over to the main base. They told me all their vehicles were out and they would find me a ride over to the main base. They told me there was a carryall leaving the lockup to take a prisoner over there. So I go over to the lockup and there is a marine guard and he had the prisoner in the back, said, "jump in the front with me." I got in and away we went half way over we got a flat tire, well you know who's going to change that, the prisoner. We are out side standing there while he changed the tire, when he thought the guard was not looking he made a break for it and started running. The marine pulled his 45 semi-automatic and said, "Halt, Halt, Halt, and then fired the 45, the guy went rolling, the guard said, "I just blew his leg off, we walked out there and the bullet went though his pants leg and rolled him, the bullet never touched the skin, powerful gun!

At Cabniss Field Base just outside Corpus Christi Texas, I seen something I could not believe to this day, 2 teenagers wanted to go to the pool and go swimming or meet girls or whatever. They were officer's kids and were told they could not go swimming until they trimmed the front hedges, a job that would have taken most of the day. But they figured a way to do it faster. We were watching as they brought the lawn mower out. It was one of those kind with a motor that you had to push. They started it up and one kid got each side of the hedge holding the mower up to the top of the hedge and walked along each side and the mower trimmed the hedge. I shudder to think what could have happened.

A funny thing that they did when a guy would be stationed at Cabniss field right out of bootcamp he was send them from one hanger to the other to get a comshaw (something built for your-self from government parts) so what they did was to take 6 elevator balance weights (they weighed 11 Lbs each) and put them in a metal box and marked on the box "1 Comshaw, Large." They also had a metal box with 4 elevator balance weights and marked " 1 Comshaw, Small." Whichever one they brought back was the wrong size and they had to go get the other one. They also had some of them try to get a bucket of prop wash, this is the air that comes off the propeller when it turns, the Navy blew that joke as they came out with some stuff to wash off the propellers with and it was called, What else, "Prop Wash." We had three hangers so there was a lot of walking and carrying going on. By the by, an elevator balance is a part that goes in the aircraft, it is a counter balance to move the elevator of the airplane. There is a lot of force on the control surface and weigh helped the pilot move the control surface.

I went in to take a shower and there was a guy in the shower. I joked around with him a lot, I got a bucket and filled it with real cold water and when he finished his shower and shut it off I threw the whole bucket of cold water on him, man did he yell! I knew he was going to get back at me so I told a few guys if they seen him getting a bucket of water to let me know. Run along a few days and a guy told me while I was in the shower that he was getting a bucket of cold water, so I started turning the shower down until it was really cold, I see him out of the corner of my eye waiting around. So now I am almost froze and I turn off the shower and pretended not to see him and he threw the cold water on me, actually it was warmer than the shower, when it hit me I said "Thanks, could you get another bucket, I missed a place on my back." I never saw such a dumb look on a person's face.

I never thought I would travel so far when I went into the Navy, went from Michigan to boot camp in Great Lakes Training Center in Illinois, to Oklahoma City, Oklahoma. To Memphis, Tenn. To Norfolk, Virginia, to The Azores, Greenland, to Port Laodie, French Manraco, Africa, went aboard ship, an A D Tender, U S S Everglades, into the Mediterranean Sea. While at sea we came to the U.S.S. Lake Champlain, an aircraft carrier the ship I was assigned to. We were about 100 yards apart and they were putting oil and fuel from the A D Tender into the carrier. I had to go aboard the carrier, they shot a line (rope) across to the carrier, which then pulled a larger line (rope) across, then they put me in a boatswain's chair (all this was is a board with a rope run thru it for me to sit on.) and pulled me from the A D Tender over to the Carrier, The waves were about 50 foot high, the two ships are moving in the waves back and forth, what a ride. The kind of thing you only see in a movie. But I was now home for the next 8 months. I was assigned to Squadron VF-81, F8F Cougars and F9F Panthers, Fighter Aircraft. I really liked these planes, I now had a new job added to the ones I already have, Tail Hooks for landing on the Carrier. And talk about living close, the bunks were just wide enough to sleep in. One of the things I had to get used to was the hammering of the ships engines at all hours of the night. I asked one of the Ships Company (guys who run the ship) what that was and he said, "Submarines get on our tail and we run away from them." Oooookkk! I really loved the job on board the carrier, I did get very tired when we went on attack mode, then I would work 18 hours at a time getting the planes up and back. I did made a couple of mistakes, but they ended up being funny, they were having gunnery practice, a plane would fly by and it had a sleeve it was towing on a long cable and they would shoot at it, the 3 inch guns were right below the flight deck and make a lot of noise, one time I walked across the flight deck and looked down at the 3 inch cannons, one fired and the concussion slapped me and knocked me backwards, it was like getting hit with a bunch of wet newspapers. The other thing that happened was I was greasing the wheels, tail hook and the nose wheel in the jet aircraft and the nose wheel well is very narrow, by the time I got done I was covered with grease, I was headed to take a shower. And I run into a Boatswains Mate (the police of the ship) they had very little to do, mostly blow their pipe every time its time for something, and they were all very cocky. He stopped me and asked why I was such a mess; I told him I had been greasing aircraft. He said, " that's no reason to be the mess I was." And he took me down to my Squadron leader (also a pilot) and said, "your people have to be in better shape than this!" the Captain asked me what I had been doing, I told him, "greasing the wheels on the aircraft, and I added with a lot of emphasis The Tail Hook!" now I'm the guy who makes sure the tail hook comes down right so the pilot can catch one of the arresting cables on the flight deck. He said to the Boatswain's Mate, "I will take care of this! And as the Boatswains Mate was going out the door he said to me, "you are going to do 4 hours extra duty" as the door shut he said, "playing cards." Anyway back to my travels: I went to Barcelona, Spain, Nice France, Athens Greece, I went ashore on a pass to these places, One time I had to do Shore Patrol duty, Navy Police, like MPs in the army. I was paired up with a Police man of Spain, we never said a word to each other the whole 8 hours I patrolled with him, he spoke no English and I did not speak his language. These women came yelling out an apartment house and I did not know what was going on, the guy motioned me to come with him. We went up about 2 flights of stairs and there was an apartment door open and the woman yelling something, we went in a there was a drunken sailor, passed out and he hadn't paid the woman for her services. I radioed the regular Shore Patrol and they took him away. After the 8 months I was transferred to the carrier U S S Forrestal, and shortly after that we headed out of the Mediterranean Sea into the ocean and home. We went by the rock of Gibraltar, I was thinking about the time one our carriers, it was the first atomic powered Carrier and was heading toward Gibraltar and it just happened to be the biggest carrier in the world at the time, the signal tower on the rock sent a message to the carrier, "What Carrier?" well it goes without saying the Captain of the carrier was a little peeved, Biggest Carrier in the world and they are asking, what carrier, he sent a message back and said, "What Rock?"

I met a guy who had been on one of the Islands and was telling about this Native Chief who had a Golden throne, the Chief had got a message that another tribe was going to steal his Golden throne, so he put it up in the rafters of his grass hut, that night it fell down and killed him as he slept. I guess the morale of the story is: "People who live in grass houses should not stow thrones." — — — — — — — Say What!

Things were at a standstill on the carrier down below where the planes being stored or repaired were setting, for the most part the lower bay was empty. All of a sudden there is a commotion and there's a sailor down on his knees with his white hat on the deck, and says I caught a Sea bat, its under my hat, when someone would peek under the hat someone would swat him on the fanny with a board, great fun for a boring time. Oh Oh here comes and Officer, "what you doing on the deck son?" he says. Well this guy with the hat happens to be a kid from New York, and they fear nothing, a crowd begins to form so the guy on the floor could escape when he needed to. He says, "caught a Sea bat Sir" the guy says, " let me see it!" the officer says and gets down where he can see under the hat, I'm thinking, they wouldn't dare, they do and someone swats the Officer on the rear, and the guy who swatted and the guy with hat melt into the crowd, gone, forgot one thing, his hat is still there, and it has his name in it. Good part, the Officer didn't want anyone to know he was suckered in and that was the end of that.

At Norfolk one time an F9F has a flameout (engine quits) and the pilot ejects out, too low the parachute didn't have time to open or for the guy to separate from the seat, hits the ground and the pilot is dead, we walked over to the pilot and the one guy from New York who was getting a real hard time thought it was the guy who was riding him, he looks at the pilot and says, " I was hoping it was Major Burns!" Bad news Major Burns was standing right behind the guy and heard what he said.

I said I would explain why I quit school and went into the Navy; I spent 3 years in the 7th grade. I was so bored with school, I was always 50 pages ahead in everything, made the teachers mad and they would fail me, Like reading, the words, the, and, that, is, was, did not exist for me, you get the picture, I was a speed reader, and when the teacher would call on me to read, I would read and then the teacher would say, " Could you read that again, and slow enough we can get it." And of course the more they leaned on me the more rebellious I became. Today they don't do that they put you in a grade where you belong. Back then you could not tell teachers anything. As today some of them forget who's paying their check. So went into the Navy and after a while they came to me and said, " You have to have a high school diploma to be in the Navy. The First Class Petty Officer who told me this also said, " You can get a GED and stay in the Navy, we will send you to school and then you take the GED test, or real sarcastically, or you just go take the test." I said, "I will just take the test!" Did too, past the test with marks high enough when I filled out some papers later on, the person who checked the paper said, " You didn't put your college scores on the papers, and by the looks of your test scores you went to college." There you go teachers!

In later years when I was going to the muzzle loading meets I ran into the same things. I would take the kids to the meets and it meant taking them out of school, they learned more about history at one meet then they did in a year of school. They had a large meeting to see about changing the dates of the shoots so kids would not have to miss school. I among others stood up at the meeting and said how much the kids learned at the shoots, there were teachers in the meeting and of course they didn't want anyone or place stealing their thunder. When the meeting dismissed we were walking back to camp there was a teacher walking behind us as I was telling a friend that my kids would still be coming to the meets no matter what the school said, the teacher spoke up and said, "I would expel any student who missed school just to come here." I said, "See here's another person who don't realize who is paying their wages!" that was the last words.

When I was waiting to be discharged, I had to go to classes to reintroduce me to the civilian world. They told me with my schooling and experience they had found 7 jobs for me with aircraft plants that wanted me to work for them. I said where, they said California, I said do they have snow out there, they said no, I said forget it. I never was a factory guy anyway. I worked a few factory jobs but I can't stand the same thing day after day. Besides as you can see I would have missed all the stuff in this book. But on the other hand I would have been retired at age 50.

Chapter 3

Back Home

I got Married just before I was discharged, and was still just a kid in that matter, and we lived with her parents. I was very seldom there. Always running off hunting and fishing, or just ramming. Thinking back on it I can't really remember all the stuff I was doing. Her folks place was in Bronson and when I got a job we moved to Coldwater. Bronson is a Polish town and of course there was a ton of stories about them. They would have a Polish Festival every year, and this one-year they could not have Kool-aid as no one could get two quarts of water in that little package. ??? Course they did help the war effort as this was one of the places that parachutes were made, the ones from Bronson opened on impact, and they were guaranteed.

There was a story about two Coldwater boys who went over to Glendale and were messing around and stole a pig, on their way back to Coldwater the police got behind them and turned on their lights and stopped them, before they got stopped the one guy hanging onto the pig wrapped a scarf around the pigs head and had it sitting between them, the cop came up to the car and asked for their license and other papers, everything was in order and they said to the boys, "Stay out of trouble." The cop got back in his squad car and told his partner, "I just don't see what those Coldwater boys see in those Glendale girls.

I picked up where I left off with fishing, I loved to fly cast, I used a plastic popper made by Weber for bass, (Weber is long out of business, just found out they were in business from 1896 to 1988) Guys from out of state would ask me to guide them for bass, there are some things that are just not for sale, and besides I have seen dude fishermen before and I would not like to be in a boat with them. I used black rubber spiders for bluegills, But I am one of those guys that has to do it all myself, so I started tying flies plus I had run into something I knew I could change. Bluegills would hit my spiders and when I tried to set the hook, nothing? These rubber spiders had rubber legs and I would see them start to disappear, after they were gone I got better hook set, Hummmmm! So to my fly tying bench I went and started tying spiders without rubber legs, instead I put hackle. Never had a problem with hook-set anymore. Then I started selling flies, I got some liquid rubber and punched some foam bodies, glued a hook in, and then I dipped the foam bodies in liquid rubber. These things worked good and were indestructible to the point that the wholesale stores would not buy them as they lasted too long. I would walk into a sporting goods shop with one of these in my hand, I would let the store guy see it then I would drop it and then step on it, and say, "I got it!" and when they seen that it wasn't hurt they would buy it. Later in life there were no more Weber poppers I found a supply catalog with just the bodies for these poppers and I started making them. When I moved up north I would go to the sporting goods shop for fly tying supplies, they got to know me. One day I walked in and one of the clerks said, "Here's the guy you need to talk to!" he was speaking to one of his customers. I said, "What's up? Turns out this guy wanted to learn to tie flies, I looked at what he had picked out and sorted out what he didn't need and showed him the other stuff he should have. I said, "Where do you live?" he told me and I said, "You are going right past where I live stop in and I will show you how to get started tying. He said, "OK". He stopped at the house and I showed him some different stuff he could tie and how to do it. He looked at some of the poppers I had made, the smaller size for bluegills; I had painted them yellow with a scale pattern on the top. He said, "Can I buy some of these from you?" I said, "sure and he bought a couple of cards, 15 poppers on each card, and he left. About 2 days later he drove into the drive, I thought Oh, Oh, this can't be a good thing. He gets out of his car just as I walked out, I said, "Hi, how you doing?" he said, "I had to stop and tell you how great those poppers are, I caught a more fish on them than any lure I ever fished with!" I'm still thinking what's wrong? Then he said, " But you have a problem with the poppers, the painted scale pattern is getting chipped off the top by the fish hitting them, is there anything you can do to prevent this?" I said, "Sure, but it will cost extra, or you could do it yourself, just put some hard as nails on them, (nail polish) but remember that will change the way they float." I then took a popper and held it above my head so I was looking at the bottom of the popper, then I said, "But consider this, the fish see these like you do when I hold it up, just the bottom, the painted scale pattern is to catch the fisherman!" he looked kinda sheepish and said, "I didn't think of that, can I get a couple more cards? My friends want some. I said "Sure and sold him some more and away he goes.

Speaking of guides I did row the boat for my Dad and Larry's Dad while they were casting for bass. Funny I never fished with them just rowed the boat for them. They wanted me to row for them because from an early age and from being with Dad I knew right where to put the boat for them to fish. And they always got the bass, there used to be a lot more than there are today. I always enjoyed rowing for them, neither one of them ever said a harsh word to me. And of course I felt it was an honor to be asked to row for them. A kid asked by an accomplished fisherman!

I also designed a frog; I took two large spider bodies and glued them together with a hump shank hook (hook has a double bend in it to keep it from turning in the lure.) I put either a white or yellow on the bottom, white for grass or leopard frog and yellow for bull-frog. The tops were green or brown, didn't matter as I was going to scale finish them were paint, this is just to catch the fisherman, see above. Then I would put green or yellow buck tail and spilt it for the two legs. This guy is a killer on bass, funny thing happened, I was out peddling my flies had all colors of spiders, black ants and these frogs. I knew this one place had a lot of fly-fishing stuff for sale and a lot of fly tying stuff also. I had built two cherry cases for carrying my flies to the shops; like my brother Randy says, "Don't cost that much more to go first class." And I usually did. Anyway went into this shop and here was a guy who looked familiar, I just could not place him. Tell you at the end of this story. I says to him, " interested in buying any flies for fly fishing?" he said, "this shop ties all our own flies and we also teach fly tying." I said, "Oh, Ok I didn't know that." He said, "Well you are here lets see what you have," Was very impressed with my spiders with no rubber legs, Then he caught a glimpse of my frogs, He said, "Did you make those?" I said, "Yes they are rubber bodied and float with the head up just like the real thing." I had some samples on a one lure card and I said, "Here give them a try." He looked it all over and said how many of these do you have?" I said, "I have 5 cards of them, 15 to the card and wholesale is $ 15.00 a card and suggested retail is $ 1.50- 1.75 ea." He says, "Can I buy what you have with you." I said. "Sure." He says, "Great, that would be $ 75.00 for all 5 cards, right?" I says, "That's right." He hollered at his employee who was standing by the cash register and said, "Give this guy $ 75.00 dollars," and he turned to me and said, "Can I have a receipt?" I said, "I'm making it out now." So I came out of there with all my frogs gone, of course I had more at home! As I left he was taking them off the cards as they had my name on the card and he didn't want anybody calling me. I was only 20 minutes from home and when I got home Sis said, "Someone called you and wanted to know if he could get some more frogs, some fly shop." By the time I called him it was 45 minutes since I left there and he had sold out of the frogs. I forgot to mention the problem with the frogs; it's impossible to find the large bodies anymore. Boy, I'm glad I bought 6,000.

Had the almost the same thing happen to me with my spider, this one sporting goods shop I went into looked at my spiders and said, "There are no rubber legs on these!" I said, Yes I know, you can hook almost all the fish that hit them because they don't have rubber legs, I put hackle instead of rubber legs, the fish come right through the hackle on a strike." When I was young I was a fly casting champion at the age of 8 and I could not figure out why I missed a lot of strikes, then I noticed that when the fish had tore the rubber legs off I hooked everyone." He says, "Why has no one else figured this out?" I said, "I guess it has to do with interest and money, people are not interested enough to figure out why they are missing strikes, they think they are at fault and the money end is that shops will sell them more spiders when fishermen see the legs are gone, But if you help them hook their fish you will sell even more." The shop always bought over $ 200.00 each time I went there and they left them on the card.

Chapter 4

Carp Spearing

Here are a couple of funny stories of when we used to go carp spearing in the lake. One day Dick, my friend and I went out to the sporting goods store for something, and there was a sign: Spearing season for the lakes and rivers opens April 15, this was odd as I knew the season was always May 15, my Dad's birthday. Dick said" I never have been spearing and would like to go". Now Dick was a funny guy, he always chewed tobacco so his one cheek was always puffed out with the chew, and also smoked cigars; I have seen Dick drink a carton of milk past the chew. Anyway we go to my place and get the stuff ready for spearing that night. About 11:00 that night we were spearing a bunch of carp, Dick says, " Are those bass right there? " I said, " Sure are and some big ones at that," Dick said, " I love bass baked in the oven, are they in season?" I said, " No but they eat the same, and they don't know about season's, grab what you want." He speared about a 7 Lb and was happy as a pig in slop. Of course I was watching for the CO as the April season bothered me. Seen no one. We got back to the shore and as we hit the shore a voice said, " You boys doing any good? " Now Dick didn't know it was the CO and held up the bass and said, "What do you think of this one? " I collapsed on the boat seat. Cost us a night in jail and $ 57.00 ea for the bass, would have been real bad, but the CO went to the sporting goods store and there was the sign. In jail we slept in the tank and when morning came a sound of metal sliding across the floor, without even uncovering his head, Dick says, " That'll be coffee and donuts. It was.

Another time my Brother Roger called me and said he wanted to go spearing that night, said Clem had never been and did not believe there were big fish like he been telling, I said OK, " I will go to blacksmith shop and make a harpoon for turtle " (you have to use a single tipped spear as it will penetrate the shell.) Now turtle are very good table fare, my Dad loved the things. Here's a little tip on cleaning turtle, Hang it by the tail, take pliers and grab it by the jaw pull the neck all the way out, cut off the head and let it bleed out, take an air hose wrap the loose neck skin around it, wrap wire around the skin so the air hose won't leak, hit it with some air and it will take the skin from the meat.

So about the time I was putting the 4 ft handle on the 4 ft harpoon they showed up, Clem said, " What's that for, Moby Dick? ' I said, " No it's for snapping turtle! " Clem said, " Turtle's don't get that big around here! " away we went to the river, I had a 14 ft flat bottom boat with a 6 hp out board and there was a waist high pipe frame on the front to spear from, I was running the motor and Roger set facing me and we were talking, we were letting Clem spear, he was like a kid in the candy shop. We had the harpoon in the back with us and I said to Roger, " There's a snapper!" Roger grabbed the harpoon and speared the turtle, nice one about 35 lbs, Roger shook it off in the boat and Clem got down to look at it. Clem said, " I will never swim in this river or lake again." Clem said, " Does that thing bite?" there was a empty cigarette pack in the bottom of the boat I took it and poked the turtle on the nose and he bit a piece out of it, I said, " This guy can bite a finger off! " Clem climbed back up into the spearing cage. The turtle kept moving in the aluminum boat making a scratching sound. Now Clem was wearing apache boots, thin leather boots that came to the knee, they laced up the front. I said to Clem, " Make sure that turtle don't bite you, it can bite right thru those boots." Clem said, "He can't get me up here." then I hand signaled Roger to tap him on the leg with the harpoon, when he did Clem let out a holler and I swear to this day he went to the top of the 15 ft carp spear pole. I laughed so hard I could not keep the boat straight. Clem still gets mad when this story is told.

One other time when Roger and I were spearing, I speared a dogfish, worthless things, I give the spear a flip to get the fish off and hit Roger in the head with the spear pole, almost knocked him out. I felt so bad. He always said after that, "that's why I act like I do.

I took my boys Edward and Robert over to Union Lake carp spearing, now Robert was skinny as a rail, sometimes I had trouble telling him from the spear pole. Anyway we are going along and Robert spears this huge carp and it starts to drag him out of the boat, I grabbed him by the belt and held onto him, there was no way he was going to let go of his Dad's spear, so here I am keeping him in the boat, he's fighting the big carp and Edward is laughing his head off. Exciting for a few minutes.

One time when Rich and I were about 12-13, we went spearing one night on Cemetery lake we had a row boat and oars, Rich was in the front of the boat with the spear and I was rowing and looking over my shoulder to see where I was going, Here come this huge fish, Rich looking down on it seen just the head and thought it was a big turtle, I yell's, "Spear it!" I seen one big whisker and though it was a huge catfish, Rich threw the spear into it with everything he had, I jumped up where he was and grabbed the spear handle with him. It twisted in our hands and fought like crazy. Finally it twisted off the spear and away it went. Rich said, "What in the world was that?" I said, " It looked like a huge catfish". Spear was so tore up we were done for the night. We both agreed it was about 10 Ft long. I told Dad about the fish and He laughed and said, " You just had your first tangle with a sturgeon." Said He seen one once that was 12 ft, long as his duck boat, said he thought it was a log on the surface and came up beside it and hit it with his paddle and it took off and almost tipped his boat over.

My second encounter with a sturgeon was on Messenger Lake, Roger and I were out casting for bass and we saw these bubble's coming up from the bottom, Roger said, "What is that?" I knew right away what it was, a sturgeon on the bottom. (They are bottom feeders) I said, "It's a sturgeon on the bottom, lets chase him out," we took one of the oars; the water was about 9 ft deep. We stuck the tip of the oar down as far as we could. I said, "Roger are you ready?" and he said, "What you going to do?" I said, "Fish cannot stand noise." And smacked the handle of the oar with one of the anchors in the boat and away the sturgeon went, talk about stirring up the bottom, mud and bubbles really came up then. I told him I was always waiting for someone to see one of these big fish, I know they would have said it was a shark.

I was out on Cemetery Lake one afternoon with my bow and some fishing arrows, and was shooting carp, they were all over the place, I seen this carp coming toward me and when his head came out of the weeds I shot, it was a monster, but it didn't fight, a fish that size should have dragged my boat all over the lake, I started pulling it in and when I got it to the boat I see why it didn't fight. I had hit it right in the brain and killed it instantly. Lucky for me, I would still be fighting it today. How big was it you say, it weighed 69 pounds.

While this is not carp spearing, it is spearing, I think? When I got out of the Navy I brought home with me a full SCUBA outfit, most of which I built myself. I took the oxygen tanks from an aircraft that was junked out, and the regulator from the plane, these regulators have impregnated "A"cloth (A Cloth is what airplanes used to be covered with.) and is good once in the regulator for 150 feet in the water, I took out the "A" cloth and made a new diagram out of rubber and it worked fine. Now I said I took the oxygen tanks from the aircraft, But! Don't ever use oxygen to dive with, Compressed Air only! SCUBA is Self Contained, Underwater, Breathing, Apparatus. One night we went out to Cary Lake and done some night diving, now Cary Lake is full of Trout, lucky I brought along a frog spear I had attached to a wood dowel, also had a mesh bag they wash socks in to keep them together, we went down about 60 feet and the Trout were all over the bottom, it was like picking up papers in the park with a pointed stick. One problem with night diving around Trout at night is they strike your mask when the light hits it. But here is how you empty the water out of your mask at 60 feet down, tip your head so the water is in the bottom of your right mask, put your fingers on the top side of the mask and exhale into the mask and the water will go out. Not as hard as it sounds. Funny for the fun we had doing this we never did it again.

Corb and I used to do a lot of diving and we had matching jackets and trapping patches on the shoulder, many people mistook us for the DNR, so we had fun with it. We went to a lake and started getting our gear out and there's this old black man fishing by where we were going in. we walked down to the shore and he asked what we were doing, we told him we had to check out the carp population and thin them out if we had to. This guy gets all excited and says, " If you boys gets a chance get me a nice carp." Carp are really good smoked, we said, "Ok" and we get our gear on and of course we had the same rubber powered spear guns they use in the ocean. It was still cold out but we had rubber diving suits, in we go and looked the place over, never even seen a fish. The old guy was disappointed.

Another time Corb and I were out on the lake fishing, it was early spring, Spearing was not in season yet, course Corb and I had our matching hats and jackets on, came round a point on the lake and here is three guys spearing, thought we were the law and pulled their boat into the swamp and jumped out and took off across the swamp. Man I bet they were mad when they found out we were outlaws just like them.

A tornado came south of Coldwater and hit at Coldwater Lake, I went out there right after it happened, they were calling for anyone with a chain saw, and I trimmed trees for a living for 25+ years, when I got out there what a mess, the guy in charge put us in a line and we went down thru there like a bunch of super termites, I cut up some of the nicest Birch trees you ever seen, I thought of how the guy whose property they came off must have tended them, now they were not even fire wood. A lady was standing on the shore and told us the tornado threw her into the lake and pulled her back out again. We got the road clear so the emergency vehicles could get thru, a friend of mine was taken out of his house and when thru the air to the other side of the lake and was hanging dead in a tree 30 foot in the air. Didn't get home until real early in the morning. Then in the spring I heard about a guy who had an old refrigerator and he had a ton of money in it, the tornado had put it in the Lake. It had been 6 months since the tornado and so anyone that wanted to could retrieve anything from the lake, so here we go with our Scuba gear, when out and anchored, in we went it was about 35 foot there and junk everywhere, I don't know why but I took my spear gun down with me. My friend Terry had seen a 14 foot long nose gar there one night, anyhow away we go, I'm cruising along and I see a glint of something and I stopped, put up my hand to stop the other guys, I took the spear gun and swung it in an arc, it hit a glass window pane, if I would have kept going I would run right into it or it would have run right thru me. That's enough of that, we got out of there. It may have been only a rumor about the money anyway.

Chapter 5

Trapping

When did trapping season open for me? After the 2nd or 3rd frost depending how cold the weather was, Dad told me animals have hair all year, but when it got cold they got fur. Sounds good to me. This one year while I still lived outside of town I spotted this river, soft bottom and to deep to wade, so when it cooled down, about 3-4 weeks before season opened I got 15 traps, the canoe, shotgun and duck decoys and set the traps in the river. Everyday I would go duck hunting, and check the traps, one day I see I had got a mink in a trap, trap and mink were gone, I could see someone had taken it by the footprints in tore up ground, of course I knew it was the CO. I always tried to set traps with no stake showing and when I got an animal the weight of the trap would drown it, this mink didn't know my plan. I checked the rest of the traps and got some muskrats, I skinned them out and put the hides in my hip boots. By the time my Son and I got back to the truck it started to rain, I told him, "Lets just lay the guns in the canoe, no sense getting the cases wet. " and away we went. About half way home the CO stopped us, He had a dippy guy from work I knew, riding shotgun as it were, Terry I believe his name was, no authority, just riding along and they started searching. My decoys were in a large laundry bag in the back of the truck. When they started searching I said," We didn't get any ducks!" They just kept looking thru stuff, I said, "We did not put the guns in cases as they were wet " they dumped out the decoys and then put them all back in the laundry bag, looked in the truck, under the hood, went back and dumped out the decoys again and shook each one to see if there was a rat or mink inside the decoy. I kept saying, " We did not get any ducks!" They put the decoys back in the bag. Never said a word just got back in the CO's car and left. They never knew how close they were to muskrats they were looking for! We went on home. That night when I went to work (I worked 11to7am) I see the CO's car parked back in the brush by the river. Now when I went to work that night I had the wife's car, Canoe was still in the truck, didn't want to park it all night someone might take the canoe. He didn't notice me in the car. Done this a couple nights, the next night I was off and called my brother Lee, I said, "Do you have a canoe?" He said, "Yes," I said, " meet me at the New Bridge," which was about 4 miles from the river I was trapping. When he got there about midnight he said, "What's up?" I said, "I am trapping this river and the CO is standing guard over it and I have to go in get my traps out." He said, "Ok," away we went. Now I have always had these night eyes and we did not take a flashlight with us. The river dumped into the lake so we paddled to it, and I started pulling traps, there's a hill over looking the river and there was the CO's car. Would not have seen it except the dippy guy was with him again and he took a large drag on his cigarette, I tapped Lee and pointed to them. Lee shook his head and we went about pulling the traps and left. From that time on I took the car to work and would see the CO setting there waiting. About 4 days I guess.

What did I do with the muskrats I got out of season? I knew the CO could search my house anytime with probable cause, they have way too much power, anyway I would skin them, easier to hide (see above.) and take them to a fur dealer out of state to the south. I'll call him Hank, Dead and gone now. Their season started earlier than Michigan. Many times he told me the CO came to his place and asked if I had sold him some fur. This dealer is making money from the furs I would sell him, he would say to the CO, "Bob stops and talks to me when he's down this way." Never said he didn't buy furs from me. This one time I took some fur down to him and he was skinning a raccoon, I said, " You are pretty fast at skinning those coon, I don't like skinning them, I figure that I am faster than anyone at skinning muskrats." Hank says," I always thought I was faster than anyone at muskrats myself!" Next thing you know there are 2 stools, 2 muskrats and 2 skinning knives and Hank's Wife standing there with a stopwatch. Hank said, "She will say go and we will see who's fastest." We sat down, She said, "Go!" and we went to skinning, we both dropped our skinned muskrats at the same time and she hit the stopwatch. 32 seconds, Hank said, "You beat me, I cut the nose off mine! " we laughed about that every time I would see him. When season would end, Hank would come to my house in Michigan and buy the fur I had. I never got less than 500 muskrats a year.

Talking about selling fur, I used to go to a sale over in another town, it was at the fair grounds on Saturday and there was always at least 3 fur dealers buying fur. I used to put my dried rats on wire rings. 50 to the ring. One Friday night I called my brother Roger and said, "Want to go to sale with me tomorrow? " well Roger always got a laugh when I was dealing with someone, so he said, "Ya I'll go." So the next day I grabs 3-4 rings of rats and away we go. Now the main thing is to just walk around with the rats draped over your shoulder for a while. The dealers would never think of stopping you, show you they were interested and they knew you could jack the price. So here's how I played it, after walking around so all the dealer's seen what you had, I would go to a dealer and say, " What are you paying for rats? " course I always knew the going price, remember Hank. They would say, "$3 dollars ea." Now bear in mind that my fur was always put up nice and they could tell it. When he said $3 dollars I would say, " You mean I can walk over to so & so dealer and he will give $3.25, the dealer would say, "Your fur is put up nice I guess I could go $3.25." I would say, "I'll be back," go to the next dealer and ask, " What are you giving for rats? " he would say, "$3.00," I would say, "You mean I can walk about 10 booths down and get $3.25?" He would say, "They are put up nice I could go $3.25." I would say, "No! I told the other dealer if no one went higher he could buy them." The dealer would say, "How about $3.35?" I would say, "I'll be back". On to the next dealer, same thing, this time up to $3.45. I had to keep Roger back as he was laughing so hard he could spoil the fun. So I would ask Roger, "Are you done here?" he would say, "Yes," I said, " Lets go home " he would say, " Aren't you going to sell your rats?" I would say, "No, I can do better at the auction at the end of the season." Then he would start laughing all over again.

However there was one trip I took Roger with me to deal. There were these two old guys called the Moore Boys, (each one of them was 80 yrs old) they had a couple of tons of stuff, they had single aisle through each room in their house, the rest of the room was piled high with anything you can think of, then in the front room where the wood heater was there was a clearance around the stove of 3 foot. And of course that's where you would find them most of the time. I had some SCUBA gear I wanted to trade off. Roger and I walk in, sit down by the stove with them. I told them what I had and what I wanted to trade for, that was the last mention of dealing for about an hour, finally one of them would say, "We have so-so but you would have to get a part for it." We sit there another hour and finally I said, " Could you throw so-so into the deal as I have to get the part?" another hour of talk about the weather and crops and such. One of them would say, "How about we throw in so-so, that should even things up?" Later I would say, I wasn't looking for so-so, how about a so-so?" another hour and one would say, "I guess we could do that if you could throw in a couple of bucks." It took 9 hours to make the deal. Roger says, "Never again!" course this is the norm for me, and later you will see I took the name "Michigan Trade Rat" for the CB.

And here is Roger, one night we were running traps and we came to a trap with 2 muskrats in one trap. They were both drowned, one rat had his front leg in the trap and the other one had his hind leg in the trap. Roger says, "I wonder how that happened?" I said, " What happened was one rat put his front foot on the trap pan and tried to spring it, he couldn't do it and says to the other rat, how do you set these traps off?" the other rat says, "you have to stomp it with your hind foot like this," and bingo, they were both in the trap. Roger says, " UN Huh! Lets get going."

My first Beaver I caught was at Kim's place, went out to set my traps out put about 3 dozen rat traps out came back the next day and they were all gone. I figured someone had a foolish moment or didn't know who I was and took them. So I go down by the edge of the river to see if there were any footprints, not a one then I get a closer look and my traps are still there the stakes are chewed off right at the water line and of course I could see the tooth marks and I knew it was beaver, so I check the rest of the line, same way. So I cut dead willow stakes and restaked them all (beaver only eat green wood.) and came to where the beaver had built a dam, what a place for mink. The first beaver I caught was a male, 60 lbs of him. I had put a slider wire at the set (Trap slides down the wire and the animal drowns) and the trap was gone, when I started to pull it in it was heavy, I had a 20 lb weight on it, that plus the beaver. I thought I had caught a deer. One night shortly after this my son Robert went on the line with me in the canoe, it's about midnight and we didn't know it but there was a beaver swimming along beside us, now the canoe makes no noise and when I hit the side of the canoe by accident the beaver swatted the water and we about jumped out of the canoe.

Talking about rats being put up, I think of the dog I had. Ringer. All you had to do was show him a muskrat board, (this a board you stretch muskrats on, you skin them, turn the flesh side out, pull tight and cut off the fat and flesh from the hide, then let them dry) anyway, I would show Ringer the muskrat board and out the door he went and would come back with a muskrat. Boy, I sure hated to loose that dog, but one day he was asleep on the floor and woke up to see Mom getting the ironing board out to iron, he jumped up and away he went, probably is still looking for a muskrat to fit the ironing board.

One day running traps I was running late, and I did not have a flashlight with me. I had some Raccoon traps back in the swamp and had to walk back to them. What I would do was, when I would skin muskrats I would carry what was left back into the swamp and put them in a pile. I would walk toe to heel to make a narrow path through the swamp. I would also make other narrow paths to the pile, then I could put traps in the paths and when the animals walked in the paths to get lunch I had them, usually Raccoon and Mink. Anyway the only thing I had to kill the trapped animals with is the barrel of my single barrel 16 gauge shot gun, wasn't old enough to carry a pistol yet. I pulled the boat up to the shore and jumped out and headed back to the traps in the swamp, got almost back to the traps and realized I forgot the shotgun barrel. Oh Well! I'll deal with what ever comes up, what came up was a 25 pound Raccoon, live and mad as a hatter. I thinks to myself, start dealing. I got as close as I could and waved my left hand at its face when it went for it I grabbed it by the throat with the other hand and starting choking it with both hands, I hung on and hung on and hung on, seemed like forever. Finally it died and my hands were numb. That incident sure improved my memory about the shotgun barrel.

In the swamp in Messenger Lake I had paddled the canoe back in as far as I could and then started walking further back in. I came to a small creek about 3 foot wide, looked like sand bottom, maybe 6-8 inches deep, the place reeked of Mink. Now like the incident prior, I always carried a 6 foot rake handle with a hook screwed into it, if a trap was deep I would just hook it out. If I needed to pull the canoe closer to shore just hooked a limb and pulled myself closer, if I got stuck in the muck I could pull the canoe over to me and pull myself out, it was also nice club for Raccoon. Having said all that, when I got back to the small creek I realized I had left the Trap hook in the canoe, no problem, where I was at in the swamp was solid, if you knew where to step. Thought I would wade up the creek a ways, I had hip boots on, stepped into the creek and down I went, above my knees, "QUICKSAND" I was in a world of trouble, back where no one could find me, not that I depended on people anyway. No one could disappoint me, as I didn't expect any thing from anyone. I was my own guy, no trap hook to get a hold of anything to pull myself out. Now bear in mind, this is late November, cold and cold water too. I had to think fast I was going down and could not pull myself out. Extreme is my business. Fell forward into the water, pulled my feet out of my boots and half crawled, half swam to solid ground, walked back to the canoe, stocking footed, got the trap hook walked back and pulled my boots out. Dumped the water and junk out of the boots and went on with the rest of my trap line. Just another day.

Rich and I one year were trapping together, had a wooden row boat, no motor, this is before we went into the Navy, I told Rich," We have to pull traps tonight as it was going to freeze up and our traps would be there until spring." We took off, we were almost done and it started to freeze and by the time we got almost back to the car there was a ¼ inch of ice and we had about ½ mile to go. We were in about 3 foot of water and all of a sudden water started coming into the boat, the ice had chewed away the wood in the front of the boat, I said to Rich, "Grab what traps and muskrats you can and head for the swamp!" He looked at me like I was crazy but he knew I could walk through any swamp. We waded about 30 feet to the edge of the swamp and I showed Rich where to come up into the swamp. The bottom of the lake where the boat went down was solid, not so in the swamp. I showed Rich where to step each step, he slipped once and could not feel bottom, he yelled, " There's no bottom!" I said, " Of course not, this is a swamp." He said, " I'm not moving off this spot, at least I know it's solid! I said, " If I have to come back there and wrap my trap hook around your head you will move!" I said, " Just go slow and step where I show you, it's only another 50 feet to dry land." We made it to land and there was a couple of ice fishing houses there, the first one I went into had a kerosene heater and a can of kerosene. We got into the house, got a fire going, and then took off what of our clothes were wet, hung them up and they dried. It was about 10:30 at night and we spent the rest of the night sleeping in the fish house, come morning we walked around the lake to the car. Now that was a fun night. Rich didn't think so, but he said, " I'm glad I had you to lead me through the swamp and not someone else."

Rich trapped again with me the next year, we had a 14 foot flat bottom aluminum boat. We were doing pretty good and then we came to this small island and there was a tree over the water. I shined the flashlight in the tree and there was a huge Possum, hide is worth about 2-3 dollars, I was handling the boat and I told Rich to take my trap hook and knock the Possum into the water and we would knock it in the head, He knocked it out of the tree alright, right into the boat with us, ever see a Mad Possum up close? But we finally got him dead.

I trapped about a 20-mile chain of lakes and a river, one day I got started late. I had a 14-foot flat bottom boat and 6 hp outboard. By the time I got clear to the other end it was dark. I still had to go back to where I started. My favorite trick was to get the boat going at a pretty good clip and then stand up in the boat.

In the middle I could steer it by shifting my weight, somewhat like a motorcycle. Things were going fine, as I started down the river, I hit a log that I forgot was there. Lucky I hit it on the sloped up end, it was just like going up and off a ramp. I flew though the air quite a ways, when it went up I just crouched down. I hit flat and kept on going, bit the bullet again. I was thinking I might try out for a James Bond part. Made it back to where I started and just threw the rats, coon and mink in the truck and left the boat, motor and oars there. I would be out the first thing in the morning and I went home. The next morning I came out to run the traps again and someone had taken one of my oars. I borrowed one from the guy who owned the place where I kept the boat. Run the line and started back, I never went on the river until on the way back. I started down the river and went slow to get a look at the log I hit last night, I knew when I was flying through the air I hit some tree limbs, guess what I seen when I came to the log? There was my oar in the tree, the limbs had pulled it out of the boat, and there it was in the limbs, 12 foot off the water! Now I knew I was going to try out for the James Bond part, that or the Timex watch commercial. Speaking of the Timex watch, one fall as I was finishing the trap line for the year, I dropped my Timex in the water. The next Summer I was fishing with my son Edward and when we came to the spot where I dropped the watch, I was telling him about it and he dove into the water and found the watch, it was still running! I called the Timex people and told them the story, they were not interested. I guess I may as well forget the James Bond part too.

There was a guy I sold fur to now and then, Ralph, one time my kids said, "There's an animal laying in the road that goes back to the woods, looks like a big weasel." I said, "Go get it!" and away they went and was back in no time. Just what I thought it was, a mink. I had to go out and see Ralph and I asked Roger if he wanted to go with me and he said, "Yes, I'll ride along." So we got out to Ralph's place and I took the mink in and asked Ralph what he would give for the mink. He picked it up and started combing it first one way and than another and kept talking the whole time, Roger looks at me, I just shrugged, Roger told me later that he just wanted to say, "Are you going to buy it or not?" but he had been on enough deals with me to know I never rushed into anything. He finally bought it. Another time late in the season I hit a big raccoon with the car, about 40 Lbs, I had all my fur put up and did not want to mess with it so I took it out to Ralph, coon were going for $35.00 at the time. Ralph said, "I'll give you $20.00 for it." I said, "Ralph, you know that coons worth twice that." I ended up taking it home and skinning it and putting on a board. Nice coon. When the time came I went to the fur auction. Seen a bunch of guys I knew, Ralph was there also. When that big coon came up they sold it by alone because it was so big. I got $65.00 for it. Guess who bought it? Ya, Ralph.

Chapter 6

Deer

DEER! someone say Deer? Now as stated in the beginning, why would people be hungry with all the game around. One night while we were hunting coon our lights shinned on a deer, I told Vern some fresh venison sounds good, all we had with us was our scoped 22's, Vern always took along this old Remington Nylon 66, cheapest looking gun you ever laid an eye on. I would say, "when you going to get a decent gun?" He would just laugh and say, " I love this gun!" Anyway, I was driving and the deer was on his side, the deer was standing next to a telephone pole, Vern shot and the deer took off, I drove away, Vern said, "I don't know how I missed." I said, "I just told you to get a decent gun, all you hit was the telephone pole," He said " Stop! You say you heard it hit the pole, lets go back". Back we went and there laid the deer a perfect shot between the eyes. I didn't mention getting another gun again. But this got me started and I went to a 22 Mag. No doubt on a shot with it. I was taught by Dad never to waste animals. He would say " If you are man enough to kill animals, be man enough not waste them." to this day I have no problem with someone taking a deer to feed their family but when I would come across deer shot and just the hind quarters gone or just the rack gone, I'm mad.

We used to get a few too many under our belts and go out and find one of those Deer Crossing Signs, we would hide the car in the woods, sneak back and take the sign down and get into the bushes and wait. Pretty soon here come some deer, they would just mill around on the side of the road and say, "Where are the Crossing Signs?" another reason the signs were there was to show the City people where to hunt.

Now one of the main problems was noise, the 22 mag is 2000 foot-pounds at the muzzle just like a 44 mag and about the same amount of noise. We tried everything, Baby bottle nipples, balloons and tape. I told the guys one night, "That's it! I'm going to build a silencer". I knew it was 15-20 yrs in jail if you were caught with it but remember we were invincible, any way I put on cotton gloves and made 2 of them, worked beautiful. The second one was even a lot better, a friend of mine named Jack, asked how to build a silencer. I said, " You can have the one I've been using." and told him to always wear gloves when handling it. Didn't hear nothing from Jack for a while, when I seen him I said, "How did it go with the silencer? He laughed and told me he really liked it but one night they were shinning and he sees this deer by a farmer's barn, 2 in the morning so he pops it. No lights came on so he guessed he got away with it, jumped out of the car and went up to the deer and it was a big goat. Jack says, "I threw the silencer in the river." Later on we became good at hunting in the daylight hrs and I threw the second silencer in the river.

This guy named Smitty had quite a bit of land and always let us guys hunt it. It's trapping time and I'm over to his place and was going to try for some Fox and Coyote, had my Weatherby 22-250. Smitty says, "If you see a deer, knock it down for me and I'll go back and pick it up with the tractor." So I'm sneaking around and there's a deer about 150 yards on the other side of the field. Got a 4 to 16 Power scope, easy shot, dropped it and when I went back to Smitty's I told him where it was. The next time I see him he said, " Guess what, that deer you shot was pregnant. Got two for the price of one."

One time at Smitty's I tried a snare, made it out of garage cable, drilled a washer in two places, bend it 90 degrees, it would lock shut but open easy. Checked it the next day, worked like a charm, except the deer fought so hard it blew it's innards out. Got a little nervous about the snare hanging there as a guy could walk right into it and he wouldn't know how to release the lock. Oh well! I proved it would work if I ever needed it to.

Speaking of some one being hungry, One of my brothers called me and said, the guy he worked with, Ralph, got a broken leg at work we need to help him. Now Ralph had 5 kids and a wife to feed, this was the call to a deer hunt. Ralph had a barn to hang them in so we agreed on a day and 5 of us showed up at Ralph's place. Ralph had a lot of land, shouldn't be a problem. A funny thing with me if I sit on a rock pile I will always get a deer. I said, "Ralph, Where's the rock pile?" He said, "right off to the northwest in the big grass field." So away I went. Now I was carrying a 12 Ga single barrel, 30 Inch barrel and on my side was my 22 mag pistol. There was a little snow on the ground in the grass field and as I went to the rock pile I tried to not step in the snow. Got to the rock pile and was just sitting down and up walks this big doe, didn't dare bring the gun to my shoulder, just shot from the hip, down she went, but was still alive and bawling. I took the 22 mag and shot her between the eyes and walked back to Ralph's to get the front loader.

Brother and I walked back to gut the deer as we waited for the front loader. I told Roger I forgot to tag the deer. When we got to the place the deer was gone. Brother said, "Sure you weren't dreaming." I showed him the blood on the ground. There were no footprints in the snow, just then about 200 yds to the west a CO's blue light came on. I didn't even know there was a road that close. We looked thru the binoculars and there the CO has 2 guys with my deer on their car. They had done the same thing, walked into the field without stepping in the snow. But the CO was searching all over the place in the field, under their car, everywhere. I began to laugh and said, "Radio the guys not to bring the front loader". Brother said, "What's so funny," I said, "The doe was not dead so I shot her between the eyes with the 22 and the CO is looking for the 22 those guys don't have." I knew when they went to court the CO would tell the judge they also had a 22 hunting deer with it. Serves them right for stealing my deer.

We were always getting deer for needy people. One year I shot 27 for people, they were hungry and we liked to shine deer, we were kinda like Robin Hoods, but this sport has to be refined or you will spend time in jail, like before you went out, if you were going north

53

you called the sheriff and said some one was shooting deer in a field next to your barn, south of town, knowing they would call the CO and then we would know where he would be. Then there's the skinning. Learned this trick, hang the deer by the head, cut around the neck, down the belly to the tail, down each leg, pull back the neck skin and put a golfball on the meat side of the neck skin, wrap a rope around the golf ball, tie the rope to the truck and the skin will pull all the way off. Hardly any hair on the meat. And what did we do with all the unusables? Same thing I did with the rat carcasses, take them to this spot in the lake and drop them in, best bullhead fishing spot ever. I learned this from Dad, also as he told me the best way to get bullheads, get a burlap bag, (heavy feed sack) and put a small beef head in it, take it to a good spot in the lake and tie a wire to it and let it down to the bottom. Anchor the wire to shore, don't put a buoy on it as someone might see it and pull it in. Wait 2-3 days and then go at night and pull it up and there they would be, the bullheads clamped down on the burlap bag and their teeth were hung up in it. Just lift it slowly and they won't let go. If you bump it they drop off. Just lift into the boat and give it a shake. This bag lasts a long time. Great for a guy who sells fish. Selling fish when I was young was not against the law unless they were game fish. Bullheads are not a game fish. Dad told me one night when he was young that He and Grandad went fishing for bullheads. Dad up in the front of the boat, making noise and moving around a lot. Grandad said, " What are you doing?" Dad said, " I'm trying something." He was too, had and old umbrella with the cloth off, had it opened and had a leader and hook on every stave. Said it tangled up so bad he threw it in the lake.

One night Roger and I was at a party and we were feeling pretty good and I see Roger doing what looked like arguing about something with some guys, just I was getting ready to go see what was going on, Roger came over to me and said, "I just bet 3 cases of beer that you could hit a 55 gallon drum with a 12 Gauge slug at 400 yards." I said, "Did you make it easy for me?" Roger said, " How do you want to do it?" I said, "5 shots." He said, "Ok!" and went back and talked to those guys, pretty soon he came back and said, "You are going to do it" Then he said, "How you going to do it?" I said,

"Simple, I will put the barrel in a lake where I can see where the bullets hit and zero in." Roger was all smiles, and I guess those guys seen him and called off the bet.

One of the things I would do when hunting deer was I never could see the rack or count the points right. Never worried about horns anyway, I tried the antler stew once and found it a little thin, anyhow Roger, Clem and I went out after deer one time, season was in, but we were hunting with center fire rifles. I had a 243 cal bolt action, course I loaded my own ammo, had hollow points, I tried these out, had a baby food jar full of water at 75 yds, had the lid screwed on when I shot the jar disappeared, looked like puff of smoke thru the scope. When I went up to where the jar had been there was nothing, no glass, no water or no lid, it was like it had not been there. I thought, this will work, so off the 3 of us go. Got to this big field and there was a large oak tree, I told the guys I was going to stand under this tree, pick me up on your way out. About the time they got to the other end of the field here comes a buck, laid the cross hairs on the shoulder and touched her off, the deer run off. Roger told me later that while he and Clem were at the other end of the field, Clem said "Did Bob shoot?" Roger broke open his gun and looked at me thru the scope, He said, "No he's just standing under the tree." When they got back to me they said, "Did you shoot?" I said, "I took a shot at a spike, said he was out in the field," when we went and looked there lays the nicest 8 point you ever seen. We took the deer to Clem's and hung it up to gut it and skin it out. When we got the hide off, what a mess, the 243 had bloodied the meat so bad it was no good to eat. I'd seen deer that were hit by a car and not in that bad a shape. Sold the 243 the next day.

Next gun was a Weatherby 22-250, now there's a barnburner. Loaded up my own stuff of course, (2800 FPS) had Roger come out to my house, had an open 40 acres out behind the house, got a 4 ft square piece of foam like they insulate with, set it out there 100 yards. Roger and I took turns standing by the foam and call the shots, you would hear the "POP" as the bullet went through the foam and then hear the boom from the gun, worked perfect for Fox, Coyote and Deer. Later after I got the hang of the gun, called Roger out to the house, asked him if was ready for a deer, said, "Sure." He brought a friend with him, Smith, we gave Smith a set of binoculars and left him at the house. Roger, Edward and my self started across the 40, we could see deer standing around, dropped down, handed Roger the 22-250, he said, "What do you want me to do with that thing?" First deer he shot in the heart, went down like it was pole axed, Roger said, "That baby is more than I thought it was," I said, "See that button buck? Take a head shot." He did and took off the top of the buck's head. Edward picked up the big doe he shot first and I picked up the buck. We threw them on our shoulders and carried them back to the house, Smith's eyes were about the size of dinner plates, he had watched the whole going's on thru the binoculars, He said "Man! It was like watching a hunting movie"

I have to stop on Deer here a minute and tell you a funny on Smith. We went over to Union City to the river fishing for sucker. Smith had an air rifle with him and started shooting birds, he got quite a ways away, I seen this small sucker laying in the water, dead for quite a while, pulled Smiths line in and hooked the sucker on and threw his line back in the river. When Smith got back close to us we hollered that he had a bite, he comes running back, grabbed his rod and started fighting the dead sucker. When he finally got it in he saw what we had done. Roger looks at the sucker and said, "Smith you are going to have to get your fish in quicker, they are spoiling on the way in."

Roger called me one time and said Lee had a deer down and was getting guys around to go and find it. I took my truck and met the guys at Randy's house. There must have been 4 or 5 of us, Roger, Lee, Clem, Dave, Scott, (Rogers son) and myself. Lee took us back to where he had shot it and we started tracking it thru the brush, it crossed the river at a shallow spot and so did we. Then it went into an open field, we still couldn't see it, we followed the tracks, blood trail had stopped, gut shot, about a mile or better was a small stand of woods and it was headed towards it. Sure enough there it was dead in this small woods. Now we had gone better than a 2 miles and it was starting to get dark, so I said I would go get my truck and drive around, Scott said, " Uncle Bob can I go with you?" I said. "Sure!" and we started back, about the time we were nearing the creek I realized that we could not go back through the woods and brush, and had to cross the creek here we would have to wade through a deep spot, I said to Scott, "Can you do this?" he said he thought he could, we get to the creek, now I knew where you could and could not wade in this creek as I had trapped it many years. We came to the spot and I said, "Here we go," in case it had not dawned on you this is late November and cold, we did not have hip boots though, just low hunting boots, the first couple of steps were a shock, I said, "You Ok, Scott," he said he was, it was up to our waist before getting to the other side. We were glad to get out of the water. I knew Scott knew he was all right as long as he was with me, that's what Uncles do. Many years later I married Scott and his wife, before the service I related this story to the people at his wedding.

Roger had another Son, funniest kid I ever saw. Name was Brent, and he was smart. Believed he could do anything adults could do. Roger told me one time Brent said he could drive Rogers car, I guess he was about 6-8 years old at the time. He kept at Roger with, " You know I can drive the car, you just don't want me to." Roger heard it day after day, one day he said, "That's it, get out there, you are going to drive the car!" Out they go Roger on the passenger side, Brent behind the wheel, Roger gave him the keys and said, " There you go, DRIVE!" course Brent had no idea how to even start the car and told Roger that he had done something so the car wouldn't start. Roger started the car, it was a standard shift, and Brent tried to shift it without the clutch and killed the engine. Told Roger again he had fixed it so he could not drive it, Roger said, "Get out," and got in the drivers side and backed the car up and drove it back to where it was. Said, "There see it goes all right you just don't know what you are doing and I don't want to hear anymore about you driving!" Years later Roger and Brent were in my truck and pulled into my yard and where I parked was right toward the house, and when I pulled in I started pumping the clutch and yelling the brakes went out, Brent turned white. Roger and I laughed at him.

I will say that Brent was not afraid of much. One day I stopped out to Rogers house, I was riding the big Chopper, pulled into the yard and Roger, Debbie and Brent came out to see the bike. Brent says, "Uncle Bob will you take me for a ride?" I looked at Roger and he just shrugged his shoulders, Debbie stood there shaking her head no. I said, " Its up to your folks." Roger said, "Go ahead." I made him put on the other helmet and away we went. Now I took it as easy as I could, which never was very easy, went about 5 miles and we came back. Brent said something like that's really neat! I don't think Debbie was ever so glad to see someone get off a bike.

There was this guy I heard about, he had some folks over for dinner. They set down to eat and one woman said, "What kind of meat is this?" the guy says, "It's venison." She says, "How could you stand to shoot it?" he said, "Come here a minute." And he took her to his freezer said, "See this, it's venison and when I shot it he never knew what hit him, dead on his feet. Now this, on the other hand, is veal (calf) they hung it upside down by it's back feet and then it rolled along til it came to this one worker who swung at its head with a big hammer, then it when on down the line and they started skinning it no matter if it was dead, dying or alive. And you think hunting is bad?"

Chapter 7

The Kids

My Son Edward was always letting his mouth get him in trouble. Now my brother Roger was at the house and in comes Edward and said, "Uncle Roger there are some geese in the back of the field. If you shoot one with the 22-250 I'll walk back and get it." Now I did not mention Roger's shooting, he was a good shot and lucky, a combination that's hard to beat. He says, "Lets take a look, about 400 yards I would guess." I handed him the gun and he rested on the porch rail and touched it off. Down went a goose. Roger says," There you go." Oh! Did I mention there was waist deep snow in the field? When Edward got back he was pooped and said, "I'm going to take a rest." I said, " Don't you have a goose to clean before you rest?" Always something like that going on.

I'll never forget when Edward had his 16th birthday, course all his friends were there, a couple of my brothers. Edward made an announcement that since he was 16 now he would not have to worry about spankings at his birthday anymore. I'm thinking: Don't say that! Too late! The guys grabbed him put him on the ground and here comes his Mother with a canoe paddle.

Speaking of Edward, he had a 12 gauge shot gun he hunted deer with and I would load up shells for him to deer hunt with, not slugs, each shell had two 69 cal balls, when you shot these the two balls were about 2 inches apart at 60 yards, So here he goes opening day, across the road to the woods, He wakes me up about 7:30, just getting light, he says, " I got two deer!" I said, "What are you talking about?" so he goes into this story, said, "I see a fork horn buck, takes a shot and away he goes, I sneak around and there he is, took another shot and down he goes, I wait a little bit and walk over and there lays two fork horn bucks." I says, "If you would wait until it got light, oh well good shooting!" My other Son Robert, skinny as a rail, He had to stand twice in the same spot to cast a shadow. I bought him and Edward 20 gauge shot guns, they wanted 12 gauge shot guns. Had two girls also, one day Robert wanted to shoot my 12 gauge 30 inch barrel shotgun, the kids called it the 'the little gun.' I knew it would send him backwards. He whined to his Mother that I would not let him shoot the 12. I finally said, " Come Here!" loaded the 12 and said, "There you go". He touched off the 12 and away he went backwards, the gun hung in the air like the roadrunner then fell to ground. He got up and dusted himself off and I heard the girls teasing him later "want to shoot the little gun?"

After I got the boys their shotguns I told them one day," Lets go for a walk. Grab a couple shells and said, "load up, keep the guns pointed up." away we go, walked a ways and came to a fence, I said, "Boys here how you do this, if I was not with you, you unload the guns, close them up, one of you hold the guns and the other go over the fence, then hand the guns over and the second guy go over the fence then reload. But I said, "As long as I am with you just unload and hand me the guns then climb over the fence." they did, I handed over each gun, and they are waving them around, I said, "Hey be careful you will shoot each other!" they both said, " The guns are empty!" I said, "Point them up and fire them," they did and you should have seen their faces when the guns went off. Sneaky Pete here loaded them while they were going over the fence. I said, "Treat a gun like it is always loaded." I know they never forgot that lesson.

I started the boys out with single shot 20 gauge shotguns, but they had to have pumps, 12 Gauge of course, Like I said before I loaded the boys shells with 69 cal muzzle loader balls, Robert went out the first time with his pump and got a deer, well riddle the deer was more like it, I said, "How many times did you shoot?" he says,

"It wouldn't go down so I just kept shooting till the gun was empty!" 5 rounds, and he hit it every time.

I showed Robert how to trap and one time he caught a mink, these things really spray a stink when they are caught in a trap, this one did and he drove back home holding the mink outside the car window as he drove back home. The CO stopped him and ask him what he was doing, he told him the mink had sprayed and he didn't want the stink in his car.

Lee and I went bear hunting in the Upper Peninsula, and we took Robert and Edward with us. We went to a place called Grand Maris, it was right on the edge of Lake Superior. Was a nice warm day as we drove along the road by the edge of the lake, of course the bays wanted to go swimming, I said, "You can go but don't stay in very long." Lee and I both were smiling. The boys got their trunks on and went running into the lake. When they hit the water they yelled and I think they both froze in the air, they got wet then came running back to the truck. For those of you who don't know either, the water is usually about 38 degrees or less.

I had a small gun shop in the basement. Roger fixed the modern guns and I fixed the muzzleloaders. Now it was a well-known fact that I had a 357 Mag revolver and would use it if I had to. One day Edward was standing in the back door talking on the phone and shooting a 22 cal rifle into the field. Some how he hit a rock or something and the bullet came back and hit him in the fleshy part of the stomach, he calls 911 and said he was shot, said he was at Bob's house, they haul him to hospital, he was fine, maybe a little scared. But the next day everybody that I knew said, " I thought you would be jail, I heard on the scanner you shot some on at your house."

Another thing Edward did, I got them both Muzzle Loaders and one time Edward came in the house with his gun and said, "It won't fire." I checked it and then gave him a real hot percussion cap that would fire through anything. He put the cap on while in the house, I yelled, " Don't put the cap on in the house!" too late, he shot right through the living room ceiling. You should have seen the look on his face, and then it dawned on him, Mother! Quick as wink he gets some putty and puts on the hole in the ceiling. Looked pretty good. I said, "Don't forget the roof, it starts leaking in your Mother's living room and Katy bar the door!" So he climbed up the roof and fixed it. He said, "Don't tell Mom." But I did, we laughed about it and I said, "It was a mistake and he learned his lesson with the worry." Far as you know she never said anything to him. She did say one time, "What's that funny colored spot on my ceiling?"

I remember one time Edward was with me in the pickup truck and as we crossed the bridge at the Hodunk Dam we looked just in time to see a kid fall into the spillway, the Father just stood there screaming, I told Edward, "Get him", Edward threw his billfold on the truck seat and was gone in a flash, dove into the water and got the kid, by then I was down there and helped Edward get the kid out of the water. The poor Father could not swim a lick. I was so glad all my kids knew how to swim.

When I hear the truck mentioned I think of the time we were over on a dirt road cutting firewood. The boys always worked hard and so I was never against a little fun. So on the way back I tied a rope to the back of the truck and dragged Robert and Edward behind truck on the snow covered road. They had a ball, downside was they had on their new snowsuits Momma had bought for them and wherever there was a bare spot in the road the gravel done its work on their clothes. But they knew Dad would ease the situation somehow, I always hoped I was as supportive as I was strict.

I built Muzzle Loading Rifles and once a friend of Edward's was at the house and said to me, " Will you make me a gun?" I said, "POOF you are a Gun!" Never did hear the end of that one. The boys were always asking him if he wanted to be a gun. The boys came home after school one time and they had seen a bunch of deer in a field while on the bus going to school, when they got home they said, "We seen a bunch of deer on the bus today!" I said, "Oh ya, where were they going?"

One thing I used to do is when the kids were older and attracted to the opposite sex, I used to help them out, Edward came home with a girl and I said, "That's not the girl you spent the night with here last night." Or when some boy would call and ask if Lori was there, I would say, " Yes" and hang up. Lori would say, "Who was that?" I would say, "Just some boy calling to see if you here." She would say, "Daaaaaaaaaad!" Just trying to help.

Then there's when Edward and Robert decide to try and make venison jerky, do they consult their Dad or Mother? Nooooooo. They cut the venison cross grain put it in the oven and dried it, they did have the right ingredients, but when they took it out their jerky was shredded wheat. But to hear them tell it, it was the best anybody ever had. Unnhunnn.

Another time I had been having trouble with someone breaking up my mail box, so I was watching and one night I seen this car stop by my mail box, only had his parking lights on. I slips out the back door with the 30-30 rifle and walks up to the drivers side, it was summer and he had his window down, I sticks the 30-30 next to his head and says, " Hope you aren't thinking who hitting my mail box." he turns around and he is looking down the barrel of the rifle, he turned white, "No he says your wife is watching my youngster and I couldn't find the drive." I said, "OK I have had a lot of trouble with someone breaking my mailbox, come on in".

Neighbor had a big dog and it would come down to our house and try to get our cat, it was a ¼ mile to the neighbor's house. One time I was home alone and I hear the cat scream and I see the neighbor's dog had the cat up a tree. I got the 58-caliber Muzzleloader and the dog seen me with it and took off running down the road. It was a blacktop, I made a perfect shot right in the dog's chest, and he went rolling down the road. I went back in the house and pretty soon here they come and got their dog, never said a word to me, there was a big puddle of blood in the road and it started to snow and the blood seeped through the snow and stood out like a sore thumb. Lois and the kids came home and when they came into the house they told me there was a big puddle of blood in the road, I said, "Ya, the neighbors dog got hit." Never said what hit him, Lois knew. I always hated to have to kill a dog because the owners were really the ones at fault. But because things are like they are, I always done the three S,s. Shoot, Shovel and Shutup!

Then there's the time I lived up north, there is a river called the Flat, now I always trapped lakes, high yield, but the lakes up north are mostly sand bottom with no feed for the muskrats. I thought I may as well give the river a shot, Why this drive to trap? You have to try it to know, always that next trap and what's in it. The river was wide and shallow enough to wade in most places with hip boots. Traps in a pack on my back. I have some Indian in me and try never to leave a track or be seen. So I would wade the river at night. This one night I was checking traps, always carried a single barrel shotgun, if you got a big coon you take the barrel off and use it as a club. I always heard something walking along the bank, bear, wolf, oh well, cross that bridge when I get to it. Anyway I went to the shore line where I had a trap, rat was caught by the head and drowned. Now when a trap jaws are not closed all the way, it's hard to open, so I squat down, shotgun trapped between my legs and stomach, and started to take the rat out of the trap, I did not know, setting right over my head was a Owl. Just as I am trying to get the trap open the Owl lets out a screech that would wake the dead. Now I'm all nerved up with whatever was walking along the bank, I'm 14 miles from town. When that Owl let out I sware the hair on the back of my neck almost knocked my hat off.

When I first seen the Flat river, I knew it was full of big fish, as I have stated before, Dad and I used to catch pike minnows for the bait shop and would see big bass and pike take minnows. So being a guy who likes a little challenge I started fishing the Flat with minnows on a fly rod, soon found out there were some bigger pike than I thought. I lived in Greenville and could walk down to the Flat river. Reminded me of the time Bill and I were fishing for pike, he hooked this beauty, gets it beside the boat and his line snapped, I said " too bad that was an nice 16 & ¾ lb pike" Bill says how did you know what it weighed?" I said, "cause he had scales on him." After I moved back to Coldwater the Flat River was on my mind. I called Roger and said how about a float trip down the Flat river ? He was all for it, now the Flat river run thru Greenville, thru Belding and ended at Lowell, and was a three day trip by canoe, we made several of these trips and was never disappointed fishing. I always was in the rear of the canoe the whole trip as I trapped from a canoe so I could handle it real well. This one trip Roger said, "Why don't you let me handle the canoe and you just do some fishing?" Felt really different in the front, but the front guy got the first shot at the good spots. Now I started with a fly rod and now fished for bass and pike with a ultra light spinning rod with 4 Lb test line. Used rapala's most of the time as they acted like injured minnows, I was having a grand time, we came around this bend and there was a downed tree, I cast up as close as I dare and a nice bass grabbed the rapala, make a few good runs and stopped, I told Roger, He's hung up on a limb of the downed tree, not so, the bass was in the middle of the river caught on something, about 3 foot of water, we got up next to where the bass was and there was the biggest pike I have ever seen with my bass in his mouth cross ways, Looked to be 6-8 foot long. Roger said "how do you want to play this one?" I said" just poke him with the paddle", he did and the pike spit out the bass and away he went. It was about a 5 lb bass, the next time we landed to eat I took the bass and put him on the cooler and snapped a picture, now as I said I knew photography so after the picture was developed, I measured the cooler, then transferred the measurement and with the pikes teeth marks in the bass figured the width. That pikes mouth was 7 ½ in wide! We made several trips down the Flat, I even took Dad once. He was a level wind casting reel guy and I had made some large casting plugs and of course Dad was in the front, He said "See that boulder? There's a nice bass behind it", was too, about a 6 lb smallmouth, I have the picture of Dad with the fish.

One time while I was still at home, we lived way out in the sticks. I had traps back in a pond about half mile from the house, one time as I was coming back from the woods I walked past a big tree full of bees. Told Dad about it and he had me take him to it, He said "Oh Boy, this tree is full of honey bees and a lot of honey, we will be back when the weather is really cold." When it got zero back we went, had washtubs, double boilers, and buckets. Now Dad was known to have a beer or ten now and then. He had been drinking that afternoon with the neighbor guy he run around with. Here was the next lesson for me. Take a foot square piece of burlap, sprinkle sulfur in it, roll it up and light it afire and put it inside the tree, the fire will go out and smolting burlap will give off a ton of sulfur smoke, the sulfur will kill most of the bees, those that are left will die in midair when they fly into the cold. Now this tree is about 3 ½ ft thru with a big split running up about 6 ft, put the sulfur in waited a bit, then took the crosscut saw and cut crossways in the trunk of the tree, top and bottom, the two swung open like opening the doors of a cupboard. There hung the Honey, 6 ft sheets 2 ft wide. Course Dad in the state he was in had to taste the honey. He licked off the knife there was a live bee in it and Dad got stung in the tongue, here we are ½ mile from home, midnight, Dad with a stinger in his tongue, his friend trying to pull out the stinger, us boys standing there laughing We had Honey for a long time, Mom used it to bake with too. But now I knew another treasure of the land.

A funny happened to Dad. He was hunting up north with some guys and they were camped by a river, Dad has a hay hook with him, he used it to hang deer in the tree, had a rope and would pull them up in tree then tie it off and it was ready for the next deer. Anyway, they were all drinking and Dad told the guys he had better put out his fish line. He took the hay hook, rope and good size piece of deer meat and put it on the hay hook and tied the end to a tree and threw the hook out into the river. He done this just to get a laugh, they drank awhile more and then went to bed. The next morning he remembered the hay hook and went down to the river to get it, when he got down to the river there was the rope or what was left of it, something had grabbed the deer meat, hook and took off with it and broke the rope. Sobering Huh!

Years later Vern and I were hunting and I found a bee tree. The way you find a bee tree is to take a baby food jar and put a little white flour in the bottom, you see a honey bee on a small flower you catch him in the jar and with the lid on you shake the jar, this gets flour on the bee, you then let her go (all worker honey bees are female) and you watch the direction its flying, take a reading on your compass and keep that heading and walk straight and you will come to the hive. That old line, making a beeline is true. I told Vern we were in for a treat; he thought I was rambling again One night when the weather turned bitter we loaded up. In the trunk, washtub, and buckets for the honey, crosscut, why a crosscut instead of a chainsaw, we didn't know who owned the land and didn't want to make noise, course Vern had his Reminton 66, I had my 22 pistol, Large spot light, had pulled traps, had them in the trunk, away we went to the bee tree. Just before we got there the sheriff stopped us, lucky Vern for once had put his gun in the case and they didn't see my pistol, when they weren't looking I hid it. Now they were trying to figure out what we were doing. We just told them we were coming from pulling traps as the temp was dropping and were freezing the lakes and then we were going to cut a little fire wood. They couldn't figure out what to do so they called the CO out and he too wondered what we were doing, course they didn't know nothing about bee trees, but they knew who Vern and I were and it had to be no good. I know they thought we were shooting deer and cutting them up and putting the meat in the tub and buckets. However they did not have anything on us, so they let us go. They later passed a law you could not have a spotlight and gun in the same car. But the bee tree had to wait until later, as we did not know who owned the land and did not want to get arrested for trespassing and we learned not to carry all the stuff at once. When we did go back and get the tree, we took Roger with us and when we cut open the tree Roger says there's what I want. It was about 5 pounds of blood red honey, it was all from a Cherry tree. Vern was living with me at the time and we took a washtub of honey home. Lori some how fell backwards into the tub and started kicking and yelling.

I bought a revolver, Hi-Standard 9 shot, made a low hung holster for it but could not get the hang of the fast draw, went and seen a movie, it was a western, in a short film they showed the Indian who taught Matt Dillon, on TV, how to fast draw. I watched as they described the process and took in every move. I could not wait to get home and try it. It worked better than they described. Now I had to learn how to hit targets on the fast draw. Vern and his Wife Betty lived with us, and I was telling him I had to learn to shoot. He said, "Come on!" And away we went. Got out in the woods and there was a tree, it was leaning pretty bad, we got on the opposite side the tree was leaning. Vern said, "hold your gun with your index finger straight across the cylinder, and point the gun a few times, then put your finger back on the trigger and remember how you pointed it." I did and I hit pretty good, shot a few rounds, got a little better, Vern said, "put your gun in the holster and pretend to shoot by pointing your index finger." I did, pretty soon he threw a tin can and hollered, "SHOOT THE CAN!" Startled me, I fast drew the gun and shot it 9 times and walked it right up the leaning tree, Vern says, "I guess you are ready. I guess I was. After that when Vern would come home at night after being somewhere he would open the door and Yell "FRIEND! FRIEND! It runs along a while and I keep practicing and it became second nature, the gun was out, in my hand and cocked faster than I could think. Not good. One night they had a wake for a girl we all knew. It was at her house where her parents lived. My Wife Lois, Vern and I drove over there and left Lois at the wake. Vern and I went to the bar and had a few, few too many as usual. We went back to pick up Lois, I went up to the door and they lead me into where the girl lay, now here's the deal. She had been in a car wreck, convertible, and had slid down the road on her face. What a mess. When I saw her, being a little out it, I got really mad, thinking why were they showing her, couldn't the funeral people done a better job on her. So we go home. Now I'm stewing, and the best thing to do is leave me alone. I strapped on the gun. Vern by this time had went to bed upstairs. I was in the front room with the lights out, street lights were the only light I had, you could see from the front room thru the dinning room, thru our bedroom to the bathroom. Lois turned on the light in the bathroom and I said, "turn out that light!" she said go to iiii." I fast drew the gun and shot the light out right over her head. That my friend was the last of the fast draw. I threw the holster away and only used the pistol when I went trapping.

This was the pistol I would take to this one tree every year and shoot the raccoons in that tree, it had a big hollow trunk and I usually got between 7 to 10 coons out of it. Vern went with me one time and wanted to shoot the coons, I said just shoot them in the head, I don't want coon with holes in the body as the fur would not be worth as much. So up he goes and I was at the base of the tree with a big club as a coon or two would run out. Now this is a nine shot revolver and I gave Vern some extra shells. He starts shooting, stops reloads and starts shooting again. A huge coon, about 35 pounds runs right to me, I got that one, here comes another, got that one, Vern stops shooting and starts reloading, that 18 coon not counting the 2 I have. And he starts shooting again, I said, "Hey don't fill them with holes!" Vern said, "every time I shoot, another looks at me. He shot 23 in the tree and there were the 2, I had got. That's 25 coons, at $ 25.00 each. We made more then one trip carrying them to the truck.

Another time Roger and Deb were at our house and I was messing around with my squirrel rifle, they were sitting at the table and Lois was at the sink in the kitchen, I had put a very small charge in the rifle then a patch, it was a 32 cal Flint Lock. I aimed quite a ways away from Lois and fired the gun, Debbie screamed and the patch that was in the gun made a half circle and hit Lois in the chest and stuck to her sweatshirt. She said, "Will you quit messing around!" and a regular person would have passed out.

I wandered off the kids a way's but like stated in the front of the book when I think of how one story leads to another. I'll have more on the kids later.

Chapter 8

My Day in Court

I had butted heads with the law before and started to put on a little better appearance, maybe I could get away with things better. Trapping is like anything, the more you do, the better you get and the more you learn. It was coming to a time when kids were seeing Davy Crockett and how he lived off the land, coonskin cap and such. How do you get a coonskin cap, trap the coon. So there was an interest in trapping, my thoughts were kids went to their Dad, and said, " I want to trap, will you help me?" So Dad would give them $ 20.00 and say buy the traps, he did not have the time or knowledge to teach them. As I said before no one can teach themselves to trap, the trial and error will kill the interest. This is not set in stone; there are trappers that have taught themselves. So here they come, see animals in my traps, none in theirs. Kids of this age are not taught to respect other's property, my Dad would have killed me if I got into someone's traps. So here it is legal trapping season, I set out my 300 traps, seen a couple of kids messing around the lake. About the 3rd day I see some of traps are moved and the fur gone. Dad always taught me to look for what's out of place to see what's going on. My trick was to set my traps with the springs facing say north, if someone stole fur and set the trap back I knew it. After I got home I called the CO and told him some kids were messing with my traps. Looking back now he probably thought I was telling him this so if I set a trap in the wrong place I could blame the kids. In

Michigan is against the law to set a trap within 6 ft of a house hole or home of animals. The next day here's the CO with a ticket for my trap too close to a house. So happen this year I had Corb trapping with me, he could not remember where the traps were, so I cut 12 ft trap stakes and put small red flags on them, helped the kids right out, normally I would have real low stakes. I could have just paid the ticket but would not for 2 reasons. One, I would have to pay for stuff they knew I done before and could not catch me and the most important was my reputation. So I went to see a lawyer I knew, Ben, about like me, worked out well, the reason I knew Ben was I loved photography, messed with it a lot while I was in the service. After I was discharged I had the GI Bill put me thru the New York Institute of Photography. And I shot pictures at 3 racetracks. Fri, Sat and Sun, and wanted a lawyer to protect me if someone I took pictures of tried to sue me. Made about $ 500.00 a weekend. And the best part was big brother got no taxes from it. I always hated a 9 to 5 job. Anyway, I told him the situation and he said it will cost you $ 300.00 for me to defend you and I won't be able to help anyway. He said, " I don't know nothing about trapping. However here is the good news, neither does the prosecutor. Here's what you do, request a jury trial in district court and tell them what you told me, your best chance." Now like every young guy I always dreamed of the Perry Mason role and here it was. So I told the Judge I wanted a jury trail in district court, he said OK and set a date, when the day came I was as pumped as I had ever been. Not knowing they were not allowed to use your past against you, in Corb and I went. Judge said where is your lawyer, I said, "I was going to defend myself" Judge said, "We'll help you," told me to call my first witness, I called Corb to the stand, they swore him in, Judge said go ahead. I reminded Corb that a trap with my nametag was found set on a muskrat house, and then I asked him, "Would you set a trap on a muskrat house? " He said, "No" I then asked him to explain why, He said, "there are from 10 to 15 muskrats in a house, if you put a trap on the house and the muskrat in a trap would tear the house down fighting the trap, then you would lose the remaining muskrats" and I said one final question, "How would you set an illegal trap?" He said, "The trap stake that holds the trap would have to be under water out of sight and you would have to be sure the animal would drown and also be out of sight, and that is not easy," I had set the TRAP and any further questions would cloud the jurors minds as they had heard about all they could soak in about trapping. So I said, "That's all the questions I have of this witness." Judge said to the Prosecutor, "Your witness," He said, " I have no questions of this witness." just like Ben had said. Then the Judge ask if I had any other witness. I said, "I would like to ask the CO a couple questions." Now bear in mind that I seen my trap laying on the evidence table. They swore him in. Judge said to me, "Go ahead," I said, "Did I call you the day you found my trap and give me a ticket and tell you someone, I thought was kids were messing with my traps?" He said, "You did." I said, "How many traps do I have out there?" he said, " A lot of them." I turned to the jury and said, "For the record I have 299 traps set. No 300 is laying on the evidence desk." Then I sprung the TRAP; I asked the CO how he found the trap. He said, "It was staked on a 12 Ft stake with a small red flag on it." Bang! The TRAP slammed shut, I turned to the jury and said, " Does it look like I'm trying to hide something here?' the Judge said, "You can't say that to the jury!" too late the TRAP had closed. I said, "I have no more questions." the Judge said to the Prosecutor, "Your witness," I took in a breath, here it comes he's going to bring up all my past. But instead he said, "I have no questions" I could have fell over. They were not allowed to bring up past offences I found out later. The Judge told the jury to forget what I said to them. But I knew it was like saying don't think of sunshine. Out they went and came right back in, the Judge asked if they had a verdict, they did. Judge ask, "What is your verdict?" the foreman said, "Not guilty!" then the judge instructed the CO to return my trap, and then the Judge called me to his bench and in a low voice said, " Be careful, you live way to close to the line!" I looked at the CO I knew I made a mistake, him having to give that trap back to me in front of all those people was like me kicking him between the legs. I was right, he really bird dogged me for the next few years, but I guess that's what it's all about, the rush of common man beating the system. And I had a run in with this judge years later.

Chapter 9

Harold

Not all the laughs in my life have been of my doing. We were to go Deer hunting opening days to a town about 30 miles away. There was Lee, Harold and myself. He was my brother's brother-in-law, none of us claimed him, I have to describe Harold, if I can. Clumsiest person I ever knew. He got this new job were he made these small metal parts and proudly bought one to show my Mother. She was eating a bowl of soup as he was showing it to her he dropped it into her soup, another time Roger was sitting at the table drinking a cup of coffee. Harold tried to walk by him and bumped Rogers arm slopping the coffee. Harold didn't say I'm sorry, he said, "I bet you are mad at me." Roger just picked up the cup and dumped the rest on the table and got up and left. Harold had to clean his shotgun, didn't have a gun cleaning kit so he put a handkerchief on a rod and tried to shove it thru the barrel, it got stuck in the barrel, so what's he do, puts a shell in the gun and fired it, the end of the barrel looked like a banana peel. Roger was closer to Harold than the rest of us as Harold was Roger's age, Roger told me of the time he and Harold went deer hunting. Harold had his gloves on and put his gloved finger thru his coffee cup handle, then here comes a deer, here's Harold shaking his hand to get the cup off so he could shoot, scared the deer away. Roger told him, "I seen some deer in that pasture down the road, lets stalk them," they about 30 yards apart. Roger told me he could see the deer ahead and Harold was heading straight for them. Harold got to where he could peek over the edge of hill and sees them. He looked at Roger and stood up and shouted, " There they are!" Roger said, "Come on Harold, let's go home."

Now here Lee and I are taking Harold hunting, we got there and found a nice spot for Harold to sit and told him to stay there and he would get a shot at a deer, stay there no matter what. We will come and get you. We walked about 30 yards away and Harold shoots, it was not even light yet. We went back and ask him what he shot, he said, "Nothing, I was just checking to make sure the gun still would fire." Uh HUH! We told him be quiet and watch for deer, Lee and I sat down about 30 yards apart and waited. At daylight here come a guy sneaking along the fencerow. I thought it was Harold by the getup, white hankie sticking out of his back pocket like a deer's tail. Branches stuck in his hat, looked just like a deer's rack, he was hunched over walking. I looked over at Lee he just shook his head. There are 2 Harolds in this world. We were later to find there is more than that. We did not see any deer, went and got Harold and went to the car. When we got to the car we looked into this field and there were deer hunters on one side and the other side walking toward each other, guns at the ready, a guy stepped out onto his porch with his coffee in his hand, seen those guys and run back into his house. We didn't hang around; we had enough for one day.

Now I did take Harold hunting once myself, my brothers and myself were master of camouflage. I put Harold in a good spot and told him to stay there until I come and got him. Off I went into a dried swamp, full camouflage, I couldn't even see me. Sit there awhile, and here comes Harold straight at me, I looked to see what I had sticking out, nothing. Harold came right to me and said, "I'm cold and want to go home " I said, "How did you see me?" he said, "You are sitting right out in the open!" Guess what? With everything else, Harold is colorblind. I looked like a black silhouette to him. I said, "OK" lets go home."

Once a few years earlier, Roger, Harold and I went squirrel hunting. Didn't see much as we wandered around. Came to a tree with a bunch of squirrel nests in it. Harold says, "How do you get the squirrels out of those nests?" We told him that we usually just shoot the nest and they come out or drop out dead. Harold says, " I will climb up and shake the nest, you guys be ready." So up he goes, shakes the nest and out runs 3 squirrel's, right down Harold's arms and legs. He starts yelling, " Shoot! Shoot! Well neither Roger or I ever bagged a Harold, although we had in fact been ready to shoot him a few times, but not today. Roger says," Come on down Harold, the squirrels are gone."

Speaking of camouflage, Roger and I went to these woods to hunt and when we get there here is his Father in law's car, Fran was his name. he was back there hunting where were going, here we are sneaking thought the woods and we seen Fran setting by a tree, we went right up by him and he never saw us. We went away quietly and then when we were thru hunting we stopped over to Fran's house and told him how many squirrels he got and told him some other details, he could not believe we were that close to him without him knowing it.

Chapter 10

Lee

Lee, my Brother, was a rush to trap with. I set him up one end of the chain of lakes I trapped, didn't know George was down stealing traps. Let me tell you about George and how I met George. In my early years I run around with Rich, quite a drinker, it killed him later in life. Rich knew this guy who owned all this land with creek on it running right into the lakes I trapped, we had to walk the creek to trap it, perfect place to trap early. So here we are setting out traps and having a drink or two, when we spots this guy coming down our trap line, looking at our traps, we confronted him, told him he was trespassing as we had the sole permission to trap there. We were about 20 yrs old and this guy is 16, we were also drinking. We told him not to be here again, he levels a 22 rifle at us and says he will go where he wants. Rich turned real friendly to George, started talking real smooth to him, all the time walking up to him, I knew what was coming. Rich was a boxer aboard ship in the Navy. His fists were like a rattlesnakes strike, sure enough he nailed George, down he went. Rich grabbed his gun and took the shells out and sent him on his way. George later called the law and had Rich arrested for hitting a minor. The fact that George had a loaded gun pointed at us meant nothing to law. We all agreed to drop charges and it was over, so I thought, for years then I run George out my trapping area. So we are back to Lee trapping and I had no idea George was still around. I told Lee about him several times, but Lee had never laid eyes on him. Then one evening, after running trap lines, we came into the fur shed to skin and stretch rats. Lee said, "I run into George today, was out in his boat checking our traps," I asked what happened. Now bare in mind Lee carried a single barrel 12 ga. Lee said, "I said to George, "come here!" George got his boat next to Lee's. Lee said, "Would you be George?" he said, "Yes," Lee said, "I am Bob's brother and you are in his trapping area again. Tell you what George, you better get to shore the way your boat is leaking." George said, "My boats not leaking," Lee said, "Yes it is, right there," and shot a big hole in the bottom of George's boat with the 12 gauge, away went George. Didn't see him for years after that.

Lee done one, one time, he wanted to trap Fox and coyotes, asked me what do you use for bait? I said, "I like to find a dead cat in the road and take it home and chop it up, put it in quart jars, about 3/4s full put the lid on loose and bury it in the ground for a month." So now Lee's looking for dead cats. I guess he didn't find any, he seen an ad, someone had kittens to give away. He went there and took them all, walked out to truck and one by one knocked them in the head. Now he has bait.

Lee and I were about as close as any, but he sure done some funny stuff. One day he calls me and said, " I shot a deer 11 times today," I said, "What were you using a Tommy gun?" No, No, he says, "I had an arrow with a sack of powder on it and shot the deer 11 times, every time I shot it would leave white mark on it, I got tired and left." You guys that say you only get one shot try this, one time. Lee said, "I'm going to shoot a deer," I said, "Big deal we shoot deer all the time." No he says, " I'm going to shoot one with shot gun, one with a rifle, one with a muzzle loader, one with a long bow, one with a compound, one with a tomahawk, one with a spear and one with a knife." He did too!

One winter Lee and I went out to Messenger Lake in a station wagon to see how thick the ice was. I mean we went out, drove the station wagon across the ice, pulled up beside a guy fishing who said, "You better get that car off the Lake!" we looked over and the water was running up out of his fish hole, away we go, didn't know about the wave that is in front of a vehicle when it traveling across the ice, if you catch up to the wave you will go thru. Bit the bullet again.

I bought chickens for my kids to tend to while they were growing up. They were Rhode Island Reds and Plymouth Rock with the barred feathers. Lee said," If you have any chickens you don't want, I would like some," Lee ties some of the finest flies in the world and I guess he wanted the feathers to tie with. One day I decided to give him a half dozen, put them in a burlap bag and went to his house and said, "You still want some chickens? He said, "Yes," and I dumped them out on the floor of his house and said, "There you go!" There they went also.

Lee has a sign in his woodworking shop, "I started with nothing and still have most of it left" He and I cut from the same piece of cloth, we both have so much stuff we don't know what all we do have.

Lee told me one time that his bathroom caught on fire, but he got it out before it got to the house.

He was putting broadheads on his arrows and he slipped and stuck the broadhead through his hand, away he goes to the hospital and into the emergency room. He told me the doctor was being Oh, so careful. He asked Lee how he done this, Lee said, "I was cleaning my bow and it went off," Lee said the doctor was not so gentle after that remark.

Lee told me one time he wanted to build a Muzzle Loading Rifle. I said, "OK, lets do it." I helped him and he built a 45 caliber, 42-inch barrel long rifle. We took it out and I showed him how to load and shoot it. We put 45 grains in the gun, which is a target load and sighted it in, 5 shots in a one-hole group. Later in another chapter "Muzzle Loaders" you may want to refer back to this, it is the common thinking that you need a large charge of powder to hunt with. I guess Lee did not hear me when I said that 45 grains was a target load. To hunt deer with this caliber I would put 55 grains of powder for a charge, couple of days later I seen Lee and he said, "I got a nice doe opening day with the 45, about a 60 yd shot, hit it in the chest as it was coming towards me and the round ball all the way to the rump, ball was still round enough to shoot again." I said, "What were you using for a powder charge?" he says, "45 grains just like you said." I started laughing and said, "I guess you didn't hear me say that 45 grains was a target load, you should use 55 grains when you hunt with the rifle." He said, "Hey, I'm not going to waste powder, 45 grains is plenty for me." And still hunts with a target load today. And as always he gets the lion's share of the deer, one way or the other.

I was telling Lee that everything you get into has it's own language, and to succeed at it you have to learn that language. Lee said, "That is the truth. How many languages do you know?" I said, "About as many as you do!"

Chapter 11

True Stories

Dad always told the story of when he lived beside a small river, there was a huge carp that hung around under the train trestle, every time the train came thru here come the carp up the river, Dad wanted to get that big carp, but knew a spear would not hold him, then he gets this bright idea, he build a fence across the river, had it set up so went the carp went upstream the fence would close behind and he would have him in the open, block the river above him when the water went down, wade in and get him. Worked like a charm only thing was Dad didn't realize how big it was, had to get two farmers with tractors to pull it out, it fed 19 families for 3 weeks. It scales were huge. Dad used them for shingles on the outhouse. That didn't work out to well, every time the Train came thru that outhouse would go to shaking and jumping. Just don't be setting in it when the train came thru.

Went ice fishing with Dad one time, we were after perch, and we found them, got quite a few, walked about a mile to the spot, we had the fish laying on the ice and after a while we got done fishing Dad says, "Lets pick these up." I didn't know what to do with them so I put them in the pockets of my coat. I was wearing a Navy surplus "P" coat, one thing I can tell you for sure and certain, perch go in a coat pocket head first easy, its getting them back out. I about froze my hands on the walk back. Another lesson learned.

We lived on the Island Granddad had squatted on, houses were scarce so we moved out there, one of the best places we ever lived. Dad always stuck his skinning knife up high in the outside door casing. Now Dad worked nights and one of my favorite things to do was get up in the morning and catch some fish, clean them and Dad would fry them for us when he got up. I knew he always liked that. But he had stuck the knife a little high up and I jumped up to grab it and laid 3 fingers wide open, Dad heard the noise and got up, when he came out and seen what I had done he cleaned and bandaged them, I never had a more tender moment with Dad, I knew he really loved me without him saying so.

Talk about selling fish, my Granddad lived on an island, river on one side lake on the other. Grandad squatted on this island in 1921. He and my Dad lived there until Dad got married to my Mother. Now those DNR guys setting behind their desk thought the river was being fished out, so they closed the waters around the island for 5 yrs. Now if people like fish when they are legal, they love them when they were illegal. Granddad had a long list of people he sold fish to and the DNR was not going to shut him down. So he would fish, clean them, walk 2 miles to the downtown bar and sell the fish. He also raised horseradish on the island, which he sold. After so long of selling fish he got the nickname of " Bullhead Dan " he always carried a basket to town with his fish and horseradish in. Dad told me he was a rough old guy, he would walk into a bar with my Dad and holler, " I can whip any man in the place, if I can't I got a son here who can! " Granddad had another side, he could get wild mink to eat out of his hand, course he would knock them in the head when trapping season came. By the by, I still have the basket Granddad carried. I still remember when I was about 5-6 Dad came home from work early and went into the bedroom and I could here him crying, Mom went in to comfort him. I later found out that Granddad had a heart attack and they found him dead in his rowboat at the island. I was too young to grasp death and was spared that grief.

I always remember Dad telling me about Granddad sitting in his boat at night bullhead fishing. Elmer was fishing a ways from Granddad, Elmer hollered over and said, " George what are you using for bait? " Granddad, said, "Night crawlers," Elmer Hollered back " So am I but I can't get a bite, throw your line over to my boat so I can see how your line is rigged." Granddad threw his line over to Elmer and Elmer said, "I see what I'm doing wrong, here's your line back." when Granddad started pulling his line back over there was something heavy on it. Granddad hollered over, "Elmer, what did you do to my line, I can hardly reel back," Elmer said, "Nothing." Grandad was getting a little hot and was ready to give Elmer the what for, when he got his line back and there was a cold beer on his line.

I always thought of the story of the guy who was bragging on the fish he caught and how big it was, way too big, Dad said this little saying, "I have a simple question, and the truth is all I wish, are all fisherman liars or do only liars fish?" Anyway, after listening to this guy bragging one of the fellows had enough. And said, "Big fish ain't nothing. I was fishing the other night and dropped my lantern over side into the water. I came back the next night to fish in the same spot with a new lantern and I hooked the lantern that I lost, pulled it up and it was still lit." The guy bragging on his fish said, " That's not possible," the guy with the lantern said, " I'll tell you what I will do, if you take 5 lbs and 10 inches off that fish I will blow out the lantern."

I had a smile. One night on the island, I was fishing for bullheads and I see and hear these guys coming down the river. They were trying to get some bullfrogs, shinning their lights around. I pull my line in, got a stick and went down by the river in some bushes. Now I could make the love calls of a bullfrog real good. When you are after bull frogs and you come toward them they will set still as long as you keep the light in their eyes and you can either spear them or gig them with a treble hooks on a cane pole, but you have to be careful and not scare them or they will jump about 4-5 times across the top of the water and go to the bottom and you lost that one. So here they come and I started my bullfrog love call, one guy says, "You hear that? That's a big one." They started shinning their light around where I was, they could not see me. I took the stick and hit the water about 4 times and one of them said, " He's gone!" and they stated cussing the guy in the front of the boat for scaring the bullfrog. It was hard to keep from laughing out loud.

When we lived on the island I climbed a tree and was looking down into the water. Here comes a big Pike and grabs a small fish, took it all in his mouth and then I seen a bunch of scales coming out of the Pike's gills, the Pike spit the fish out then grabbed it again, turned it around and ate it. I was telling Dad about this and he told me that Pike take a fish in their mouth scale it then spit it out to turn it around and then eat it. Would have been a great movie.

Across from the Island was a spring where we got our water from. There was a 2- foot pipe on the end that the water run into. One night I had to go get some water, jumped in the boat and rowed across the river to the spring. I missed it by about ten feet and when I got out of the boat I was in some muck, almost like quicksand, I had to think fast. I had the only boat we had and there was no way anyone could help me. Took the bucket and pushed it down into the muck and I could lift one foot at a time, kept that up until I got back into the boat. Went and got the water and went home.

Climbing Trees, I was 40 feet off the ground trimming a tree. Roger and I trimmed trees for several years. Here I am 40 feet in this tree, climbing belt, hooks (tree climbing spikes) and a small chain saw hanging from the belt. I hollered down to Roger that I was having a problem, my whole left side was going numb, one of the signs of a heart attack. Roger told me later he was saying in his mind, "I have no way to get him down!" I finally one handed got down. I told Roger I was going to take the rest of day off. He said, "You ought to go to the hospital and get checked out!" I said, "No, I don't like hospitals, I'm just going home." So I did. About 3 hours later and the nagging of the family I went to the hospital. They put me right in a room and hooked all these wires and tubes up to me, wouldn't even let me go to bathroom. I told the nurse, "OK I just won't go at all!" She got a hold of the doctor and he said to let me go by myself just stay outside the door in case. No problem. They kept me all night and the next day I told the nurse I was going home. She said, "Wait a minute I'll get the doctor." When he came in he said he wanted me to take a stress test. I said, "Ok, I am just laying here anyway." So they took me down to the lower floor and put another set of wires on me and put me on a treadmill. Now I walk about 6-7 miles per hour, average person walks about 5 miles an hour. I asked the guy, is this all the faster this thing will go? They had warned me that I might have a heart attack just walking on the treadmill. So he turns it up a bit. I said, "This is a Sunday walk in the park." He calls the doctor in and then turns it up all the way, I said, "Still too slow." So they inclined it, I said, "Can I go home now?" The doctor ask me what me what I do, I said, "Trim trees with ropes, trap and walk when ever I can." He tells the attendant, "Send him home!"

One time I was fishing for some catfish along the river and was doing pretty good, had about a dozen, threw them up in the grass behind me, and then I caught a dogfish. Worthless things. I threw it up on the bank and fished a little longer, no more bites, time to go anyway. I grabbed my burlap bag to throw the catfish into, and they were gone. I looked all over for them, it was a moonlit night and I see something moving in a tree. Shined my light up in the tree and there were my catfish, the dogfish had chased them up the tree. I told this story to my Wife and she said, "You are retarded!"

I can go you one better than that. Early one morning I was sitting on the bank of the island bass fishing, went with just 2 night crawlers, have to go tonight and get some more, caught a nice bass and there went my crawlers. I wanted to fish some more, but no bait. While I'm sitting there I took a little snort out my pint, looked down and there was a snake with a small grass frog in its mouth. Now there is not a better bass bait than a frog. I grabbed the snake and took the frog and put it on my line. The snake lay there, it looked real unhappy with me. I thought what a thing to do, I took his breakfast, so feeling sorry for the snake, I poured a shot from my pint bottle into his mouth, at least I felt better, sitting there waiting for a bass to grab the frog and I feel something hit me on the boot looked down and there was the same snake with another frog for me.

When out to the sporting goods store and they were having a sale, a pair of binoculars caught my eye, they were $140.00 marked down to $ 80.00, sounds good to me so I bought them. Took them home and the Wife says, "What did you pay for those?" I said, "I haven't figured it out yet." So I takes pen in hand and figures, they were $80.00, I will have them for at least 20 Years, Lets see, 365 days in a year, 3,650 days in ten years, 20 years would be 7,300 days, divided by $80.00. HEY! That's only 1.3 cents a day, What a deal! I told

her the good news and all she did was raise one eyebrow???????
Kinda wished I had looked around to see if there was any other good
deals.

There was a news report on TV today about a guy who had been
broken into 2-3 times and he put a sign in his yard " Wanted, Dead
or Alive, the person who broke into my house." When the news
people talked to him he said, " I don't really mean it." Wrong, out
of the mouth come the intentions of the heart. How do I know this?
One year somebody stole some of my traps, now there are a lot of
dishearting things, but to have your traps stole is bad. I went of to
the local sports shop, Ray owned and run the shop, "Dancin Bears
Sporting Goods". Now Ray and I go way back, we worked together
a long time in the alumuim extruding plant. Ray was quite a character, Bout 280 lbs, always run around bare footed, had a heart of
gold, very slow to anger. Anyway, I went out to his shop and said,
" Ray can I put a notice on your board?" and he said, " Sure", I put
up an 8 x 10 paper, which read: $100.00 Reward for one shot within
200 Yds at the person who stole my traps! and I signed it, and meant
it. Funny no more than put it up and a sheriff's deputy came in the
shop, looked around a bit, read the sign, looked at me and left. Rest
assured the law knew who I was. And I had been around long enough
to know there was nothing anyone could do about the sign, besides
it gave the shop character. But everybody knew I meant what it said.
Us boys shooting ability was well known here.

My Uncle Elmer wanted me to come out west and help him dig
a well. I was small and he could lower me into the hole. I would fill
the bucket and Uncle Elmer would haul it up, going along pretty
good, down about 30 feet. I heard Uncle Elmer yell to get into the
bucket. I did and he pulled me up and said, "Come on to the root
cellar, there was a huge wind storm coming." We went into the cellar
and stayed the whole night, when we came out the next morning we
could not believe our eyes the wind had blowed all the dirt from
around the well hole and there it stood 30 feet in the air. Well I want
you to know Uncle Elmer was not one to waste anything. He cut the
hole into fence postholes and what was left he sold a guy for donut
holes.

Kim, a friend of mine, told me about some guys out by his place who hit a deer with their van, jumped out, threw the dead deer in the van and took off. Suddenly the dead deer was tired of the ride and jumped up looking for the closest exit and some of the guys were in the way. They were glad to escape.

Kim thought I was the greatest mountain man that ever lived. I don't know why. Kim had sugar diabetes real bad, his eyes were about shot and he had a mountain of trouble with his feet and legs. His records at Ann Arbor (Medical center) were almost 5 feet high and were wheeled around on a two-wheeled moving cart. In fact he had to have one of his feet amputated and he told his Mother when he had to go to get it done just to stop at my house and I would do it for him. I probably would have too. I caught my first beaver off his place. (See Trapping).

Chapter 12

Fish Story

I remember one morning Roger and I came into Ray's shop and were talking to Ray and in comes this guy with a real bad case of the ornery, snarled at Ray, " Give me 2 dozen Crappie minnows," and handed Ray his minnow bucket, guess he didn't know you could not rattle Ray. The guy looked around for something to beef about and spotted one of those huge hooks made into a fishing fly with the hook about a foot long mounted on a board. He snarled at anybody who would listen. " Now there's a waste of time and money, what good is that thing, just a thing to hang on the wall!" Oh Oh, he just stepped into my area. I said, " Hey don't knock that fly. I gave it to Ray a while back. I used it while I was in Texas. I caught a big fish with it, got back to shore and the CO was there and told me the fish was too small and I had to throw it back, took 4 of us guys to throw it back in the lake. The guy knew he had been had." As I recall, didn't do much for his attitude.

When Rich and I was about 14-15, we used to hunt rabbits all the time. We get 3-4 and go to my place and clean them, and then Rich hit the couch for a nap while I cooked them. I always made Baking powder biscuits while the rabbit was cooking. I would parboil the rabbit, then roll it in flour and fry it. Every thing was going fine, but when I took the biscuits out something was wrong. I had used baking soda instead of baking powder, boy were they sour, I took a piece of one in and woke Rich and said, " Taste this," he took a small bite and said, "Ugh! Bad!" And went back to sleep. I made a new batch of biscuits finished the rabbit, set the table, and went and woke Rich. We set at the table and started eating, Rich took one of the biscuits, buttered it and took a real small bite, then he looked at me and said, "I had a dream you made some real nasty tasting biscuits. I could almost taste them when you woke me up." Needless to say I doubled over laughing.

Course, on the other hand Rich and I had some laughs together. We were about in our 30's and we both worked at this aluminum extruding plant on the afternoon shift and there was this one guy Joe we always had fun with. He was very gullible, one day we came to work and Rich says to Joe, " Bob's the luckiest guy I ever seen, ask him about when he went hunting today." Joe says, " This is not another joke is it?" Rich says, "Just ask him". Joe comes over to me and says, " Heard you had a good day in the woods." I says, " Sure did, I never had such a day, went after squirrels with my 22. I sit down under this big oak tree and shot 6 squirrels with out getting up." Joe says, " That's pretty good." I says," That's not the half of it, up walks a 6 point buck and I dropped him with one shot between the eyes." Joe says, " That really is good!" I says, "You haven't heard the best of it, as I was getting up to leave I leaned on my gun to stand up and the stock slipped off something, there laid a fat billfold, had a wad of money in it" Joe says, " Wow how much was in it?" I says, " Don't matter, it was counterfeit, just like this story I told you." I had to run to get away from Joe.

There was another guy, who worked there, Doug, he was either afraid of girls or bashful. Never did figure which, but if you teased him about girls he went Red and sky high, As I said, I was a photographer and started asking around at the shop if anyone had a picture of Doug, one guy said, "I have a year book with his picture in." I said, "Great, bring it in I want to use it." He brought it in and I took it home and took a picture of his picture, then I got one of those girlie magazines and took a picture of a guy and gal in a compromising position, no clothes of course, I took the negative and made a picture of the magazine picture all except the guys face, then I took the negative of Doug's face and put where the guys face had been. Looked just like Doug was there. Doug was the shipping clerk and after I showed the picture to the guys I put it in a manila envelope and laid it with his papers on his desk while he was gone and we all watched as he opened it. He looked at it and jumped off his stool and started yelling, "IT AIN'T ME! IT AIN'T ME!

One Mother's day Dad came over to my house, had his new wife with him. We decided to go fishing for a while and went out to the lake with our fly rods. We took along a milk can, one of those kind they hauled milk from the farm on the truck. We started catching blue gills and throwing them in the milk can, we had put it about half full of water, we kept catching them till our arms were wore out. Dad says, "Think we got enough?" I says, " As long as they biting lets keep fishing." By the time we got done fishing it was dark. Oh! Oh! We are in big trouble, gone all day on Mother's Day; the ladies didn't say anything, for about a month!

Roger said to me one day, "How do you hit birds on the wing?" Well sir, since I loaded shells we went out shooting the next day, I told him, "You get first shot," I shot a few birds he missed, morning doves, rails and misc. but this one shore bird came flying over and I said, "There he is!" And I drew a bead on it and since Roger had not shot, I fired and hit it. As it was falling, Roger shot it again, I said, "No, No, shoot them while they are alive, anybody can shoot a dead bird!" Whoa Nellie! Did that get him? I don't think I got another shot that day. Roger got real good at wing shooting, said to me one day, " How hard is it to hunt ducks?" Sounds like a hunting trip to me, next picture you see is Roger and myself heading into the swamp with the canoe. Showed him how to set up the decoys and told him when I hit the duck call if some come over don't look up as ducks can see the whites of your eyes. Bout that time here comes a hen mallard, I hit the call and said, "Hello," she said, "Hello," then I hit the feeding chuckle, she banks into the wind, set her wings and flares to land. She's just hanging in the air, I said to Roger, 'There you go!" He pulls up and shoots and down she comes. Roger looked almost disappointed. "Said, "I thought you had to shoot at ducks while they are flying really fast?" I said, "Not when you speak the language." We went out another time on Messenger Lake. While I was pushing the canoe up in the marsh grass Roger was loading his gun. About that time I heard him say, " Here comes three ducks!"

and he starts shooting, down came two ducks, and I see what they are and says, "Unload, we are done for today," he says, "What" I says, "You just shot two wood ducks and they are 90 points each, both our limits." The next year he goes into a swamp a little ways from his house and build a nice duck blind, you could wade right out to it. Early the next morning, opening day, he sneaks out to the blind, when he gets there its gone, seems as tho the muskrats liked it so well they took it and build a house. I don't think he ever went duck hunting again.

Randy came to the house, we were going duck hunting, it was opening day, we went to the Hodunk dam, then went up river a ways and there was a nice stand of cattails, eased the boat up into them, pulled out the camouflage boat cover and of course we were in camouflage gear. We sat there a while and I got to thinking that this year the season didn't open until noon. I told Randy, "We have to leave and come back just before dusk." We got already to pack up and here comes the CO on shore, I told Randy, "Sit real still." CO looks all around, he wasn't more 50 yards from us, and a credit to our camouflage he never saw us there. He left and we waited about a ½ hour and we left. Randy still laughs about us being in the CO's river and he couldn't see us.

Here is how to cook up ducks. I break the first rule. I skin them, guys don't skin them as the skin holds in the moisture and ducks are dry anyway. But lets skin the duck, get some of those bags you can seal for the oven, put a quarter of an orange inside the duck, put it in the oven bag, put in 3 spoons of butter, and 3 table spoons of wine for each duck and of course the seasonings you like, bake for a hour and a half at 350-degrees. The duck will melt in your mouth and the whole thing will be moist too. Now I have shared this way of cooking duck with a lot of people and I can tell you that not all ovens are created equal, nor the way some people cook, just find out how you like them and that's the right way. The guy who trained my dog, Amos, Jim Tanner the elder, for pheasants, was bringing his Wife and himself to our place for dinner. I had shot 6 ducks and cooked them as above. When they got there his wife said she did not like duck. But she said she would try it, she ended up eating most of the duck. Here's a smile. When you hunt ducks, you hunt them with a shotgun and every now and then you would find a lead pellet, well done of course, but one time my Wife asked me why I didn't just shoot them with one pellet? The Beverly Hillbillies I'm not. Once Jim, his son and myself went into the top of the old school to catch some pigeons to train the dogs with, what a mess that place was, I done that twice, first and last.

Now of course if you want to cook a Coot, some people call them a Mud Hen cause its like eating mud when you eat them. How ever here is a foolproof way to cook them. Get your pot of water, enough to cover the duck, put in all your spices, onions, potatoes, what other veggies you want, put a fist size stone in the pot, cook until you can get a fork in the rock, throw the coot out and eat the rock and veggies.

Roger and I done a lot of pheasant hunting. One year he shot the same 8 shells, I just kept reloading them for him. I got another dog we would hunt behind. I say another as the first dog I had I lost, Champ. Good dog too. Would stay on point as long as the bird sit. We were hunting with him the year before and he went on point, the bird flushed, went down again, flush, go down again. The bird just kept that up until the bird and the dog were out of sight. We could not find the dog, we looked several times, no luck. So anyway I gets this new dog, a setter, named him Amos Moses after a man of the cloth. He also was a very good dog. We were hunting the same area we had lost the dog Champ the year before. We were about 20 yards apart, I came upon a sight I could not believe, there was Champ on point, well his bones were and about 10 feet ahead of him were the bones of a pheasant, still sitting.

Speaking of pheasants, I always like this little poem:

There once was a very elegant pheasant,
His disposition wasn't very pleasant,
Then someone kicked the H out of him
And now he is just a peasant.

There is a River 10 miles north of Coldwater called the St. Joe River, it used to be a good river for pike. Wanted to go one afternoon and could not find anyone to go with me. Oh well, took the canoe,

3 hp motor, motor mount, (I had built this mount) and my fishing gear. What I would do is put the motor and mount in the bottom of the canoe, drift with current and when I was ready to quit for the day I would go ashore and put the mount and motor on and motor back upstream to the truck where I had started. Gets the motor on, starts it up and it started running full bore, throttle was stuck and I was going to crash into the other shore. I quick turned the motor to one side, bad idea, it rolled the canoe over. There I stood in 3 foot of water and the motor kept rolling the canoe over about 4 times before the water killed the motor. Every time it rolled over the propeller blades went past my head. See the Lord loves me, it missed every time. I'm still clear down the river with a wet motor, it would have to be taken apart to get it running again, I had to paddle all the way back against the current. At least I was not up a creek without a paddle.

This same river one time I see a commotion across the river. I walked over the bridge and down to where something was going on. There was a Pike, little over 30 inches long and he had a 14 inch Pike stuck in his throat. His eyes were bigger than his mouth. I knew before, that Pike eat each other, but never seen anything like this.

I was always good at picking locks. When my younger brother Randy got married we decided to bell them. In case you don't know what belling is, its just harassment all in good fun, when someone gets married. We went to their house and when they seen us pull up to their trailer they run into the bathroom and locked the door. We went into the house, got into their cupboards and took all the labels off their can goods. We then went after the two of them. I walked up to the bathroom door, messed with it a minute and then said, " You got a good grip on the door handle?" he yells out, " Yes!" I said, "Give it a pull!" he did and it came off in his hand. I had picked the lock from the opposite side. We grabbed them and us guys took Randy with us and the gals took his Wife, Karen with them. We had agreed to meet in Coldwater in about two hours. Poor Karen didn't know where they were taking her, she had never even heard of belling. When we got back to town we had Randy push Karen thru down town in a wheelbarrow. In those days a little fun didn't bother the cops, they just laughed with us. I would hate to try that today. Anyway, we took them home no less the worst for wear. Randy did mention after that he had a few surprise meals from his canned goods.

Chapter 13

Varmint Permit

S ummer again, Fishing, more trapping, I got a license to trap all year long. Legal! The DNR gave permits to trap and do animal control. Woodchucks, Coyotes, Skunk, Beaver and any other animals doing damage. When I first heard about this Varmint Control permit I was surprised as it is the responsibility of the CO's to take care of varmints. Then I got to thinking. I could picture all these CO's sitting around a table having coffee One says, "You know, we have 40,000 trappers in Michigan. If we would give a permit to trap nuisance animals they could collect money trapping in the off season and we could sit here and have a lot more coffee." Indiana decided they would like to watch Beaver, so they turned a bunch loose. Most of them came to Michigan and they call them dumb animals? A guy called me and said he had talked to the CO and he gave me your number. He lived at Hytke lake, said he mowed his yard last night and when he got up this morning he had over 2 inches of water where he had mowed. I said, "You have a Beaver by the sounds of it, I'll be out this afternoon". When I got to his house sure enough, a small creek running beside his house into the lake. He asked what I charged to remove the Beaver, I said, " 20.00 a beaver, but I think you only have one." I went up the creek and sure as shooting a Beaver dam, pretty good size logs, meant I had a big Beaver. Now Beaver have a funny way about them, they control the water at the left side of the running water looking down stream.

And that's where I would have to put my trap under normal trapping rules, remember the permit, put a trap anywhere you want, anyway way you want. So I tore a hole in the dam and put a 330-connibear trap there. This is frame spring trap that if you stick a broomstick in it will break the stick in 3 places. Set another trap further upstream just for insurance, this one was a No 3-jump trap with teeth. Put a 25 lb weight on a wire so when the animal got in, it would slide down a wire hooked to the weight and it would drown. Came back the next day and there was the beaver, dead, all 81 lbs of him, (by the way, Michigan record is 105 lbs, Canada's record is 140). I went upstream to check the No3, and it was gone, weight and all, I see a trail through the swamp grass where the weight was dragged, also found some tracks, Bear! But he got hung up on a log and pulled out of the trap. I forgot to mention under the permit you could not keep the hides. They were not any good any way. I did keep some of the Beaver meat, great for Coyotes.

Had another guy call and asked if Coyotes would get his dog. I said, "How big a dog you got?" he says, " 10 lbs" I say that's just breakfast for a coyote. He asked what I charged to remove them. Said he had $4,000 in the dog as his Daughter was hearing impaired, dog told her when the phone rang, and everything else she couldn't hear. I said, "$20.00 each one," I said, "Let me come and look your place over to see if there are some around." He said, "OK." Went out there, asked him where he owned to, half of one side of the lake and big woods. There were plenty of Coyote signs, one very big one. And signs everywhere. I went back and told him, "You got them," I said, "How about this. I will take all the Coyotes out for the permission to hunt here and that way I can keep an eye on the place for any new Coyotes that may come in." He said, "Fine with me." The first Coyote I got from there was the big one. I pulled up to set in my jeep and there he was hunched up to get me when I came near. I pulled out my 22 cal pistol and shot him between the eyes from the jeep, 46 lbs and 6 foot 8 inches. And a beautiful coat at that. I put these two animals in first as they were the biggest I ever caught.

The I gets a call from a guy on the other side of the same Lake and asked if I could take out some Beaver. I told him I would be out that afternoon, had to check the other traps across the Lake anyway.

So he takes me back in this swamp where there was a small creek running into the Lake. Boy did he have Beaver. He tells me it's hard to walk thru this swamp, too late, I was gone into the swamp. When I came back he said, "You have Indian in you don't you?" I got 8 beaver out of there.

I was trapping this lake with my canoe, this one trip I got 3 Beaver, 5 coon and about 20 Muskrats, and I pulled my traps as it was going to freeze up. Want to know what the weather will be, ask a trapper. Anyway, coming across the lake the wind was blowing real good. It was in my favor as I could paddle on just one side of the canoe by using a back stroke, took me a while. When I get to the landing where the truck was, there stands this guy. He said, "How did you do that? I watched you come across the lake and you only paddled on one side." Well, if the guy had to ask I knew it would take longer than I wanted to explain it, so remembering what the guy said when I first came out to this lake I said, "Guess it's the Indian in me." He was happy with that.

One year they were having trouble with Beaver at Silver Lake. They had built a dam 125 foot long across the creek that was the exit of the lake. When the water came up on the lake most of the septic tanks backed up and of course there was nasties in the lake. I was called out there and took the Beaver out, got big male 60+ lbs, a female and 3, 20-pound kits. Then tore some the dam apart to let the water thru, they wrote of incident in the Coldwater newspaper, " Local man catches the Dam builders." The story did not go over very well, too many animal lovers, well they are animal lovers until they have to put up with them. Then it's "Help!"

Wood chucks, I had a ball with these critters, charged $5.00 ea to take them out. Used connibear 220 right at the holes. I charged $20.00 ea to take them out with a live trap. I just took the live trap when I got one and threw it in the river till he drown. Got in one day and I had a call about woodchucks, so I called back and it was a lady. She said, "How do you catch woodchucks?" I said," I use a 220 killer trap" she said, "Can't you catch them alive?" I said, " I sure can, cost a little more." Oh great she says, "Do it that way," I said, "Ok, where do you live? I will come and remove them." she says, "I don't have them." I said, "OK where do you live?' she says,

"Why?" I says, "So I can bring them to you when I catch them." she says, "I don't want them!" I says, "Now we come to problem, neither does anyone else!" and I hung up. Come to find out she was from the animal rights.

The thing I hated to get in my Fox and Coyote traps was a cat. Those are the wildest things. Almost got bit a couple of times. I finally got to where I would just shoot them. Then I found out Coyotes loved cat meat. I would take a cat, chop it up. All but the head, put it in quart jars about ¾ full put the lid on loose and bury them in the ground for a month or two. Coyotes also loved Beaver meat I would do the same with it and the Beaver castor and glands I would put in a jar with water and let them set in the sun for a couple weeks. Mixed these in different ways. There's a saying if you don't puke at your first three sets the baits no good. The thing with cats that people don't understand is that they are killers. You feed them at the house, let them outside and they go on a killing spree, seen this a few times. One time the neighbor had a cat and knew he fed it. My Mother had a peach tree tipped over in her yard. I said, "Mom why don't you get rid of that tree?" she said, "There is a nest of rabbits under it. When they are gone I will have one of you kids remove it." We walked out there just in time to see the cat kill the last baby rabbit. Didn't eat them, just killed them and left. Did I mention that 220 killer traps work great for cats!

Speaking of domestic animals, one Saturday morning I got a call from the DNR. He says, "Are you one of us?" I said, "One of us who?" he says, "You have our Varmint control license, don't you?" I said, "Yes!" He said, "Do you have a varmint rifle?" I said, "Yes, it's a Weatherby 22-250 with a 4 to 16 power scope." Then he said, "Can you come up south of Lansing if we need you?" I said, "Sure." he says, "Ok, I will get back to you one way or the other." and hung up. This was about 8:00 in the morning. About 3:00 that afternoon he called back and said, "We won't need you to come to Lansing, We got him." I said, "Him who? " He said a lady had one of those nylon play pens for her baby and she had it on the front porch of the house with the baby in it and was just sitting there watching the traffic. Her German shepherd dog lay there on the porch. She wanted to run over to the neighbors a minute and figured no one would mess with the baby with the dog right there. When she came back the dog was gone and all that was left of the baby was its head. They tracked the dog down and shot it and the baby was in its stomach. Knowing German Sheppard this is no surprise to me. About a year earlier there was a woman in Battle Creek who had one and it was about 9 yrs old, she had got it when it was a pup. She was 80, she could not walk down the street to the grocery store and would put a basket in the dog's mouth and he would go to the store and the grocer would put whatever she had called and wanted. Loaf of bread, quart of milk, whatever. Then the grocer had not seen or heard from the woman in a couple of weeks so he called the police to check on her. When they got to her house the door was locked, they looked through the window and seen her lying on the floor the dog next to her, they broke down the door and when they went in they could not believe their eyes. The dog had ripped her throat out! Like I have always said, "You can take the animal out of the wild, but you can't take wild out of the animal."

Randy was with me when I was trapping the small river behind his house. The place was full of Raccoon, had a few rats and mink. But I wanted the coon. They were pulling down the corn in the fields that belonged to Randy's Father-in-law. I had made a special brew for them. I took some fish and put them in a glass gallon jar, put water on them, put fine netting over the mouth of the jar to keep the bugs out and set it in the sun for 3 weeks, then skimmed the fish oil off the top, done the same thing with some Beaver glands, they were rotted pretty good, what was left of them made a good base. Then I got a blender and mixed them together good. While I was blending Edward and Robert were about a mile away hunting deer. When they came back to the house they asked whet that stink was, they smelled it a mile away. Imagine how far a coon could smell it. Anyway, Randy was with me when I was setting the coon traps. I would put a little dab at each set. Randy says, "You sure don't put much lure on each set, what is I?" I said, "Just some special stuff I whipped up." He said, "let me smell it," I said, "OK just don't smell too deeply." Guess he didn't hear me, took a big whiff and I had to grab him as I thought he was going to fall in the water. He says, " That's terrible!" I said, " ya, I know, its great!" smiling from ear to ear.

Chapter 14

Motorcycles

First let me say my Mother hated motorcycles. It was bad enough when I was riding stock road machines but when I got the Chopper she would not even look at it. Called it a beast that was going to kill me. But it didn't.

I really liked motorcycles, got in a world of trouble most of the time. They were building a freeway, I would go out there and open them up. Figuring the fines I paid I own a pretty fair piece of that road. All the bikes I had would keep up with traffic. Cops got after me once, I did not have a driver's license, no insurance, no registration. Plate was 10 yrs old, but it was the right color. Anyway they chased me home. I had it in the garage and was sitting on the porch waiting for them, hauled me to jail, went in front of the Judge the next day After the Judge read the ticket, no license, no insurance, illegal plate, speeding, eluding and reckless driving. Judge said to the cop, "How fast was he going?" The cop says, "My squad car will go 132 miles an hour, it was doing it and he drove away." Judge says, "I guess 140 miles an hour sounds good. 3 days in jail and $ 115.00 fine." My boss where I worked was also a deputy. I asked him to put me in for sick time at work. So I got $11.00 an hour while I was in jail. Boy! I sure needed the rest.

Jack and I were headed to Bronson and I looked up, seen a tornado headed right at us. I told Jack and we pulled off the road and got into the ditch. I had my Indian and Jack had his Harley. We lay down next to our bikes and the tornado went over us. People say they sound like a freight train, baloney! More like 6 trains! Anyway, it went right over us and after it had passed we got up, I asked Jack if he was alright he said, "Sure, how about you?" "I said, "Fine." We got our bikes upright and started them up to drive them out of the ditch and mine acted funny, I guess so, it had a flat rear tire. We got it up on solid ground and I put it on its stand and took the tire off and we took it into Bronson to get it fixed. I figured I had run over something in the ditch. We got to the repair shop and the guy checked it out and there was nothing wrong with it. He even put it in the water tank to check for a small leak, nothing, the only thing we could figure was the tornado took the air some how???????

Every time I hear people call motorcycles bikes I think of the guy who showed up every morning at the border with a bicycle, had a bag of sand on the handle bars and a bag of sand draped over the rear fender. The Guard at the border would make him dump the sand out and he would go through it, the guy with the bike would put the sand back in the bags and cross the border. This went on every day for 12 years. One day when he showed up with his two bags of sand the Guard says to him, "Well guy, this the last time I will be checking you out when you cross the border. I am leaving in a ½ hour, retiring. Would you grant me one request? When you get across the border this time please tell me what you are smuggling. In 12 years of knowing you I promise not to tell the new Guard, let him go thru the sand every day as I have done." The guy said, "I will." He got across the border and turned to the Guard and said. "I'm smuggling bicycles!"

Used to race Motocross on Sunday. This one weekend I took my Wife and kids, Edward, Robert, Lori and Lisa and away we went. About 90 miles away. Got home around dark fed the kids and was getting them ready for bed. Heard a knock at the door and there was a cop. He says, "You weren't home today?" I says, "No." He says, "You got two boys about 12 and 14?" I says, "I do." he says, "Can I see them?" I called them to the door and the cop says to them, "Did you tell your Dad what you did while He was gone?" They just looked at each other. The cop says, "I will tell him. They went across the street and waxed the neighbor's windows." I says, "Boy, you sure can't trust kids, here they were with me 90 miles away, they take the keys to the car, drive back home and wax windows and drive back. I didn't even know they were gone!" the cop says, "Oh they were with you?" I says, "That they were" Cop says, "OK" and starts to walk away. I say, "HEY! Don't you have some boys to apologize to?" He didn't say a thing just keeps walking away, I said "you — — — — —-, that's why kids have no respect for the law" and I slammed the door.

Moved out in the country shortly after that and almost the same thing happened again. Edward was not interested in bike racing so he went with his friend Steve, to Steve's house and spent the day. Monday morning here comes a state cop. I asked him to step in, it was raining. Just about the same thing, only this time Edward was supposed to have smashed some gauges on a bulldozer down the road. I had talked to Steve's Dad on the phone to see if Edward was going to spend the night or did he want me to come and get him? He said, "He would like to spend the night if it was ok?" I said, "Yes." I asked what the boys had been up to, Steve's Dad said, "They were here all day. No problem". I says to the cop, "Who seen Edward smash the gauges?" He says "Oh I can't tell you." I slammed my fist on the table and said, " I know where Edward was all day and it was 10 miles away, don't you ever dare step onto my property again unless you have a witness with you!"

I never have been able to understand how they come around accuse a kid of something and another kids out raising cane and they appear to look the other way. Like a kid come speeding past the house and I couldn't get to the gun. I looked and he turned around and was coming back, I figured I didn't have time to get the gun so I grabbed a big limb I had trimmed off the tree, run into the road and stood there like I was up to bat. The kid seen me and skidded to a stop. I asked him what he thought he was doing, this is not a racetrack. He said, "Don't worry about it there is nothing you can do about it." I smiled and said, "I now have your license plate number, could not have got it if you hadn't stopped, I said, "Of course I would have took your windshield out if you didn't stop." I said, "Bye!" and went into the house and called the cops. The sheriff deputy stopped and told me the kid was in a little trouble, he had been driving his mother's car when I stopped him.

Jack and I went riding towards the west and when we came into Bronson there were people lined up on each side road, some even had chairs and were watching the road, I said to Jack, "They heard we were coming this way and are waiting to see us." We went on a little further and there was a parade starting to go through town. Rained on my parade again, as it was.

Chapter 15

More on the Kids

The Boys were good boys and the cops are trying to ruin that. Like Robert, the youngest of the two, he didn't take any guff from any one, I remember one time for some reason Robert, who was in grade school, had to ride the high school bus that Edward, who was in high school, rode. Anyway, someone give Edward some trouble. Edward was pretty easy going, But Robert! Some one was giving Edward a hard time and shoved him BANG! Robert nailed him, right cross I believe. So after that as a punishment Robert was dropped off a half mile from home and had to walk the rest of the way home. He wore his walking home as a badge of courage of protecting his brother. Now bear in mind that I was a go to schooler if there was a problem. Robert comes home one day and tells his Mother he did not want to go to school anymore. She told me, we were both surprised. We asked him why and he said, "He was being made to sit it the lunchroom all day," I said "Ok go to school and I will check on it." Next morning I called the principle. You will never believe who he was! The judge when I went to court for the illegal trap the CO had to give back to me. (Chapter 8) I said I would be there in a few minutes and hung up on him. When I got there they had Robert and another kid in the office. We all went into his office, turns out that the other kid had kicked Robert in the ankle so Robert threw the ball at the kid. Robert said he was the only one being punished. I said, "Why?" he says the coach didn't see Robert get kicked just seen him throw the ball, I said, "Poor excuse." So I asked to have the kids removed. After they went out I told the principle, what's this about making Robert set all day in the lunchroom? He says, "That's the way we punish kids." I says, " Not my kid you don't!" I says, "If you made me set there all day I would playing with myself." I said, "From now on if you have a problem with any of my kids call me and I will take them home and they can work. I have a big pile of dirt I have to move and I don't care if the dozer does it or the kids move it." Well, the next thing that happened was Robert came home and said he was expelled from school. I called the principle and asked what was going on. He would not talk to me, so I called the school board and asked for a meeting about Robert. Now Robert is in high school, 10th grade if I remember right. Turns out that the kid who kicked him was in his car (Volkswagen) in the school parking lot. He calls Robert over and when Robert bent over to talk to him he sprayed Robert in the eyes with wiper solvent and tried to drive away. Robert smashed out the back window of the car with his fist as he did. So here we are at the school board meeting, the principle says, "I tell kids if they don't want to be here go home, and after what Robert did to the kids car window, he don't belong in our school." It was my turn to speak and I said, "Did you take Robert to the nursing station to get the solvent out of his eyes," he said, "No." I told the board," With an attitude like the principle has it's a wonder there are any kids in school. And the board is letting him do it. But I'll tell you what I'm going to advise Robert to do. He wants to go into the Air Force when he graduates. I'm going to tell him to do this, quit school, go in the Air Force now. They will see that he gets a high school diploma and whatever other education he wants. Then when he comes home again he can come to the school board meeting and laugh at all of you." And that's just what he did, came home from the Air Force with a high school diploma, and started a college career in law enforcement in the Air Force and he was a forth degree Tae Won Do. I knew he had it in him. Proud of the boy, I was. While he was in the Air Force he was stationed at Kokomo Indiana, Robert was in the Military Police in the Air Force and once a month they would drop him on one side of the base at night and he had to get to the other side without getting caught. He would go by all the aircraft and other restricted areas and he would leave behind him a trail of mitary police handcuffed to their cars and embarrassed one way or the other. He said they only caught him once all the time he was there. Bear in mind, these guys were carrying loaded guns, and to them he was a spy or worse.

And Lori, a child after my own heart, the oldest of the two girls, she didn't take any guff either, just a little more mild mannered than Robert? One day she comes home and says she don't want to go to school any more. We asked her why, she said, "They were making her sit in the hallway on the hard floor." I told her to try it one more day. In to the school I went, right past the principle's office to her room. There she, and about ten other kids, sat on the hard tile floor in the hall. I got her up, we went into her room and I told her to get her stuff from her desk. Her teacher said I could not come into the room. One glance from me told her she was wrong about that. She cleaned out her desk and now we go to the principle's office. I said, "Why are they making those kids set in the hallway?" she says, "We are trying for a school record to get a reward of computers for our school, the best behaved school will get them." I says, "How stupid, I'm taking Lori to another school so she won't have to put up with this foolishness." Principle says the school bus will not bring her to school if she's not going to this school. I said, "We will drive her every day, small price to pay." And we did, Lori was no backdowner; She always took Lisa by the hand when they walked. One day she comes home and said, "I had to smack the kid down the street, he pushed my little sister." I said, "OK, you alright?" she said "yes." I thought that was the end of it. Pretty soon there is a knock at the door and here stands a cop. He says," Your kid hit the boy down the street and give him a bloody nose." I said, " Ya, I heard about it." he says, "Can I talk to your child about this?" I said, "Sure." And called Lori to the door. The cop took one look at Lori and said, "I guess that's all I need to know," and left. Didn't surprise me. Oh did I mention the Boy she hit was almost two heads taller than her! I would guess she had to jump up to smack him. I remember once we went to National Shoot, Lori went with me to a lot of the shoots. I left her there and went home to work and came back the next weekend. I asked her if she had any trouble, she said no, "I had my knife with me the whole time." I remember one time later on, her boy friend had a girl at his house and Lori went over there and when he came out on the porch she slugged him in the nose.

All though Lori was a tough kid she did have her down sides. One time when she was about 15 she had a mountain of trouble. I really don't remember what it was now but I knew the solution, a two day float trip down the Flat River. This river at the time was one of the most pristine places around, of course like all things man can destroy that and he has. But at the time it was the best therapy for any problem. We would go along and I would say to her, "Cast right over by that rock." She would and the water would explode when a small mouth bass hit her lure. Catching big fish was an everyday occurrence with my kids. Puts a whole new meaning on "Take a kid fishing."

Once when we were over to Randy's the kids went down by the creek, No, no one fell in but my girl Lori stepped in, and right into the muck, her shoes were a mess and when her Mother asked her what had happened Lori said, "I took a foot wetness."

Lisa was the youngest, had more fun with this girl, she never had much trouble at school. One thing funny she did I still laugh about. I got chickens for the kids to take care of. So, one day I was going to town and she wanted to go. It was fall and the farmers were hauling corn from the fields and as always were dropping some along the road. I told Lisa, "When I see an ear of corn I will stop and you can jump out, pick it up and throw it in the back of the truck and we could feed it to the chickens." She thought it was great fun. I would stop, she would jump out, pick up the ear and throw it into the truck bed, and I would hear it go clunk. We did this several times and this one time she jumped out and I didn't hear the ear hit. I says, "Didn't you get it?" she says, "it was just the wrapper", meaning it was just the husk. She always kept her room neat as a pin, I would go into her room and her shoes were always lined up under her bed. I would move one about an inch. When she came home she would go to her room and pretty soon she would say, "Who has been in my room?"

I said Lisa never had any trouble in school. When she was going to Girard school, I think she was in 4th grade, they called us to come over and get her. She was on the window ledge walking around, Outside! Just like her Pa, no fear!

Tina, the joy of Grandpa's heart. She is Lori's daughter and she has the same stubborn streak as her mother. She used to go to town with me in the truck and would stand up in the seat so she could see everything. One time she was so tired and kept falling asleep standing up and I would try and sit her down, then she would wake up and be mad because I was trying to set her down. She is a very smart girl. One time, when she was about 8, she asked me how my muzzleloader worked and I told her all of the details just as I would any adult. When I finished she said, "Oh, that's easy."

As I said earlier, Robert went into the Air force and when he came home on leave he was a 4th degree Tae-won-do and he was sitting in the front room and the parakeet got out of it's cage. As it flew by, Robert picked it out of the air and said, "Mom, your bird got out!" and she come and took it from him. But where I was going with this is, he taught Tina some of the kick moves he knew. A little later Tina, who is all 7-8 years old comes up to her Mother (Lori) who was sitting on the couch, and says, "Mom I am going to kick you in the chest and there's not a thing you can do to stop me!" Lori got already to say something and POW Tina kicked her. Lori grabbed her and warmed her rear end. Course Grandma got into it and said, "Robert showed her how to do that, get after him!"

When we still lived in town, Roger and I went deer hunting out to Smitty's. Roger said, "lets go to the back of the property, there's a nice grass field back there." I said, "Is there a rock pile?" As I stated before, if I can sit on a rock pile I will get a deer, He says, "Sure is!" so we go back and I get on the rock pile, Roger was east of me, the wind was blowing west to east so my scent was blowing toward him and his scent was blowing further to the east. A buck came between us and started screaming, he wanted to cross but would have to go thru my scent. When deer get upset like that they can scream just like an eagle. He finally could not stand it anymore and jumped the fence and came right by the rock pile I was sitting on. I had the 12 gauge with the 30 inch barrel, shot just like a rifle, perfect shot right in the heart. Went about 50 yards and dropped. Few minutes Roger came to see if it was me that shot. I said, "There is a deer laying right over there." We went and looked at it, a nice 8 point, not a big rack but nice shape. Roger gutted it out and we dragged it out to the truck. Now the kids were young and when I got home and hung the deer in the tree I told them I had shot Rudolph. Talk about a house in an uproar for a while. I finally said, "It wasn't him as the nose was not red." That was a little better.

One day my Mother called me and told me that my Son, Ron, had been to the house and wanted to see me. Ron was my boy from my first marriage. I had three kids with her, Dodi Lynn, Ronald, and Joel. She had taken the kids and went to Ohio. Anytime I would go down to see them she would say they were away with someone so I didn't get to see them. When Ron had come to my Mother's he said, "I want to see my Dad." It had been 28 years since I last seen him. So we made arrangements and we all met at my Mother's place. It was halfway between where He lived and where I lived. I knew his Mother told him that I never paid support, but the kids found out different. Anyway while we were talking Ron said he wanted to build and fly a model airplane. I said, "We can do that." When I got home I called the hobby shop and had them send him a model airplane kit, and engine and a radio. As he built it we would talk on the phone and would help him out. I decided to drive to his place and see him and the family and also how he was doing on the plane. He had made a mistake on the wing and we cut it apart and fixed it. He still had a bit to do on it when I headed back home. About a week later he called and asked if we could put the plane in the air. I said sure so up he comes to my place. We went to the field and an instructor helped him get the plane up, as he flew it over me I looked and on the bottom of the wing in big letters, "THANKS DAD". Touched my heart and I was so proud of him.

Dodi was kind of a wild child, I seen her a few times, but just too many years apart. Same with Joel, he was exactly like my Dad.

Back to the motorcycles, I didn't have the respect for them I should have had. I had a big Indian that was top heavy. For some reason I loved to ride this bike in the rain, never got in any trouble with this one. I did one day fall asleep on it, came to a curve and went straight, lucky there was a gravel road there, it woke me up. I bought a new 250 cc Harley new. That bike was a joy to ride, used to have a small hill I liked to climb with it. Got home from the hill one afternoon and had to run to the store, still had my leathers on, a car run a stop sign and hit me, my leg slid along his bumper till I hit the license plate, went into my leg, spun me around and I slid about 120 feet down the highway. As it was sliding, I got on top of it. When it stopped I rolled away from it and took off my helmet, always was afraid of fire, there I laid in the middle of the road. A friend of mine seen the whole thing and stopped his car by me so no other cars could hit me. Man was he mad, I had to cool him down, I was laughing about the whole thing, here comes the meat wagon and took me to the hospital. I asked my friend to take the bike to my house. I gets to the hospital and the guy says, "I will have to cut your leather pants off," I says, "You try it and you will see how well a one legged guy can fight." They didn't try to cut them, I give $ 180.00 for them. They ex-rayed my leg and said I had a hair line crack in my leg bone, nothing serious, put a cast on it, gave me a pair of crutches and sent me home. Got a pretty good settlement out that deal.

Then there was the Harley 74. That thing was always getting me in trouble, the thing always flooded. I was about 8 miles from town and it flooded while I was moving and then caught afire. A guy came along with a fire extinguisher and put it out. Just had to put some of the wiring back. Another time I was riding down the highway and something went wrong and it quit. Burned the cylinders, took it to a guy who built racing bike engines and he bored it out. Now instead of 1250 cc it was over 1500 cc, never had a speedometer last more than an hour after that. Wild machine, I stripped it down and it would fly. I would put it in gear, turn the front wheel and gun the engine, pop the clutch and it would go down the road a ways on the hind wheel. I would pull over tighten the chain and go on my way, by the by, this was the bike I got 3 days in jail with, judge said I was going over 140 miles an hour. My youngest Brother, Randy, came to my house one day. I had just put in a new speedometer cable. I asked him if wanted to go for a ride. He said, "Sure!" I put him in front of me on the bike and reached around him and got it going down the road. Then I let him drive it, it was in the highest gear and he poured the gas to it. I was laughing so hard I could hardly see. I reached up and pointed to the speedometer, it was bouncing around 110, he did slow it down a little. In later years he became a very good dirt bike rider, wore No 1 for quite a while. He still takes long trips on his bike around the Upper Peninsula. Course, the Harley would keep up with traffic. One day I pulled into my Mother's house, I took off my helmet and hung it on the bike and put on a soft cap I carried. There was this guy there, a friend of my brother's, Jim, and he came out to the bike, put on the helmet and said, "Lets tear up the road," I said, "Jump on." He had never been on a big bike before, pulled out onto the road and headed north, when I got over a 100 mph I leaned over and showed him the speedometer. He said, "What would happen if we spilled?" I said, "They would pick us up with a sponge." Last thing I heard from him. We got back to the house and he took off the helmet and walked away without a word. He was kinda of a white color. He did ride with me again. I was over to another town about 10 miles away and he asked me if I could run him over to get his car. As we came into town, a two lane highway, there was this kid on a bicycle riding in the road, all the cars went honking at him, now bear in mind that I had two car horns on the bike, I says to Jim, " Get ready and slap this kid on the back as we go past," we got up to him, Jim slapped him on the back and I hit the car horns. You never heard such a scream as that kid let out, as he went up to the sidewalk to ride his bike.

Chapter 16

Photography

J ust before we moved out of town I started taking pictures at the Butler Motor Speedway Saturday nights. Shot pictures of the action on the track and then a picture of the Flagman giving the winner the checkered flag to driver of each race. After I was doing that for a while I added the track at Manchester, Friday night and the one at Angola, Indiana on Sunday night. I sold the 8 x 10's for $ 1.50 and the Billfold size for a quarter. I made about $ 500.00 a weekend. I had messed around with photography (it's a chore just to spell it) while I was in the Navy. And after I started shooting the racetracks I had the Navy send me thru the New York Institute of Photography. Got all 99% out of a 100% score. I had to take a Portrait, Landscape and Action Shot. The action shot was 3 racecars going about 100 mph and was at night. You could count the lug nuts in the picture. The portrait was of Lori. I built a camera out of a shoebox, black taped a lens in, I got the lens at a yard sale for 10 cents, after I took the picture I took the lens and built an enlarger, printed the picture to an 8 X 10. That was one of the pictures I sent for my final exam. The kids at the racetracks loved the billfold size pictures, for a quarter they could afford them. I put a notice on my display board that the best display of the billfold size pictures would win a free billfold picture each race night for the rest of the year. For kids they had some nice displays. The kid I picked as the winner had a board that folded out and out and out and out Etc. Said. " I don't have much room at my house, so I had to make them fold up." I told him he did a wonderful job.

Every 3 years I would take an aerial of the tracks. I would pay a guy at the Coldwater airport to fly me over the track. Had to get the same guy, as he was the only one who would remove the door. I hate shooting thru Plexiglas. He would fly over the racetrack and then roll the plane over toward my side so I would not have the wing strut in the picture. There is a lot of vibration in the plane so I would have a 12-pound weight screwed on the bottom of the camera. I used a large format camera, 2 ¼ X 3 ¼ Graflex Speed Camera, its like you see in the old time movies. About 10 X 10 X 8-inches, I would then come back to racetrack. This one time I came back at intermission and there was a guy looking at my display board and when I walked up, he said. " Was that you in that airplane?" I said, " That was me!" he said, "you didn't have no door on the plane and when it rolled over you were hanging out of the plane, what would have happened if your safety belt came loose or broke?" When he asked that stupid question, all I could think of was the guy sitting on a newspaper on the bus and someone asked him if he was reading that paper or the guy laying on his back on an icy sidewalk and someone says, "Did you fall?" So a stupid question deserves a stupid answer. I said, "Nothing, see how big this camera is, I would have just stood on the camera until it was a foot off the ground and then jumped off." He walked away.

Once at Manchester I was standing at the curve where all the action was and here comes a wheel with the axel flopping. Coming right at me, I took a picture then stepped out of the way. The drivers liked these pictures for some reason. Pretty soon here comes another wheel with axel flopping. When the axel broke on these cars the remaining part would still be bolted to the wheel. I shot the picture and stepped out of the way, it hit a telephone pole and it put a dent in the wood about ¾ inch deep. Then I decided it was not my night and went up by the finish line, you guessed it, and here comes another wheel and axel. I thought this was enough and went and sat in the car. Here comes another wheel and axel, just missed the car. I went back to the curve where it was safe.

I worked at the Regional Center as an attendant nurse for the mentally handicapped and I would come in to work and would have my tanks, developer and film from the 3 tracks, the tank was light proof and I would develop the film and dry them, when I got out of work I would go home and start printing pictures. I always had a 1000, 8 X 10 pictures and 2000 billfold pictures with me, plus the special orders. They would come up to me and say, " Remember that night 5 weeks ago that cars flew over the fence, do you have them?" I would say, "What was the number on the car?" they would tell me and I would dig the picture out they wanted.

A car came around the No 3 turn and rolled over. When it did, the drivers safety belt broke from the floor mount and threw him out, well out to the end of the belt that was around his neck, killed him, broke his neck. I shot some pictures, one that showed the safetymen taking him loose, you could see the guy's wrist watch well enough to see the time. Now we are coming to why I went to see Ben, the lawyer, He said the best thing to do was to sell them in complete sets in manila envelopes and not display them, I knew who the first persons would be buying them, the Insurance guy. I sold a bunch of them, but not to the kids.

Sis always liked Ansel Adams, he done all black and white photographs. She wanted to try black and white photography so I got her a 35mm camera outfit and some black and white film. One winter the snow had melted and then froze, Sis got up early and asked me where her camera was, I told her, she said, " You should see outdoors, its beautiful looks like a thousand jewels." and away she went. About 2 hours later she came back and said, " Wait until you see the pictures I took, I had to lay on the ground to take some of them." I was awake then and I said, "What camera did you use?" she said, "Mine!" I said, "There is no film in that camera, I didn't want to put it in until you were ready to take pictures." You always keep film in the refrigerator until you are ready to use it, keeps best that way. I said, "You can take my camera, its got film in it." But she said, "No the moment was gone."

Chapter 17

Larry

Larry, a guy I grew up with, was one of the best shots I have ever been around. We were hunting Pheasants over by Bronson. His Grandmother had some land and we went walking around, up went a pheasant and Larry shoots him out of the air, don't sound like a big deal, Oh yeah, he was hunting with a 22 cal rifle. He made two great shots that day, shot a pheasant out the air, later we wandered down by the creek that run thru his Grandmother's land. He found an old bottle and threw it in the water across the creek, pulled up and shot while it was floating, hit the screw lid and spun it off without breaking the bottle, course he said it was just the way he planned it.

Larry and I were out fishing one time and he said, "Wish I could learn to fly cast." Now I had taught my self when I was 7, used to sneak Dads fly rod out and cast until my arm felt like it was going to fall off. By the time I was 8, I was casting in tournaments. They had round plastic rings, like a hula-hoop only smaller, you had to lay the fly in the ring the first cast. Anyway, I says to Larry, "Here hand me your fly rod." He did and I took the fly off his line and handed it back to him and said, "There you go." He said, "What?" Then I said, "You want to learn to cast or fish?" One comes before the other, with no fly you won't have to worry about hooking a fish, just casting." I then had him put his billfold under his arm he was going to cast with. I did this so he would not use his whole arm, showed him the 10 o'clock to 2 o'clock position with the rod and told him to stay on time, any where past these the line bunches up and falls out of the air. Then I showed him how to back cast. People, when they try to fly cast, don't let the line get behind them and they have a pile of line at their feet, or it cracks like a bullwhip and snaps the fly off. Here's how you do it, when you back cast say in your mind, "New York is a good place to be from." Then you can forward cast. Larry was sharp, he was casting in about ten minutes. I said, "There you go." Put your fly back on and let's fish. That was about 47 years ago. I know he is still fly-casting. Told me he just fishes for bass now.

Talk about a fast bike, Larry, asked me if I would go to Battle Creek and drive his car back as he had to pick up his Harley. They put a ¾ race cam in the bike, it was already fast. So away we go, get the bike and I followed behind him, he pulled over once and said, " I never had a bike with this kind of acceleration." This bike as I remember was painted pink, I guess later in life I figured out if someone would get on his case about the color he would leave them in the dust. One day I had a chance to see what he meant, he said, "Jump on and I'll take you home." Memorial day, traffic on the two lane was bumper to bumper on both sides, so we got on the center line, it's hard to describe the noise cars make going by you on both sides. Larry says, "There's a cop after us." now Larry had the same problem I had, we got a cereal box and motorcycle instructions mixed up, you know where it says tear along dotted line????? Anyway, we were running about 80 MPH and we cut off to our road, someone in a car pointed the way we went to the cop, we were going down a hill where the cop could not see us and Larry stopped the bike and we both jumped off. When the cop came up to us he said, "OK who was driving?" Larry and I both pointed to each other and we both said, "He was." There was nothing he could do. We waited a while to make sure he was gone before we left.

This was right by the cemetery where we used to ditch the cops all the time, come roaring down the road, up into the cemetery, straight back to a small path that went down the hill across a small dirt road that led to a paved road. A car would have to back out of the cemetery, go all the way around to the paved road. I showed this path to my Wife in 2007 and it still looks used.

Here's a smile. Larry, Vern and I decided to go fishing at Messenger Lake. No man in his right mind would go on the lake dry, so we stopped at the local pub and had a drink or two, maybe more, can't remember, Anyway, gets to talking to the owner of the place and he had heard our plans to go fishing. Said, "If you boys get more fish then you want, bring them in. I'm so hungry for some fresh fish." Now this guy was German. So while we were still able to, we left for the lake, All three of us was raised on this lake so getting a mess of fish was easy. The main reason we were going was in hopes of hooking into some nice bass. We start fishing, get a nice mess of bluegills, about half a 5 gal pail, and I ties into something, fought like crazy, knew it wasn't a bass, more like a Catfish. Finally got it up to the boat and it's a Dogfish, about 18 inches long, nothing more worthless. Vern whips out a 38 Revolver and shoots at it a few times while its still in the water. I guess the people around us didn't like Dogfish either, they all pulled up and left. Now the normal thing to do was to get this trash fish in the boat and slit its throat and throw it back in the water. But I get it in the boat and I looked at it and told the other guys, "I never thought I would catch a German Brown Trout out of this lake." They looked at me like I was crazy, and then we all broke out into smiles. It was time to go get a drink, this fishing makes a guy thirsty. Back to the bar we go, bucket of fish in hand. The owner seen us come in with the bucket and said, "You guys get some fish?" We showed him in the bucket and asked him how many of them he wanted, He said, " What ever you don't want, what's that big fish?" We told him it was a German Brown Trout and you can have them all for a couple of rounds of drinks, couple of rounds! I don't even remember leaving the place. We had to drive, we were to plastered to walk.

One time when Larry and I lived up north I didn't have a bike at the time. This guy said, "You can ride with me." Harley Sportster, that thing had gas lines the size of garden hose. Away we all go out on this highway just rolling along and a car tries to run us off the road. The guy said, "You ready?" I says, "Let her roll," away we went, passed the car, got way ahead and turned back toward the car. We were going over a 100 mph and I reached into my jacket pocket, got a handful of steel ball bearings and as we passed him I tossed them on the pavement in front of his car. And we went on our way. Oh, did I mention Larry and I worked at a station in town? The next day here's the car for a new radiator. You should have seen the holes those ball bearings made.

We had more fun at that gas station. Once two cars pulled in at the same time, these were the days when an attendant put the gas in for you, washed the windshield and checked the oil. Things have sure went down hill since those days. Any how, we are both checking oil at the same time, we look at each other and then start sword fighting with dip sticks. The guy who owned the station was a dip. One time he changed the oil in this 58 Chevy, now these cars had about one inch clearance between the air breather and the hood when it was closed. He drains the oil, puts the oil plug back in, lifts the hood, removes the oil cap, laid it on the breather, put in the new oil and slammed the hood, Opps! For the oil cap put a nice dent in the hood.

One time Larry was into the sauce, gets on the kids bicycle and away he goes uptown. He was gone about half an hour and here comes his Sister Betty and his brother in law Wes. I said, "I will go and get him." There he was on main street riding along, the light turned red and I jumped out and said, "Your Sister is at the house lets throw the bike in the trunk and go to the house." We did, and just as we got back in the car the light turned green. Now I hate to be held up and always try not to hold anyone else up, dropped her in gear and took off. Course I squealed the tires and there was a cop right there, he pulled me over and asked if I was trying to get away from him. I told him what I was doing and he seemed ok with that then Larry says, " If he wanted to get away from you, couldn't get him if you tried, this car is faster than any thing you have seen!" I said, "Larry is a little under the weather and I was taking him home." Cop says, "That's a good idea, just take it easy." Thought sure Larry was going to get me a ticket. The car was a 50 Ford, Larry and I souped it up, in fact I set a track record at the drag strip that will never be broken, it was a 8cylinder flat head, 2 Stromberg 97 carbs, with an slush box (automatic shift transmission) got 98.7 in the quarter mile. There was a 53 Chevy with a 6 cylinder, with a stick shift, that could have raced me, but he would not come out so I went down the strip alone.

When I headed to the pits they waved me back unto the start line, there set another 50 Ford, had header pipes hanging down, rumbling pretty good. I was running Sportsman class which meant when you looked under the hood it looked like a stock engine, the other Ford was a higher class. They give me a length and half start on him. I had taken it easy when I went down alone. I decided to pour the coal to it and see what this guy had. Away we went, he beat me by inches, we pulled back into the pits and here he come, growled, "What you got in that thing? You are supposed to be running Sportsman," I said, "Other than a little work inside the engine that's all." He said, "I should have left you at the starting line. I'm running a Buick V8 overhead valve engine, twice the engine you got and I was lucky to beat you!" He was a pretty decent guy when he settled down. He said, "I'm glad you are not running my class, if you can get that stock Ford to run like that". Larry and I did good.

There was this guy that was out of his skull, had a Harley with a car engine, small block Chevy V-8 as I remember and took 4 guys to hold it up until he got going. He would always go off the end of the track trying to stop that thing. Had it painted candy apple red, trailer he hauled it on was candy apple red, and the Corvette he pulled it with was candy apple red. Sharp! One day after the drags I was headed home and I see a bunch of cop cars and an ambulance on this curve. There was the guy who rode the bike, he lost it on the curve and rolled over several times and he was dead. I thought man, after all those hair-raising trips down the track and he gets killed in a car.

My brother Roger came up to spend a few days and we took him with us when we went out drinking. When we came out of the bar we decided we were too drunk to drive. Roger could drive. Now he was the smallest of all us boys, and we got him going down the road, this is the same Ford as I just mentioned. He was so small he could not see over the dash. We told him, "Just look up and keep it between the trees". We made it home. Speaking of the dash, I had taken it out, painted it white, when it was dry it took a coke bottle with fuel oil and rag hanging out of it, lit it and smoked streaks on the white, then put a few coats of clear over it, looked sharp.

Seemed like Larry and I were always getting someone to try and catch us. Up north there is a lake, Baubese, and we used to swim there and there was this life guard who thought he was the law. Him and his stupid whistle, always-telling people not to cross his rope he had out. He said, "I can catch anyone." He had an 8 -foot aluminum boat with a set of oars. I was a SCUBA diver while I was in the Navy and always could swim like a fish. I told Larry, "You drop me off at the beach and I will swim to the other side of the lake and you can pick me up." So here I go down the beach with a large pair of swim fins. I swim out to the rope and over it and then I hear the whistle, just kept going, the guard jumps in his little boat and starts after me. I just waved bye and started swimming for the other side, I let him get close a couple times then swam to the other side, took off the fins, waved bye again and got in the car and away we go. Larry could hardly drive he was laughing so hard.

I had another run in with a lifeguard at Messenger Lake, We were fishing in the early morning and I was casting by the swim-ming beach. There were no swimmers around. Here comes this life-guard and yells that I can't fish there. I said, "Boy, I was fishing here while you were still crapping yellow." That was the end of that. What's with these guys.

One night Larry and I were bar hopping and about 2 in the am he takes me back to my car. He gets me out of his car, stands me up and lets go of me. I fall face forward without even putting my hands out to catch myself. He picks me back up and says, "For a minute there I thought you were to drunk to drive, but you hit the ground without missing." Stuck me in my car and away I went, about half way home I either passed out or went to sleep. Lost control of the car and it rolled over in the ditch, the place where I sat was the only high place in the car, just like a bubble, the rest of the top was smashed flat with sides. When they hauled me to the hospital, there was Larry, and his wife. A spider had bitten one of their kids.

Larry and I also played in a band at the bars, he is a real good lead player, and I played rhythm and was a lead singer. We could keep them out there on the dance floor as long as we wanted with Johnny Cash's Folsom Prison Blues. We had a lot of jam sessions at the house too.

Country Music, one time I tried something. I put a 45 RPM record on the player, only I had the player so it would play the record backwards, this guy got his truck back, his Wife back, his money back and his girlfriend back. And his dog.

Speaking of bars, Larry and I went into a bar and was having a beer or two, minding our own business. We always had the barkeep bring over a card of those dried fish to the table, we eat what we wanted and they would charge us for what was gone. After that, we would have a cigar while we were drinking. In comes this guy we knew (Travis) and he sat down at our table with us and ordered a round for the table. Then here comes another guy we knew (Richard) and sat down with us and ordered a round for the table. Travis said, "Hey, bring a double round for the table", Richard said, "Make that another double round and bring me a case of beer to go," Travis said, "Another double round for the table and a case of beer to go." When all this got to the table they each drank one beer and said, "We just stopped in for a case of beer to take home." And away they went. You could not even rest your elbow on the table there was so much beer. Did we let it go to waste? No way. But I don't remember leaving or even getting home that night or morning, which ever it was.

Chapter 18

Ice Fishing

Rich and I used to hunt the railroad tracks for rabbits and would end up at the Cement Plant, at the Lake. I would open my coat and there were two small ice fishing poles on each side. In my pocket were mousies, small tackle box in my other pocket along with some plastic bags. There were always some open fish holes where someone had been fishing. We made a day of it and would come home with rabbits and fish.

In later years I would build ice-fishing houses, both 4-foot by 6 foot and 4 foot by 8 foot. Usually built 3-4 a year, guys would buy them from me right off the ice. Two guys could fish the 6 foot house, while the 8 foot would hold 3 guys. Anybody I would invite would wonder what the new house looked like this time. One year I built a 8 footer and painted it all white, then while I was at a yard sale I bought this curtain, all fancy lace type, I tacked it to the front of the house, covered the whole front. And I painted it red on the front of the house, took off the curtain, Well you had to see it to appreciate it. Sold that one off the ice for $ 200.00. I guess I should tell you about the inside. Propane stove, coffee pot, radio, electric lights, 12 volt tail light bulbs for lights, had a shoot built by the door so you could send your fish out unto the ice without opening the door and letting the cold in, your coat would be hanging on a hook in the house. Never had any windows in the house as I didn't want the CO to know what I was doing. If I went out alone I would have 4 lines in the water, limit is 2, if the CO knocked on the door I would pick up 2 of the poles and touch the lines against the heater and it would burn them off, better than a ticket. Also had two buckets that one fit inside the other, still looked like one tho, nice for carrying extra fish, maybe even a bass or two, they are awful good in the winter. They, like the rest of the fish, are a lot firmer in the winter. And this was the time I was building Muzzle Loaders and I had scraps of the Tiger maple and I made ice fishing pole handles out of the wood. Fancy and of course they caught more fish.

I had to learn the hard way about having vents in the peak of the house at both ends. Went fishing, came home, that night I woke up and could hardly breathe. Bad, I went to the hospital and they put me on oxygen right away. The fumes had burnt my lungs and the cold air didn't help either. I was in the hospital a couple days. I enjoyed all I could stand and told the nurse I was going home, she says," You can't go until the doctor releases you!" I hadn't seen the doctor since when I first come in. I said, "Well tell you what, I will eat lunch and then if the doctor has not been in to release me I'm going home." She said, "ya, okay". She thought I was kidding. Right after lunch here she comes down the hall, I am dressed and on my way out, She said, "Go back to your room and I will get the doctor!" She did to! Doc comes in, looks at me and signed my release.

You have to watch the cold, one night it was so cold I put a bucket of hot water on the back porch and it froze so quick the ice was warm, even colder the next night, we would go out to the ice fishing house and would have to open the fish holes as they had frozen shut. We would go in the house, it was real cold, clean out the holes and light the stove, about 20 minutes later when it warmed up the words we had spoke earlier would thaw out and interrupt what we were saying at the time.

Dad gave me his ice spear, lot smaller than the one we used for carp. It's actually a spear for Bluegills, used to be able to spear them in the winter. Dad bought the spear in 1921 and its hand forged, had to pay a dollar for it. Back then Dad was working for a quarter an hour. Anyway, I built a spear house and tried spearing. The house has a 2-foot square hole in the center, you have a decoy, either live or wood and when a Pike came in after it you spear them. I speared a 38-inch Pike and took it over to Dad. Never did spear again. I just wanted to do it once. It was quite the thing to do. You can set and watch all kinds of fish come thru as long as you want to watch.

I remember one year Dad bought a deer hunting shack up north, got it cheap as they build it the wrong way. It was 14 foot by 36 foot and they had build it so the that the long way was facing north, right where the coldest wind would blow, and Dad said, "We'll drive some poles in the ground and swing it around so the end will face north, be a lot warmer." We took a huge power auger to bore the holes for the pilings to swing it around, had to have two guys hanging on to it all the time, things were going good, then Mom called us in to eat lunch. We just left the auger in the hole and went in. After lunch we came back out and the auger was froze in the ground, Dad said," Better have three guys hanging onto the auger." We grabbed it and Dad started the engine. When he put it in gear it was froze so hard that it spun the lot the house was on 90 degrees, Dad said," Well I guess that takes care of that!"

One time Corb called me up and asked if I was going ice fishing that night, we fished at night for crappies, used small minnows. I said, "Guess we could", He asked if I had an 8 foot house on the ice. I said, "Sure do, Brand new one!" he said, "Good, I got a guy I want to go, names Ray, he's never been." I said, "OK stop out to the house and we will take my truck as I had a very heavy duty battery for the house lights." Ice was thick enough to hold a locomotive, they get to my house and away we go. Driving on the lake out to the fish house, Corb says to Ray, "Right there is the house." Pointing to the fish house, Ray says, "Sure close to shore!" Corb says, "we been on the lake for 5 minutes." Ray jumped out of the truck. He thought it would fall thru the ice. Do I need to mention that Corb and I had a good laugh? We get settle in, Corb on my left and Ray on my right, I always set in the middle so I could tend the stove, coffee pot and radio. I showed Ray how to put the minnows on the hook so they would stay alive. Corb said, "Those voices I hear sounds like so and so," I never had windows in my houses as I didn't want the CO looking in. If I went alone I would have at least 4 poles in, law says 2, if the CO knocked on the door I would grab 2 poles and put the lines against the stove and burn them off, see, 2 lines in the water. Anyway, Corb thought he knew who was out there and stood up to try and look out the vent in the peak of the house. While he was doing that I reached over and set his 2 poles in the corner of the house, you could not see the lines. Corb says, "I guess it wasn't who I thought it was." and he starts to set down, then he sees his poles are gone and thought the fish had pulled them in, lets out a yell you could hear downtown. Ray and I started laughing and He knew what I did.

Al and I were fishing at the Narrows one night and a guy he knew showed up after we got there. They passed the pleasantries, and then don't ask me how or why he knocks his bucket of minnows over and started scrambling to pick them up. Al could say things with the driest humor you ever heard. He says to the guy, " Why didn't you count your minnows before you left home." Had another instance like this, kind of funny. Casey was fishing at the narrows, chops himself two fish holes, this was back when you used an ice spud, a little harder than the augers they have today. Anyway Casey is baiting his hook and guy walks right up in front of him and drops his line in one of the holes Casey had just cut. Casey never said a word, he just picked up his ice spud and cut the guys line, the guy just looked at him and then walked away.

Casey told me one time that a job he had in the winter he would leave in the morning and he always forgot his gloves. One of the guys that he worked with told him to try tying a string around his finger. Casey said he tried it but his hands still got cold!

Al was my Father-in-law for 24 years and he would do anything for a smile no matter how much work it took. His sister-in-law went on vacation and while she was gone he went to her house, last house on a dead end street. He took some wood stakes and orange ribbon and made a double row of stakes through her yard and left. When she got home from vacation she seen them and called Al and told him. He said, "Looks like they are going to make a turn around through your yard so cars can drive back out." She says, "We'll see about that!" she called the city dept and they said they didn't know anything about it, she calls the county garage and they didn't know anything about it. Finally calls the highway dept and jumps all over them, the guy says, "Hang on lady, what does it say on the stakes?" she said, "I'll go and look and call you back!" she calls them back and says, "It's a 33S backwards!" the guy says, "Lady I think someone is pulling a joke on you." And hangs up. Al said he could hear her coming a mile away.

Corb came over one day and said that a guy just opened a Sporting Goods store and he had Mickey Mouse boots. I said, "Great, what are Mickey Mouse boots?" Corb told me that were boots cut off a flight suit, and that they had valves to compensate for the pressure up high and they were like a thermos bottle. I said, "I seen a pair of them a while back," Terry and I went to a lake and the ice was thin around the edges and Terry stepped thru and got his one foot wet, it was 6 degrees and I worried that Terry's foot was going to freeze. I kept asking him if he wanted to go home and get some dry socks, he just kept laughing at me, he finally said, "Come here!" and I went over and he pulled his boot off and his wet foot was warmer than mine. I didn't ask him what kind of boots they were, but now I knew. So here we go, I came back with a pair and have never been without these kind of boots since. While we were at the store the guy showed us a muzzleloader, explained how it worked. I guess you have gathered from what you have read of this book that I was a very self sufficient, and to make your own untraceable ammo was right up my alley. When I got the money I went back and got a 50 cal. It was a Hopkins & Allen under hammer. I was amazed at the accuracy of these things, I started to go to the meets where they shot these in competition. And I found a new way of life, these guys were great to be around. And I see some of them brought the stuff to sell and done real good at it. This is the life. I even ended up at the nationals.

Chapter 19

Memorial to Vern

I first met Vern when I was in high school and I still remember the incident. First let me describe Vern. He was small and wiry, strong both of body and will. I always felt sorry for Vern as he was raised without a Dad, or let me say I never met his Dad. Vern did talk about deer hunting with his Dad and that's all. And that may have been to his advantage for surviving but I can think of no greater loss. He did mention his Dad once in a great while. Not to take away from his Mother who raised him. He loved her dearly, she was a great person. I worked the same place she did and had occasion to talk with her many times, both at work and in their home. Anyway, back to the incident. It was on the steps of the high school, a very large kid, LaVern was giving Larry a bad time, in steps Vern and landed a knuckle sandwich on LaVern's chin. I still say to this day that Vern had to jump up in the air to smack LaVern. But it was over in seconds, after that I only seen Vern a few times until we were older. We became very good friends.

Vern and Larry used to go to the movies when they were teen-agers and shortly they would hear over the loudspeaker, "Vern, come into the lobby." They would go and there was Vern's Mother and she would say "Give it here!" and he would reach into his pocket and hand her the pistol he was carrying. They would go back and watch the rest of the movie.

Later years we were over in Bronson at a bar playing pool. Vern had an impossible shot. Vern says to me, "How do I play this?" I said to him, "Hit the nine ball into the seven and that will knock the three in the pocket." Vern said, "OK" and lines up for the shot. One of the guys we were shooting against said to me, "That shot is an impossible shot, can't be done!" I said, "Shhh! Vern don't know that." We were playing for a case of beer each and the guy says, "You just lost 2 cases of beer." Vern shot and the balls and did just as I said they would, three right in the pocket. Got real quiet.

Another time we were shooting pool at another bar, the guys we were shooting against started getting a little rowdy, said, "They would wait for us outside," course Vern would rather fight than get up in the morning, he says to me."Watch this." And he leaned over the pool table to make a shot, nudged his shirt just right and his pistol falls out on the pool table. It got real quiet again.

One time Corb and I were going to Crystal Lake in Sturgis, Michigan. It was clear, about 50 foot deep in the deepest place. Vern wanted to go along, we said let's go. I had my flat bottom boat on the truck and we put it in the lake so Vern could watch us under water. We went to the bottom and after while Corb signaled he was going up and I stayed down for a while. Corb got into the boat with Vern and they were watching me down below. I was at about 40 feet, I done my drill I usually done. I would go through the procedure as if my SCUBA went bad. What you do is take off the gear down below and come up on your last breath. Here's what you had to do, come up a ways, stop and let a little air out, go up, stop, let a little air out. You had to do this as you could get the bends in some instances. Bends are the nitrogen from the compressed air. They get into your joints and expand when you come up too fast. Anyway, Scuba tanks will float to the surface when you take them off. In fact, you had to wear a lead belt to stay down. I took off the tanks and let them go and they went up near the boat. Now Vern had never seen the drill and when my tanks came up and I was still down there, Corb said Vern went crazy, Yelling, "how we going to get him up, he clear down there and his tanks are up here!" but Corb told him I was alright and would be up shortly. Vern was so impressed he went and bought a Scuba outfit.

After Vern got used to the SUCBA outfit Corb and I took him to Coldwater Lake just off the swimming beach. There was a black hole there a ways out and we wanted to take a look at it. So down we go, Oh! Did I mention that Vern did not know how to swim! I told him with his fins on he could keep himself above water all day, had him try it and he was pleased to find how well it works. But I told him to practice without them as he may get in a spot where he is in the water without his fins. The hole proved to be very deep, about 30-35-feet down. Vern goes ballistic on us and we had to get him back to the surface. Corb and I started back down and we stopped at 85-feet, so we still have no idea how deep it is.

After I was discharged from the Navy Vern and I got together and picked up where I left off when I went into the Navy. Vern had a 53 Chevy and we turned the headlights up so when sitting at the base of one telephone pole you could see the top of the next pole. We used this setup to hunt Raccoons at night, this one night we broke up over this hill and there was a bunch of eyes in this tree. We stopped at its base and started shooting raccoons, we had 22 cal rifles, some of them after they were shot would hang up in the tree limbs, so after we thought we had shot them all I climbed up and started throwing the dead raccoons down. All of a sudden Vern starts shooting while I'm in the tree, I said, "What are you doing?" Vern said, "There's a few more above you and I'll shoot them so you don't have to climb back up. " That's the way we did, fear nothing. We got 21 coons out of that one tree.

One day I was driving the car down the road and Vern said, " Drive across that field." I said, "No" and he emptied his 22-auto rifle in the floorboards. We both got a good laugh about that. Vern was a good friend, and in later years my little Girl could not say Vern and called him Tern. I told Vern about the guy who hated birds and used to go down to beach and throw stones at the birds, " He left no TERN unstoned!"

Vern and I went fishing on the Flat River. It's a 2-3 day float trip from Greenville to Lowell. Now Vern was good at casting on the lake but was way out of his element on the river. I don't know how many times he got hung up. This was after I had accepted the Lord and was trying to steer Vern to the Lord, now Vern and I were cut from the same piece of cloth as far as being our own person. When I accepted the Lord I was so headstrong and so self reliant that I did not know how the Lord got along without me and was always getting ahead of the Lord. I don't know if you have ever tried that but it goes like this, one step ahead and 10 steps back. Praise God I have got over that. Anyway I was trying to lead Vern to the Lord and he would keep trying the Lord, like this. One time he cast into a downed tree, we were using rapalas, (casting lure) and they were quite expensive at the time. But when he cast into the tree he said, " If you can find that lure, I'll know there is a God!" I told him I could find the lure but not to tempt God.

Vern always like to go with me on the trap line, one time I told him I was trapping Beaver on Silver Lake and he wanted to go along, these were the Beaver mentioned earlier and the one I got was the big male, Vern was so excited when he seen it in the trap. Another time he went with me when I was trapping Fox and Coyote, he said he would like to trap a Coyote as he wanted a tanned Coyote for the back of his sofa, I said, "I'll show you how to catch some Fox and Coyote and you can run my line for a few days while I trap on the lake, Fox and Coyote are caught on dry land. Here's a brief line about how these critters live. They hunt mice, ground squirrels and birds, including pheasants. They have hearing beyond belief, and will hear a mouse in a grass field and jump into the air and come down on the mouse almost every time. They hunt until they are full and then hunt some more, anything else they catch they bury in the ground until later, here's where the trapper comes in. You let some meat get tainted and then dig a small hole and put the meat in, stick a small stick about the size of a pencil and then cover up the hole and pull the stick out and it leaves a small hole so the animal can smell the meat, set your trap in the ground in front and off to one side. There you go, Oh! I forgot to mention you have to be very careful not to leave any of your scent at the set. So here's Vern running the line and I'm at the lake. A couple of days after he started the line I'm paddling back to the truck and here's Vern with his truck down by the lake. First thing I saw was his smile almost as big as the lake. Here's a big male Coyote dead and rigid leaning against the front of his truck. Never seen a guy so happy.

One of the places I trapped we also hunted deer. This was the guy's place with the hearing impaired daughter. Vern hunted deer with me there also, but he had this Chevy S-10, 4 wheel drive and he claimed it would go anywhere, no biggie to me I always had Jeeps, they climb trees. When the weather got bad we had to drive back about a mile to where we hunted, usually took Vern's S-10, not much place to haul a deer in the Jeep. And this little truck went though snow and ice, thru the fields. One time while we were back in the hunting area I told Vern I wanted to see how the 4 wheel drive was tied in, he lifted the hood and guess what? The four wheel drive wire was unhooked. Here he had been driving thru everything with 2 wheel drive. His faith that the 4-wheel drive was working took him through. This was such a deal that I preached a sermon about it.

Vern and I had our little disagreements, but our friendship like all the friendships I have is not about disagreements, its about forgiving and going on, besides we were having so much fun it didn't matter. I can still see Vern in his Model "A" or "T" I can't remember, but I can still see him, hung over from the night before, cigarette and breakfast roll in one hand and a beer and steering wheel in the other hand headed for work. Funny, Vern gave up smoking for ten years before he died, He died of lung cancer, and He told me I give up smoking and die of what I give up. The last time I went to see him he was in the hospital. He was so glad to see Cora and I. I kissed him on the cheek to show him the love of our friendship. Somehow I knew it was the last time I would see him. I never did get him to the Lord, after he died Angel told me that he led him to the Lord. Praise God! If you are working on someone to accept the Lord, never give up. The seeds that you plant will blossom. The Lord said, " but my word will not return void."

He loved my Mother, as does Cora, but we stop at Mom's and set and talk a while, pretty soon Vern would say, " I have never been to a house where they did not give me a cup of coffee!" Mom would make some coffee. It was like she was waiting for him to say it. Usually we got something to eat as well. Vern done something, he would take a cup of coffee right out of the pot and drink it down. Would have burned me alive. To this end, Roger and I headed up north to finish a deal I had going We took our thermos bottles full of coffee and I would pour myself a cup and stick my finger in it, Roger would say, "What are you doing?" I said, "If its too hot for my finger its way too hot for my mouth."

Vern always had to stop and buy some of that nasty smelling jerky when we went hunting. And of course some soda pop, I always drank tea out of my thermos. This one time we were headed to the guy's place with the 4,000-dollar dog, daughter was hearing impaired. And it was the last day of shotgun season. I had my bow and he had a 12-gauge shotgun with slugs. I got in my tree stand and that's where I shot the big doe at 70 yards. After I got the deer I see a hole someone had dug to hunt geese and didn't fill it back in so I was filling it in and here comes Vern, no deer, he asked if I got one. I said "ya." Then he asked what I was doing and I told him. About that time here comes a doe out of the woods, I told Vern get down there will be a buck right behind her. Sure enough but Vern could not get a shot until it was clear up on the hill, he took a shot and away it run, I said, "We could go look but that was an awful long ways." We walked up to where it was standing and it was about 165 yards, and there it lay about 25 yards away, shot right in the heart. So we had a pretty good day.

Chapter 20

Muzzleloaders

At these meets I see a lot of guys build their own guns. At home I had about $8,000 dollars in wood working tools, so I starts picking brains, for the most part guys would help you along. First advice I got was to get a stock blank and throw away everything that did not look like a gunstock??? And I learned where to get Wood, barrels, locks and triggers. I'm still building today. And shortly after that I started a gun shop in my basement. Roger worked on the modern guns and I worked on muzzleloaders. You know how I am with the law. I'm in a new area, so the first thing I do is call up the Feds. I had heard horror stories about the Feds coming into your business in the middle of the night. The guy I got a hold of says, " I can't get over to see you for a year, what is it you need?" I said, "We are opening a shop and want to know the ins and outs" he says, "is that all! I will be near your place Tues and will stop in". When he shows up my first question was how often do you guys show up at gun shops, he laughed and said, " We have so much to do with "K" marts and other stores selling guns to guys who can't have them that unless you make an appointment you won't see us." When we said goodbye to him. I was rubbing my hands together, we got this made. We did all the paper work and kept the surface legal. Guys would try to buy handguns with no papers, truckers mostly. We would tell them they only get one shot and then everybody knew they had the gun. We stayed away from things where other people could get us in trouble. We did well enough ourselves.

Corb came over to the shop one time with a black powder revolver, 36 cal and wanted me to put a German silver front sight on it for him. Easy enough job, got it on and then went outside to see how close it was. Let me give you some facts about revolvers. When interest really peaked in black powder the companies wanted to reproduce these handguns. They went to the patents to get permission. They said "fine," however they did not want them modified in any way. For those of you who don't know, these were made with front sights set for 100 yards. I found this out in a very amusing way. I was at this shooting meet and two guys were there and they both knew everything. So they have to prove it. One has a brand new Calvary hat and said, "Bet you can't hit this hat with your revolver," he had a 44 cal, guy with the gun says, "how far?" guy with the hat says, "100 yards and to help you out you can have 6 shots." So the guy loads up and the other guy takes his hat to the 100-yard range, back he comes and said, "There you go." Course, all the activity stops so everyone could watch. The guy walks to the firing line, puts percussion caps on his gun and starts firing, third shot he nails the hat. The bullet went into the headband, ruined the hat. Guy who owned the hat said, "I have a revolver like that and I can't even make it group at 25 or 50 yards." The shooter says, "you should have tried it at 100 yards, that is what the sights are set at when they come from the factory!" One of the guys did know something. Anyway back to Corb's revolver. Took it out and it hit right on the money. Now here's the thing with revolvers, they have a long cylinder and the thing you don't want is cylinder travel, meaning you want the round ball right at the front of the cylinder so when fired it goes right into the barrel, this is how you get the best accuracy. Trouble is the powder charge alone won't put the ball at the front of cylinder. So here's what they do, they pour in the powder charge and then fill it up with cornmeal, then press the ball into the cylinder, right at the front. Having said all that, I says to Corb, "I have always wondered why handgun shooters don't mix the powder and the cornmeal together it is 50-50 mix." He says, "I don't know, try it." I did just one shot, when I fired it, the gun almost jumped out of my hand. Didn't hurt the gun, then the light went on, what I did was make a burning space between the powder grains, the worst thing you can do in a muzzleloader, this is why guys have bulged barrels, they didn't have the ball seated and there was an air space between the powder and the ball. Always have a mark on your loading rod to make sure the ball is seated. I really don't care for revolvers, as they are a mess to clean up.

Let me say a word about the accuracy of a muzzle loading rifle. At the meets, your first target is at a double bitted axe, it's stuck in the end of a log with a blade facing you, on each side of the blade there is a clay pigeon, you have to split the round ball on the axe blade and each half will break a clay bird. Then your next shot is at a playing card edge ways, and then the targets get hard! Did I mention that all these targets are at 25 yards? One of the matches I always liked was what they call a blanket shoot. Each shooter puts an item on the blanket, best shot gets first pick and right on down the line. Another I liked was the loser's shoot. Each station had what looked like a blank paper target, on the back was an X, randomly placed and the shooter did not know where it was You shoot 3-5 shots and the scorekeeper turned them over and the winner was the one scored closest to the X. I always shot a flintlock and would shoot the gun upside down in this match. To shoot a muzzleloader upside down you put the top of the stock on your head so you can see the sights. You are wondering about recoil, when loaded correctly there is hardly any, (I will get into the proper loads later.) One time at my house a newspaper reporter came to see me and do a story on building muzzleloaders. He traveled around the state and talked with craftsman, and we went out in back yard and he shot my gun. Then he wanted me to shoot. I turned the gun upside down and hit a 3 inch target. I went to the drive up at the bank the next day and the teller said, "We seen you last night on TV, my husband shoots those black powder guns and when you turned the gun upside down my husband says, "That flintlock will not fire" and it went boom and he said, "upside down."

Wasn't long until I was at the National Muzzle Loading Association at Friendship, Indiana, rented a booth to sell out of and made pretty good money. I got into Blacksmithing and made fire iron sets, and fire steels, for starting fires with a flint and steel. Made other wood and leather things for shooting. Sold a few of the guns I made. And always had a good time. They have a modern shooting line on one side, 300 stations, that's where the modern campers were. On the other side was what they call the Primitive side, guys dressed in early American clothes and stayed in teepees, tents and lean to's, kind of an early trappers tent. And they also had a range on that side, along a trail. Each side also had a Black powder shotgun range. And on each end of the where the association stopped was a flea market. There was about 100,000 people came through there in the 11 days the shoot was on. It was twice a year.

I always liked to help out and soon became a Range Officer. I can't even describe the first time I had the whole range under my control. A lot of responsibly with 300 shooters, I had to do it to be a Range Officer, but after I became a Range Officer I went to the other side where the primitive shoots were. I also collected the booth rent, even cleaned the bathrooms.

At the Nationals 2 guys and myself went over to the cafeteria for coffee. They had the deal where you walk along the food tables and get what you want and pay for it at the end. Had hand rail opposite the tables with the food. I was sitting against the rail and was telling a polish joke to the guys, I feel a hand land on my shoulder and looked around and there was a giant of a guy. He said, "I don't appreciate those polish jokes!" I thought he was kidding and I said, "Don't take them personally." He said, "I do take them personally, I'm polish! And I don't want to hear anymore!" Away he went and sat down at a table and started drinking his coffee. We sat down and I notice he keeps looking at me. He finished his coffee and came over to our table, sticks his finger in my face and said, "This is not the end of this!" and out the door he went. I told the guys, " That guy is sniffing something." We finished our coffee and went out the door, there he stood with a Razor in his hand, course he didn't have any place to plug it in.

One meet our club went to every year was the Lansing club at Looking Glass River. We went there one year and they had a club shoot, three guys from each club shot as a team, we had a higher score than all the other clubs combined. When we broke for lunch someone moved the sights on our rifles. We took it with a grain of salt, all good fun and they wasted their time as we had them marked in case they got bumped traveling.

Roger, Clem, (the spear pole guy.) and I went to Lansing Club at the Looking Glass river. Clem had never been to a Muzzle Loading Shoot. Roger was just finishing up a long rifle and needed to lap out the barrel, this is where you get some abrasive, put it on a oil soaked patch and run it in the barrel a lot of times, it has to be tight, takes out the rough spots that would rip a patch, plus it is easier to load. We stopped in town to a place where they made grinding wheels and got some of the dust off the floor, worked perfect, I still have some. I told Clem I would have running water in the teepee, he didn't believe me, had a wooden barrel with a spigot. About dusk I said, "Lets go wander around camp." First thing we saw was some guys playing music, Upright Bass, 2 Guitar's, Banjo and really sounded good. Clem said, "Those guys must be in a band together." I told him this is the first time they played together. We listened a while then wandered along. Heard someone yell, " Hey, Wolverine," (my Indian name) I see who it was and told Clem, "Don't drink out of those little brown jugs." Did he listen? No! When we got over there we passed the pleasantries and then sat down with them to talk. I introduced Roger and Clem, and here comes the little brown jug. They said here is water, it looked like water when they poured it in Roger and Clems cup. Pure Moonshine. They sipped that and made it last a while when they were done with that, they said, "Here's the good stuff!" another little brown jug, Roger declined, not Clem, tipped up the jug and drank too big a drink, face turned red, then white, he's gasping for breath, the guys said, "Good huh!" Clem, when he could talk again, said, " What was that? The guys said, "105 year old wine."

I went to the meet at Dorr, just south of Grand Rapids. Of course I got into the woods walk, you had to be dressed in pre 1840 clothes to shoot this meet. At this one station they had eggs at 30 yards sitting on a cone. I stepped up to the line and scorekeeper said, " All you have to do is hit an egg and you will get 10 points, if you miss you can eat a raw egg and we will give you 5 points." Let me say that on a woods walk you got a score at every station and there could be 5 to 10 stations, so points were important. Anyway, I threw my rifle to my shoulder and fired, splattered the egg, the score keeper said, "Do you ever take time to aim?" I said, "When it came to me eating a raw egg I'm an excellent shot." On these woods walk you also had to throw a knife and hawk at a block with playing cards on it.

It was my turn to set up a woods walk, at our home club in Union City, there are from 5 to 10 stations on a woods walk. And you get 10 points at each station. I would set it up and then have a club member at each of the stations. One would be where you throw tomahawk and knife. You had to have your own tomahawk and knife, a lot of times 3-4 guys would share one tomahawk and knife, not under my rules! They would go running back to camp to get their knife and tomahawk and of course I made it hard. National rules say the tomahawk and the knife have to make a complete turn before hitting the target so I set it up so you were too close to the target and you yourself would have to judge how far back you will have to stand to make it turn over once. Then I set up a turkey target, there is a target on the market with just a turkey head so you can shoot it with your shotgun and count the pellets that hit the head. I took the target and cut out the head and put it on one end of a 4 foot 2 x 4, then I drilled a hole in the middle of the 2 x 4 and run a large screw through it and screwed it to the back of a tree. Then I hooked a big rubber band I had cut from a truck inner tube so it would pull the head from behind the tree to the left. I then hooked a camouflage duck decoy line to it and run it to the shooting station. Here's how it went, the guy would load and be ready to fire then he would say, "Turkey or Gobble." And I would relax the decoy line and the head would pop out to the left and he would try to hit it, the shooter had 10 seconds to locate and shoot. Now bear in mind there was no indication of where the target was until it popped out. Still with me? Good! I only allowed one shooter at the station at a time so the next shooter would not see where the turkey head was. This one fellow with a chip on his shoulder sets up to shoot, (these are mostly young or new shooters, the targets mellow them out) he said, "This looks simple enough." (As you have seen in this book when a guy with an attitude comes along, he is in my area) I said, "When you are ready to fire either gobble or say Turkey." And the turkey head will pop out and you will have 10 seconds to hit it. He said, "Ok!" he said, "Turkey!"

and I relaxed the decoy line and he is looking all over for the target and when he finally seen it he fired so fast he missed it, was he hot, he said, "This is not a very fair target!" I said. "Hey, I can give you another shot if you like." He said, "That's more like it!" he loads up puts his gun up and said, "Turkey." I pulled the decoy line tight and the turkey head came out on the RIGHT, he shot where he thought it was coming out on the left. Did I forget to mention that by pulling the decoy line you could make it come out on the opposite side?

Then there was the fire starting. I was pretty good at this. You carried a flint and steel, some stuff for the nest and char. For the nest I usually used sisal (rope) and the way you make char cloth was to take some cloth, I used sheet blanket, cut in round pieces, put them packed tightly in a metal can, I always like a 100 foot 35mm film can, have holes punched in the lid, from inside out so the smoke can escape, put the can in a fire, it will smoke out the holes then a flame out the holes, when the flame went out you took it out of the fire and let it cool, a few hours, Do Not Open Until It's Cool or The Cloth will Just be Ash! Ok, lets make a fire, take the sisal, make a birds nest, lay it on the ground, take some char cloth, pull it apart a little and lay it in the nest. Then you take the flint and steel and strike the flint against the steel and sparks would come off the steel, hopefully into the nest, you drop the flint and steel and grab up the nest and start blowing into the nest and you should get a fire. I could do it in 9 seconds. That's the only way you lit your campfire. One time I was timing the fire starting, you have a stopwatch and when the guy made the first strike you hit the watch, when you saw fire you hit the watch, that was the guys time. This guy comes up and gets his stuff ready, he struck, I hit the watch, seen fire and hit the watch, 1 second and ½.

Another way the fire starting was done was to have the guy start a fire with flint and steel, walk 10 steps and light a candle. I seen some burnt hands on this one, new guys tried to carry the fire in their hands. The way to do it is to carry the fire in the tin box you kept your fire making stuff in.

Flint! I always shot Flintlocks and it wasn't long until I was making my own flints for the gun, flint knapping isn't hard, just takes some practice. After I made flints for the gun it was time to make some arrowheads, you have a piece of thick leather on your leg above the knee to Knapp flint. Lets back up a little, say you got a flint nodule, this is a lump of flint around 8 inches thru, you first need to break it in half. Take a mall and make a depression in the ground big enough for the nodule, put it in the ground and strike in the center with the mall, it will break in half, now put it on the leather pad and strike it on the edge and sliver will come off, now you can then make a gun flint or an arrow head. You use a piece of deer horn, lay the flint flat on the pad and push down on the edge and flakes will chip off. (Be sure to wear safety glasses as flint flies fast and hard.) Turn it over and do it again, arrowheads are easy, just chip off everything that don't look like an arrowhead. The best thing to do is go to library and get a book on flint or look in some of the Muzzle Loader magazines. By the by there was a doctor in California who had to have surgery and he knew about flint so he made a full set of instruments for his operation, Why? He knew that flint is sharper than any steel blade that's made.

Lets talk about the proper loads for the muzzleloader. It should be around 1600 feet per second. You are probably thinking that's awful slow for a rifle, consider a 12 gauge shot gun with a slug is 1200-1300 fps, a general rule is one grain per caliber, 50 cal = 50 grains of black powder. A very interesting thing I come across, if you lose your powder measure, lay one of the lead balls you are shooting in your palm, make your palm as flat as possible, pour black powder over the ball just until it is covered, this is awful close to your regular load. I have a 50 cal and a 54 cal, in the 50 I shoot 59 grains and in the 54 I shoot 65 grains,. The reason you want 1600 fps is that if the load is any faster it will strip out of the cloth patch. A guy by the name of Bob Wolf taught me this, he said, "don't take my word for it, try it yourself." And he gave me a formula for figuring this and it will be included in the Appendix. You can try it too, just start loading your gun and put more powder each time, try 5 grain increments, and try different distances also, with too much powder you will see a ball whip. You can also pick up your patch and look at it, it should not be burned through. Another way to see if you are over charging is shoot over snow when the sun is shinning in the spring, every grain of power that did not burn will melt and make a black spot, another way is to shoot over a white bed sheet. Now bear in mind that I only shoot patched round ball, these new inline guns are no different than a modern rifle. (Refer to Chapter 10, Lee) Be glad I don't make the laws. It would be like Pennsylvania patched round ball, and flintlock only. Over the years I have seen some things that I have come to hate, one is the tc gun co, they made a lot of half stock rifles. I'm going to open myself up to a suit, but what I say is true, like I said earlier my Brother has a sign that says it all " I started with nothing, still have most of it left." Shortly after getting into muzzleloaders I met a man who had a black powder shop, name of Roy Keeler, in fact he is the one who got the black powder season for deer in Michigan. First time I met him I called him MR Keeler, he says, "You call me Roy or Pa, no Mr." That's the way he was. He was also the most safety conscious guy I ever met. So one day I was at his shop and he was fuming. Turns out a guy was shooting a tc rifle and it blew up on him, 50 cal. The idiots that built these put in their instruction that you could use up to 120 grains of powder per charge. That's twice the powder, anyway the gun blew, he didn't get hurt, and he had bought it from Pa. Of course Pa made it right with him and sent the gun to tc factory wanting to know why it blew, they sent him a replacement with no explanation. The next time I went up to see Pa he had another tc 50 cal that blew, tells me this story. A buck skinner had the 50 cal at a Boy Scout meet, explained the history, how it worked and let each kid shoot the gun. He down loaded it to 35 grains, after the boys left the Scoutmaster asked him how much powder can you shoot in that gun, the buck skinner said, "The instructions said 120 grains, the boys were shooting 35 grains, here I'll put 90 grains in it and you can shoot it." he did and it blew, the trigger guard was all that was holding it together. (Didn't get hurt) Another gun Pa had sold, course he made it right. So he is showing me the gun and said he was going to send it to tc (note I put tc in lower case letters that's where they belong). It was quite a while before I got up to see Pa again, whenever I went to see Pa we talked a lot. After a while I remembered the blown tc, I said 'Pa what did you find out about the 50 that blew at the Scout camp?" His face got red and he said, "Wait until you read the letter they sent me." While he was getting it out of his file he was telling me," I sent it to tc and they sent a new gun, that's all. I called them and said, "This is the second gun that blew and I want to know what's going on." They said, "We sent you a new gun." Well! He says. "The last gun I sent you I had photographed and notarized, and I can proceed to someone who would be interested in this situation." They said, "We will send you a letter!" And Pa says, "Here is the letter" I started reading it and it said; We make 1000s of guns and if one or two blow we don't feel bad. I could not believe it. Needless to say Pa was unhappy. I don't know what he did but I never heard of another one blowing. He was a real stickler about plastic sabots, the problem was that would not stay seated. Remember what I said about an air space between the powder and the ball? Pa found out about this the hard way. He went on a bear hunt with his 50 cal, heavy barrel, and 1 ½ inch, more than a 1/3 thicker than the standard. He wanted to try out the sabots. Loaded his gun, walked around a while unbeknownst to him the sabot was creeping up the barrel. When he shot, the barrel bulged, if it hadn't been a heavy barrel, Katy bar the door! Pa was into the national's big time, in fact they wrote an article about him in their book, Muzzle Blast, so sabots were never allowed at the range.

Had a lot of smiles at Pa's place. One time there were about 6 guys arguing about how early the peep sight was, Pa listen to it for a while then he went down his gun vault and came back with a match lock from the 15th century. He says, "Boys see this little tube above the lock on the weapon? What its for is the other end of the wick or the cord, they lit both ends in case one went out, and stuck the loose end in the tube to keep it from falling down and setting off the lock, guess what they used the tube for went the gun was converted to a flint lock?" That ended that!

I got into building Bedford County flint lock rifles, all the old rifles were referred to by the county they were built in Pennsylvania. The Germans were the biggest in building guns and when they came over to the USA they settled in Pennsylvania and each county had its own gun makers. The Bedford is a long slender rifle, if you seen one you would know why they had women's names. It had a bunch of German silver inlays, and Pa had all the reproduction parts. One time I was up there and he said, "How you doing on the Bedfords?"

I had built a few of them, I said, "Pretty good." Pa says, "Next time you come up bring one along." I said, "OK" so the next time I went I took one along. Pa said, "You are doing a fine job on these, did you ever see a real Bedford?" I said, "No" and away he went to his gun vault, came back with a Bedford in real nice shape for its age. He laid it beside my gun and they looked like twins, I was really proud. Pa says," Pick up your gun and shoulder it, then pick up the original and shoulder it." I did and when I put the original to my shoulder it felt like it was made just for me. My gun felt like a broomstick, I now had a new goal, it took a few years but I got it, I can't even explain what it is.

Pa passed away a couple years ago, sure is missed. And he took a mountain of information with him. I have been in his shop when a guy would ask for a hammer for a musket, tell Pa the model and Pa would bring out a wire ring with a hundred hammers on it, Go right to the one the guy needed. He could answer any question you had and was glad to do it. This man, God bless him, was one in a thousand.

One of the meets I went to was on a personal invite, came up to me and handed me a letter, Indian's called them the talking leaves. Anyhow it was from the Turtle Clan, I knew they had been watching me, I guess I made the grade. Anyway at the meet they had a John Colder run, John Colder was with a bunch of mountain men and a bear charged him and tore him up real bad, they left him for dead. One of the things mountain men did was if someone was killed they took everything they had, no sense of leaving it to rot or rust. And I mean everything, his gun, tomahawk, knife and even his clothes, and left him, didn't bury him cause he was still breathing. Away they went. Pretty soon John sat up, then got up and walked back to nearest Fort several days away. He made it who knows how. But this was the way of life on the frontier. He came stumbling into the Fort with no clothes on. So the club had the John Colder run and this is how it goes. You put a prize on the blanket, took off your clothes and run 100 yards and back naked, first one back got the pick of the prizes. The next day three older ladies on 4 wheeler's got lost and ended up in our camp. The Turtle Clan owned the land. They didn't know what to think. Thought they had went back in time. I got to thinking if they had got lost yesterday and run into 30-40 naked guys running thru the woods they would have thought they were in heaven. I took a guy with me, had the 16 foot teepee and plenty of room, now this was a 3 day meet. I made coffee after the camp was set up and here's how you do it. I had a gallon coffee pot, filled in half full of water, when it got to boiling I threw in a hand full of coffee grounds and let it boil some more, next I broke 2 eggs in the pot, let it boil some more, and then filled it with cold water, the eggs would be hard boiled and most of the coffee grounds would be in the eggs, take the eggs out and there was your coffee, we drank the same pot of coffee for the 3 days.

One meet I went to in South Bend Indiana was a real family meet, had things for the kids to do. And had a very interesting deal, I told you before about fire starting. So here's how it went. The man had his fire making kit and they gave his woman a small container of pancake batter, she also had a pan. Put them on a line, when the scorekeeper said go they run 25 yards, stopped, the man started a fire, remember I said you had to blow on the nest to get the fire going, not much breath left after running. He got a fire going and the woman cooked the pancake and the man eat it, then they had to run back to the start line and the scorekeeper stopped the watch. I don't even remember who won, I was laughing so hard and some of the men ate a mighty sloppy pancake.

Another meet I went to Touched my heart. After the events of the day they would have a large fire and all the people would set around it. The guy who was in charge was called a Booshway and he had a staff in his hand, called it the "Talking Stick" and the only time you could talk was when you had the staff in your hand. (I often wondered why this method was not used at meetings or even school) he would walk around the circle of people and if you wanted to say something you stood up when he came to you and took the stick. He came to me, my Indian name was the Wolverine, and I would say something like a greeting to the people like, " the Wolverine has traveled many miles to sit at the concil fire with his friends and hopes for many more council fires for them." he took the stick around and a young couple stood up and took the talking stick and they said, "Our baby son died and is with the Manitou, (God to the Indians) and has only the clothes on his body and we wish to put this pair of moccasins in the fire and send them up to him for his feet." And they put a small pair of moccasins in the fire. Boy that was powerful!

One of the best rib ticklers I ever had was from the actions of a guy named Dick Smith. He was the one who made my 16 foot teepee, he would always come around to make sure I had it set up right. People would ask me "how long does it take to set up" I would say, " by myself half hour to forty five minutes, with help two hours." Dick was part of the Turtle Clan, and Dick is hard to describe, he had to be experienced, he wore a human finger necklace. Anyway, the way this whole deal got started was the Turtle Clan left Kalamazoo in a convoy to go to Dorr, Michigan for a four day rendezvous (I'll explain this word later) there was a lot people in the Turtle Clan, so here they go down the road, on the way a guy driving ahead of them hit a deer, course the Clan stopped so see if they could help. That's the way muzzle-loading people are. The guy was out of his head as he thought the DNR was going to arrest him for killing the deer. The Clan tried to assure him he was in no trouble and the CO would give him the deer to eat, he says, "You eat it, I'm out of here." and away he went. Now this is perfect, a four-day meet with deer meat to eat. They put Dick Smith in charge of it, the deer was a pregnant doe, so the next picture you see is Dick Smith, camp set up, he's in full costume, sitting by the fire with the unborn fawn on a spit over the fire, not a care in the world. Now right across from club grounds was a KOA campground. Here comes this young boy and walks up to Dick and says, "What are you cooking?" Dick says, "DOG! Sioux always eat their dogs," now Dick always sounded gruff, The kid looks down at the ground and says, "I'm looking for my dog, he run over here somewhere." Dick says, "Walk to the back of the camp and see if anybody has seen it." The kid walks away and Dick is saying to himself, " I'm going to jail", "I'm going to jail," then he hears a voice like thunder say, "Have you seen my kid? he is looking for his dog." Dick looked up, up and up and here is this giant of man. Dick is thinking "I'm not going to make it to jail!" Before he could say anything to the guy here come the kid with his dog, Dick says," I almost collapsed on the spot."

I had my teepee set up at Dorr one time and was inside getting ready to cook dinner. I hears something going on behind my teepee and went around and there three guys, they had dug a hole, put some hot coals in the bottom and was putting some meat and veggies in the hole, they had them wrapped in something. I went back inside and it got quiet. I went back out and they were gone, didn't even leave a track behind. Later that day I heard something out there again. I went back to look and there they had dug up the meat and veggies and the hot coals had cooked the meal for them and they were sitting around eating with their knives, no self-respecting mountain man would carry a fork with him. They said, " Would you like to eat with us?" I said, "No thanks I just ate." I went back in, the next morning I looked back there were they had been nary a track or any sign they had been there.

RENDEZVOUS, a meeting place, the mountain men would have meet in the mountains with the fur buyers when Beaver was the fur to sell or trade. They done mostly trade as the mountain men had no where to spend money and needed supplies. They traded for a lot of gunpowder and lead, salt, coffee, etc. And of course mountain men from all over would show when the wagons loads of trade goods arrived. Then one thing would lead to another, like my Betsy gun will out shoot any gun here. Then the shooting matches would begin and you would hear, I can hit a playing card with my tomahawk or knife from 10 paces. This is way the meets started and continue today. To camp at one of these meets today you have to have a camp, clothes, and gun from before 1840, there is always a place for the tin (Modern) campers too. And today they have costume judging, these guys have some pretty fancy duds. I had Sioux outfit, beaded deerskin shirt, pants, belt, and moccasins. 175,000 beads and of course I built my own everything. When I would describe my outfit, you had to describe everything so the judges knew you had the knowledge. I would say, " Everything you see, I built." I also had a trapper's outfit, this one was comfortable, and I had a Rogers Ranger's outfit, Brown Bess and all. Rangers were from the 1750s era. This Englishman named Robert Rogers went to the Queen and said, "If you will give me a elite bunch of men we can stop the French at the New York area." Now bear in mind that in these days they did not fight in the winter. Rogers was going to change all that. Here is the thing, when they were not fighting in the winter the French would bring in all their supplies across Lake Champlain in New York when it was froze. Rogers was a think ahead man and had several blacksmiths with him. The smiths made ice skates for the men and they caught the French in the middle of the Lake and sank their supplies. If you want a small glance at the Rangers see the movie, Northwest Passage.

I think this was about the time they put a herd of cows into space, it was called the, "Herd shot around the world!" ??????

Can you imagine fighting in the winter, the Rangers had long bayonets, as did the French and would run these though the enemy in the middle. Think about that, did you ever stick your tongue on metal in the winter? This is the same thing only the guys innards would stick to the bayonet and when they pulled them out everything came with it. Reminds me of the torture some Indians done, cut a small slit in a tree, make a small cut in the stomach of their enemy, pull out a small part of their intestine put it in the slit in the tree and make them walk around the tree till all the innards pulled out or they died in the process. I heard about the Apaches and what they would do to their enemies. Strip off their clothes, cut off their eyelids, and then cut off their heels and turn them loose in the desert. Tip toe thru the tulips?

A guy named Jim had a Black Powder shop we used to go to, he also had modern guns. Now this guy was a blast. Out behind his shop was a valley with a pond at the bottom He had a target set up across the valley, I would guess the target was 100-200 yards away. He had a picnic table he would set at and shoot across the valley. He had what they call a "clang" target, and that's the sound it made when a bullet would hit it, you would know you hit the target if it clanged. He used a pistol to shoot at the target and he never missed once. At least that's what I thought. I later found out he had a button under the table that he pushed when he shot, and the target would clang, wonder if he ever really hit the target?

My brother, Roger, had a 22 caliber revolver and the thing went off in the hostler and hit him in the knee. Now Roger could fix any gun but this one he could not figure out. I says, "Why don't we take

155

it down to Jim's shop, he is pretty sharp and might be able to figure it out." Roger said, "If he can't figure it out I will sell or trade it to him." Away we go. Gets down to Jim's and told him what the pistol was doing. Jim looked at it and then started loading it, Roger and I both yelled at him not to load it in his shop as it might go off. He just laughed and shoved some shells in it and closed it up, when he did it went off and put a hole in his shop door. He opened it back up and took the rest of the shells out and studied on it for a while, he says, "I have no idea, you want to sell this gun to me? I want to keep it around until I figure it out." Roger said, "Sure, but I have quite a bit in it and would like it back out" Jim says, "No problem" and bought the gun. Never did hear anymore about it.

I did a funny at Jim's place one time. He asked me if I wanted to play handles with him, I mentioned throwing tomahawks and this is what he meant You flip a coin to see who goes first, the first guy sticks his tomahawk in the throwing block and the other guy or guys try to hit the handle and cut it up. The guy with the most handle left is the winner. I did not say anything about this before but at the national meets they had a cross stick in front of the throwing block, it would hit your handle and knock your tomahawk away. So after seeing that I learned to throw the tomahawk and stick it upside down The other benefit to throwing this way added some distance to the throw, so I was first. I threw the hawk at the block and it stuck in the top of the block upside down, the handle was in the air and to throw at it you had to throw above the block and over the block, if it did hit the handle it just glanced off, Boy! Was Jim frustrated!

I heard about these two guys. The one was a hunter and other never did hunt. One day the hunter asks the other guy, " Want to go hunting? I have a gun you can use." the guy says, "Sure, I'll try it." So he takes him to the range and let him shoot until he got the hang of it and they went hunting. They got to woods and the new guy says, "What are we hunting for?" The hunter says, "You know, game!" and they separate, and pretty soon the hunter hears a shot. He goes over to see what the greenhorn shot and there lays a woman. The hunter says, "Did you have an accident?" the other says, "No, why? I seen the woman sitting there under a tree and I asked her if she was game." and she smiled at me and said, "Yes." and I shot her.

Somewhat like the two that went into Canada hunting for Bear. Of course they got lost, step off the road 10 feet in Canada and you are lost. Anyway the one says, "we are lost and no one will ever find us," Not so, says the other guy, "I read up on hunting up here, you get lost and all you have to do is fire three shots in the air, and the ranger will come and find us. Go ahead fire three in the air." he did and they stood around for quite a while, the one says, "Are sure that's what you read?" "Yes it is, fire three more in the air," so he did, they stood around for a long time and the one guy said, "You read that wrong, the three shots in the air don't work." "Yes it will, fire three more in the air," the other guy says, "I can't, that's all the arrows I had with me!"

Back to Muzzleloaders, one of the hardest targets I ever saw was the quarter target. At 25 yards there is a cross bar with a 2 foot string and a quarter hanging on the bottom of it, below the quarter was a empty coffee can The idea was to shoot the string and drop the quarter into the can. This is all freehand shooting, no rest. And the problem was this, shoot too high the quarter would fly back at you, too low and it would fly behind the target post. And this is the first target of 5 you had to shoot. Then you had the double bitted axe with the two clay birds, you shot the edge of the axe and split the ball and got both birds, every time I see this target I think of when the our Club put on a demonstration shoot one Memorial day. I had built a rifle special for this shoot. The people would watch, as the members would shoot the axe target and break the birds. They all thought it was the best shooting they ever saw, then here I come and said," You can do that too! I have a rifle here and you can try it. I will load it for you and you can shoot." There was quite a few people who shot, they all broke both the birds, and I never did tell them they were not shooting a round ball but a smooth bore with birdshot. I was the one who put on the fire starting with the flint and steel, up comes a guy and said, " I can start a fire just as fast with a kitchen match' I said, "Well lets give it try, Oh! We have to go stick our fire making stuff in the river, bring your match." We went over to the river and I dipped my flint and steel in the water, he put his matches in the water and we went back and I started a fire, he didn't, his matches were wet. I guess I should have told him that flint and steel fire hotter when they are wet. That's why you will see a flintlock shooter wet his thumb and wipe the frizzen before he shoots. (The part of the gun lock that the spark comes from when the flint hits it). It also cleans off the residue from the prior shot. As I said before my flintlocks would shoot upside down, but the lock had to tuned like a fine watch.

I made my own Black Powder a couple of times, never came out right, its easy to make and kind of dangerous, all it is, Charcoal, Sulfur and Salt Peter. (Potassium nitrate) You mix these wet as they can blow up dry, then you make them into small cakes and let them dry. Old guys dried them in the sun, then you put the cakes in a container that can't spark, I always used a gallon glass jar with a wooden lid. I put some lead round balls in and then had small motor with a long belt that turned it when it was well mixed you open the jar and put in some Graphite to make it flow smoothly and there you are. If you want to grade it you put in through different size screens, smallest grains would be 4F, then 3F, 2F and the largest would be 1F. This is how they are used, 4F is the priming powder used in the pan of a flintlock, 3F is used in guns up to and including 45 caliber, 2F would be used in the larger caliber's and 1F is used in cannons. When I said it never came out right I meant 25 grains would shoot like 40 or 40 grains would shoot like 25. I didn't need to make it. I just wanted to try everything. As I said one of the ingredients is salt peter (Potassium nitrate). During the civil war people would have a chamber pot by their bed and the soldiers collect the urine and dehydrate it and the crystals are potassium nitrate.

I also cut my own trees for my gunstocks. Here's some important information on how to find the Tiger Maple used for stocks. Tiger Maple is called that as it has lines in the wood. The lines are hardwood and between them is a softer wood. But here is how you find them, at the present time they are 1 in 1,000, if you look at 1,000 maple trees, 1 will be Tiger. They are the trees that are exposed to the westerly wind and will lean to the East. Go up to the tree you think might be Tiger and look at it what you can see of the roots and lower part of the tree. You will see in the bark lines running horizontal on the tree, that's the one you want. I got so good at it that one time I found one going 60 miles an hour down the road, I bought it for $10.00, cut it down, hauled the logs to mill they cut them into 2

½ inch planks and kiln dried them. I took what wood I wanted and sold the rest, it was about a 75-80 foot tree. I got over $10,000 for it. Course you have to deduct cutting and drying at the sawmill. Now Birdseye Maple is something else. They think the eyes are from the tree starving at some point of its life. When you go to buy a Birdseye stock look at both sides, the eyes are only where it starved not thru the whole thing, so look at both sides. Here's another tip when you go to buy a Tiger or Birdseye stock. Carry a cup of water with you and ask the seller if you can wet it down to see the grain. Sellers with nothing to hide will let you and those who won't you don't want their wood anyway.

Roger and I were hunting deer on Smitty's place one year and we were walking thru the woods. I stopped, "Roger, right there." He said, "What, a deer? I said, "No that tree right there, it's a Tiger Cherry.' Roger says, "Did you bump your head or something?" course Smitty said, "You can have that tree, just don't leave a mess." From this tree among the guns I built was a Brown Bess, these were the guns the British had when they came at us in 1775. They are 69 cal, 46 inch barrels, course they were flintlocks. Anyway I got $10,000 for this gun. Sounds like a lot of money, but I had 1500 hours in the building of it. I had choked the barrel (this was not done to the originals) and it shot like a rifle, these guns are smooth bores and you could shoot birdshot in them also.

Roger Mendenhall and I planned a Bear hunting and Fishing trip into Canada, in 1969. What he didn't tell me until later was he had two guys he wanted to take along. I said, "What the hay," What I didn't also know was that I was going to chaperone the one guy. But it ended up Ok. He wanted to be an outdoorsman but had never been around anyone who was. I took my 14-foot flat bottom boat, my canoe and Roger had a v bottom boat. We were going to try and catch some Lake trout. Roger had been in this area before, I was always further north, and this was the Ranger Lake area. We had to motor up a small River, drag our boats over a dam, that's why he wanted 2 extra guys. Any way, I had no idea how little this guy, we'll call him Kurt, knew about fishing. We got into Ranger Lake and going to troll for the Lake trout. I tells Kurt to put a swivel on his line, he says, "What's a swivel?" I thought to myself O-boy; I got to thinking what a shame no one ever took the time to help this guy out. I forgot to mention that I was the laughing stock for the other two guys. I had brought my ultra light fishing gear. But I had the last laugh. I caught a 10 and 11 ½ lb lake trout, the other guys, Zip! I don't think they even had a hit the whole time. We fished a couple other spots and got some Brooke Trout. There is nothing like fresh fish fried in the wild. We stopped at the edge of the lake to cook the dinner and of course, I had to look around. I came across a tree a Beaver had tried to drop, the teeth marks were wide, meaning the Beaver was huge. The chew marks were 4 foot off the ground. Now I knew they had caught a Beaver in Canada that was 140 lbs, but a Beaver that could chew 4 foot high on a tree had to be around 250 lbs. I took pictures of everything. And I really had a rough time with this big a Beaver. I'll tell you at the end of this story about the beaver. We finished lunch and went to fishing again. We got back to camp late that afternoon and decided that no more fish than we were catching, we may as well been hunting for bear, we all had our bear license. So the next day was the first day of the hunt, Roger said, " The best time to hunt them is in the afternoon and we should check our guns out tomorrow before we go." Roger knew where there was a dump with Bear everywhere. Slept in the next day, eat a bite and decided to shoot the guns. You should have seen their faces when I pulled out my 54 cal flintlock, 42 inch barrel. But the laugh was on them when we started shooting. They never saw a gun that accurate. Here comes Kurt with a 30-06 bolt, 3 x 9 scope, he had borrowed the gun and I assumed the guy had showed him how to use it, Nope, Kurt says, to me, "How do I load this thing?" I showed him and he turned out to be a pretty fair shot. I drove my ¾ ton Chevy truck with a big camper, and the other guy, I think his name was Dave, had a 4-wheel drive carry all, they call them SUV's today. So we decided that we would take the carry all to the dump site, so we get to where we were going to hunt and I went down the path, they were still getting there stuff around, I knew they would not be very far away if I needed help. I get a ways down the trail and there are Bear paths everywhere. Glad I had loaded before I started out. I found a big tree blown down and got up in it about 12 ft off the ground and sat down. I had brought my tomahawk just in case. I sat there from 1:00

in the afternoon to 5:00, and never seen a thing, and had not heard any shots, strange surely somebody should have seen a Bear. I gets back to the 4 wheeler and there's all 3 of them guys asleep. Glad I did not get in trouble, they had not even loaded their guns. Some Bear hunters! The next day we were going to hunt by a River we had fished at, lot of Bear sign there. It was a big curve to where we were going to hunt and I told Roger I was going to walk a straight line thru the woods to where we were going. I should be there about same time they got there with the carry all. Now bear in mind that I did not know how to use a compass, didn't even have one with me. And buddy, you get lost up there you are really lost. I have always been good at getting where I wanted to go. Besides outdoorsmen never get lost, turned around maybe, never lost. So I got out of the suv Kurt says, "I want to go with you." I knew he had no idea how lost you could get up here. So I tells him, "If you lose sight of me for a second you start hollering as loud as you can until I find you and I am serious!" To his credit he stuck close. We were following some fresh Bear tracks headed the same way the carry all was going to be. I slowed a bit in case he was too far ahead of us and the other guys might get a shot. We got to the road and there they were waiting for us, I said, "Did you see that Bear?" they said, "Yes it run right across the road in front of us." I said, "Did you get a shot?" They said, "No we forgot to load our guns." I have been hunting with some crack-erjacks, but these guys take the cake. We came home, no Bear. Kurt told me he was sorry for all the trouble he had been, I said, "Not at all, I enjoyed helping you out." Oh yah, the Beaver, Did you figure it out? The beaver was sitting on some snow when he chewed on the tree.

Randy and I took a trip to Quebec, Canada in 2003 to hunt Caribou. It was 1635 miles to where we went. I took the 54 flintlock and the 30-06. This time I had to stamp numbers in the barrel of the 54 as there was no serial numbers on it. We had booked a hunt with a lodge. They had guides, meals, and rooms. We went in December which was really supposed to be real cold, the first morning Randy I went out of the lodge and I said to him, " It sure doesn't feel very cold, I would guess about 20-25," He said, "Yes, don't feel bad at all." We would go ice fishing when it was 7-15 degrees and I didn't even put on gloves. When we seen the guide I said, "I thought it was supposed to be cold up here!" the guide said, " This is the warmest winter we have had in quite a while." I said, "What is it 20 degrees?" He says, "its 35 below!" It was so dry you could not feel the cold. We got on snowmobiles and went about 35 miles back in looking for Caribou, you could shoot 2 on the license we had. I told people when we got back home if they wanted to hunt Caribou they could practice by sneaking up on some farmer's cows. Those Caribou are the stupidest animals I ever did see. I couldn't take the 54 flintlock as it was too long to manage on a snowmobile. We came to a rough place and the guide had to take my snowmobile thru for me, then he came back and I got on the back of his snowmobile and he took me across. It was so rough I lost my breath and flew off his snowmobile and in the deep snow. I could not move for a few minutes and Randy thought I had a heart attack. But we got going again and I was sitting on a hill while the guide took Randy to a lake he said always had Caribou. I already had 2 lying by me, I hear this snowmobile come tearing toward me and it was Randy. I could not figure out what had happened. He said, "My gun won't fire the shells I got, have you got any shells?" I said, "I do, but they won't fit your gun." I had fire formed them for my rifle and although we both had 30-06s my shells would not fit his gun. I said, "Here take my gun and shells." Away he went and I heard a shot and here he comes with a Caribou. We had small snowmobiles and the guide had a large one, so Randy and I dragged one ea while the guide dragged two. When we got back to lodge Randy said when his Caribou went down about 40 more come to see what was going on. I told him, " While I was sitting on the hill Caribou came out of the woods all around me. This trip was a flop as far as hunting goes but it was great to go with my brother. I would never hunt Caribou again. Like I said it was like shooting a farmer's cows.

The first trip Randy and I took to Canada was around 1967. We didn't plan anything, just took off, had our fishing gear with us, and had my truck with the canoe on top. We stopped at different places to look at the lake and such. We found a small lake and decide to give it a try. It was quite windy and I told Randy, "You fish and I will handle the canoe." His lure no more than hit the water and he had a fish on, turned out to be a Pike, and we could not believe our eyes. There was a Pike on each side of the one he had hooked trying to get the lure out its mouth. We didn't keep any fish, no way to keep them cold. We had a nice trip and on the way home we run into a road block and had to go through this roadside park. Looked ahead and there the Rangers (like our Cos) searching all the vehicles for over limits of fish. There was a truck with a camper on it, also had a boat hooked on the back. We walked up so we could hear what was going on, here these 3 guys had 3 coolers full of Walleye fillets, only about a hundred fish over their limit each. They told them there is the line to United States cross it, leave everything here, truck, camper and boat. And one of the Rangers said to one of the guys, "Give me that knife you have on your belt. And then you can walk home!" They are rough in Canada.

Reminds me of a story I heard about this same thing. A guy in Oregon lived a short ways from Canada and said, "When I retire I'm going hunting in Canada for Bear," he had heard there were a lot of Bear there. So he retires and buys a new truck, new gun and whatever else he thought he would need and away he goes to Canada after Bear. He gets one and starts home, when he come to the check point before United States border, Ranger says, " How you doing." The guy says, "Real good, look at that big Bear in the back of the truck." The ranger says, " Nice bear, you got a bear License?" the guy says, " A license! I thought bears were a nuisance and you could just shoot them." The Ranger says, "You have to have a license, and the bad news is I have to confiscate (big word for steal) all you gear including your truck." The guy says, "If that's the law, so be it." The next year into Canada he goes again, he really wanted a bear mount, new truck, new gun and gear. Gets another bear and is heading home and stops at the check point, it's the same Ranger, they recognize each other, the ranger says, "I hope you have a bear hunting license this time, another nice bear you got there." The guy says, "Here you go!" and give him the license. The ranger says, "And the papers to export the bear to the United States." The guy says, "What are you talking about?" The ranger says, "Canada is another country and you have to have an export permit." The guy says, "I don't have one." The Ranger says I hate to tell you this, but I have to confiscate all your gear, including your truck. The guy says," If that's the law so be it." Next year here he comes again, new truck, new gun and gear to the check point, Guess what, same Ranger, looks in the truck and says, " That is a giant of a bear, I sure hope you have all the paper work This time," The guy says, "Sure do!" and gives the Ranger the paper work. The Ranger says, "I sure hated to take your stuff before, but it is the law." Guy says, "Hey I ended up with a bigger bear anyway, you are just doing your job." The Ranger says, "I have to ask you something. Every bear that you got was shot right between the eyes, you are some kind of a good shot!" the guy says, "naaah, when they looked into the bright light how could I miss!"

You know how Canada got its name? They could not agree on a name so they put a bunch of letters on pieces of paper and put them in hat, and then drew them out, first one C,aaaaaaaa,N,aaaaaaaaa,D ,aaaaaa. Funny,aaaaaaaaa?

I had a 32 cal flintlock long rifle that I built. I shot 23 Grains of 3F in it. I took it squirrel hunting and was sitting under a tree. I guess I had 3-4 squirrels, and here comes this button buck; this one would be good eating. I wondered to myself would this 32 knock him down? I knew the way to find out and I did, took him right in the heart. I just sit still for a bit and was getting ready to go find the buck when I hear the rustle of leaves. Looked and here come two nice Raccoon. I shoots the biggest of the two and the other one just stood there. I loaded up and shot the other one. Now I get up and go look for the buck, didn't go far and I could not believe the damage the 32 had done! It looked like he was hit with a 30-30. Tell me about those heavy loads, they just are not necessary.

I had a smile. One time I was hunting out behind my brother's house, he had a bunch of deer in the woods there and I had seen this nice buck. I took a 58 cal Hawkins I had built, it was a half stock. The early Hawkins were full stocks. And this gun was heavy, anyhow I'm sitting there waiting, I knew that big boy was going to come thru there. I heard a snap, it sounded like it came from my rifle. I tried the hammer and it was loose and would not cock. I reach into my possible's bag and got a screwdriver, took the lock out and the mainspring of my lock was broke. That was the end of that hunt for a day. I got to thinking about it, had I been a mountain man way back when, it would be weeks before I could get another mainspring.

One time I went squirrel hunting with my brothers, Lee and Roger. They had 22 magnum rifles and I had a 25 cal flintlock I built. I shot 12 grains of powder in it. I went off into the woods, they went another direction. I shot 3 squirrels and then I heard these shots like there was a war going on. I slowly walked that direction and there they were, shooting fish in a creek. I looked and there over their heads was squirrel watching them. I shot the squirrel, and they looked around and said, "What did you shoot?" I said, "there was a squirrel watching the fooliness going on and I shot him."

Another time we went squirrel hunting, again I had my 25 cal, and this time I was dressed in my 1830 buckskins. I said, "I'm going to hunt right here," and away they went. Sit down and shot 4 squirrels and it begin to rain. I got a little chilly so I got out my fire making stuff and started a fire. Just sit back to enjoy the fire under a deadfall and there's another squirrel, I dropped him and shortly here they come to where I was. They said, "We thought we were back in the 1700s when we see you sitting there by the fire. And most people can't even start a fire in the rain." They said, "You really ought to get a decent rifle, you might even get some squirrels." I said, "How many squirrels did you two get?" they said, "We heard a few but couldn't get a shot." I said, "There lays my limit in squirrels." Never heard anymore about a decent gun.

One year I was trapping behind my brother's where the mainspring in my lock had broken. This time I was carrying a half stock, it was a 50 cal. And as I came around the bend in the river there was two nice geese. I had never shot a goose before and here was a chance. I shot the head right off one. Finished running my traps and went home. I had never cleaned a goose either. Pheasants I just skinned, but I thought Geese had to be plucked, so that's what I started to do. In minutes the kitchen looked like it had a snowstorm come thru. But I did get it plucked. It was then that I was glad I had not shot the other one too! Haven't shot one since.

Chapter 21

Indian Sticks

My whole family, well at least the male part of my family, has always shot and built Bows and Arrows, (Indian Sticks). When I was young we used to have homemade bows and cattails for arrows. Cattails were everywhere so we had an unending supply. I remember, when I was about 12, of standing on a curve on the highway, one foot on the road and I would shoot into the grilles of cars as they came at me. Everybody has to have a hobby. When I was 14, I built a Lemon wood bow with a drawknife. I had no vise so I held it between my legs. Bow came out nice. Shortly after that I built a 16-inch bow and some 3/16 arrows, looked the real thing only smaller, Dad had a great time with it until he cut his knuckle and that's all he wanted. I was proud to give Dad the good time he had with that small bow. I used to take the Lemon wood bow and come into the yard on my bicycle and shoot while on the bike, got pretty good at it to. Shortly after this is when I asked Dad for the gun and bought the bow and arrows. Then when I turned 17, I went into the Navy.

After I got out of the Navy, it was a while before I done any bow hunting. My brothers were into it a lot more than I was. I really had no interest in building bows again. Lee made some really nice bows, Roger made premium Arrows, Buzz my brother I have not mentioned, built Knives, Custom Knives. He was written up in Knife World magazine twice. It was funny how he got started. We worked at the same aluminum extruding plant and one day he found one of the big circular saw blades that had a crack in it, he asked the maintenance man if he could cut it for him and that's how he made his first knife. Buzz always had a fascination with knives. As a kid he carried a large Bowie everywhere, that and 12 Ft bullwhip. Lash Larue was the big thing in Saturday movie. It was 5 cents to go to the movie back then. Buzz called himself "Shane" after the movie with the same name. He got hurt one time, stepped thru the ground that had a fire burning under it, burnt his foot real bad and they took him to the hospital. They called Mom and said her son Shane had got burnt real bad. She said, " I don't have a son named Shane. Oh wait a minute, yes I do." She always wondered what they thought of that statement. Buzz had to have skin grafts to fix the burn. The knives, Buzz and I would fight with knives and the fight was over when the point touched the other guy's body.

Buzz got his name from me, when I was small I could not say brother and said, "Buzzer" so from then on he was Buzz. His real name is Rolland.

Course all us boy's hunted deer with bow and arrows. Roger shot more deer than anyone else I knew, and legal. No matter where he sat or stalked he seen deer. Lee shot a few too. I related earlier how he shot the same doe 11 times with an arrow with a flour bag on the tip just to see how many times he could hit the same deer.

There was an old Indian Chief who had two boys, Falling Rock and Running Wolf. He had to decide which Son would be Chief after him. Here's how he did it. He told the boys to go and trap furs for 1 moon, (1 month) and the one who got the most fur would be Chief. He told Falling Rock to go East, and Running Wolf to go West, after a month Running Wolf came back, had a fair amount of fur, Falling Rock never did return. Sad story, last year while I was in Canada I seen where they were still looking for him, signs every-where, "Watch for Falling Rock".

We also shot Carp, Garpike and Dogfish with harpoon tipped arrows. One time Roger and I took the canoe over to Union Lake where it dumped into the river. There was a big swampy area where the carp would wallow. We were pushing up thru the spot and I shot a huge carp, maybe 35-40 lbs, and it started dragging the canoe around. Roger said, "Will you quit playing with that carp." I said, "He's dragging us around so you can get a shot." About this time a pickup truck with a camper pulled up and parked on the edge of the road about 50 yards from us, two kids got out of the back and the Mom and Dad got out of the cab. They stood there watching us. About this time I am getting a little tired of the carp dragging us around so I pulled him up to the canoe and hit him in the head with the tomahawk we had with us. Carp are junk so we would just kill them and throw them back in the water. When I pulled that big carp up out of the water to hit him the family got all excited when they seen the fish. They jumped in their truck and away they go. About 20 minutes back they come, all had fishing rods. They thought they could catch these carp. They don't bite in this stage, they have females on their mind, a male would get on each side of a female and hit her in the sides and her eggs would come out of her. Then the males would fertilize them and here's this years crop of carp. We didn't have the heart to tell them. You can catch them in the river in the spring and summer after they were thru bumping. Guess what you use for bait? Kernel corn.

There used to be 8-10 of us guys that done a woods walk twice a month, 2 guys would set it up each month, we took turns at it. One time Roger and I set it up together. Coldwater is where the plant is that makes the artificial turf for the football fields. It comes in 4 foot square pieces about 4 inches thick. Hard foam and there is not an arrow around that would go thru it. Not even a crossbow! So I takes this piece that is white, it also was made in green and black, and I cut a deer body from it and painted it brown. I put a set of 8-point deer horns on it, where the tail would be I put a spring with piece of the white foam for a tail, and then I made 4 legs out of wood slats and put a pin through the body where the legs should be. I took a 2 X 8 and hooked the four legs to it, next I took two rubber bands I cut from a truck inner tube and hooked them on the deer's chest and to the 2 X 8 in front, here's how it worked. You pull the deer backwards so that its body was on the 2 X 8 and there was a clip on the 2 X 8 that held it down. When you released the clip the deer would jump up, tail wagging. Ok, now we took this to the woods, set it up in some knee high grass, pulled it down and run a piece of camouflaged duck decoy line on the clip up the shooting station. We only let one guy at a time come to the shooting station, we would say, "See that deer laying down in the grass? Take your best shot at it." You could just see the head, horns and a little of the back, they would draw back and just before they shot we would pull the string and the deer would jump up, tail flying and most of them missed, but Clem, from spear pole climbing fame, drew up and when the line was pulled the deer jumped up and Clem shot into the tree tops.

The guy I mentioned earlier who had the property at the lake and was worried about his dog getting eaten by the coyotes, I was there hunting with a bow and just couldn't get a shot. I was shooting an 80 lb Golden Eagle with 24-inch arrows, 165-grain heads Late in the afternoon a doe comes across quite a ways out. I figured about 60 yards out. I pulled up and let fly, got her, she run off and I stayed put for a while and then went and looked for her. She went over a hundred yards, and I don't know how. I paced off the distance and it was over 70 paces from where I shot at her, blood spraying out right where she was standing when I shot and almost all the way to where she laid. Hit her in the femoral artery, could not have been a better shot and she was bled out. I got this kind of shooting from the meets we had. There were 8 of us and each week 2 guys would set up a shoot thru the woods. And then when Roger and I started the Gun shop we also sold arrows for a while, and we would put on a shoot each month, 1st prize was a dozen arrows. One of the shots you had to make was a 100-yard shot and of course we tried out the targets first to make sure it could be done.

Roger had a cookout at his house one time and, of course, all the guys and Wives were invited, we brought our bows. Roger had a nice range to shoot. We played around for a while and someone said, " Hey lets see Bob and Roger shoot against each other." We put an aluminum pop can up end ways and each shot 6 arrows. When the smoke cleared there were 12 arrows in the bottom of the can, it ended there. A little later Roger said to me, "I'm going hunting tomorrow and I want to check my sights on my hunting bow." I said, "OK I will stand by the target and spot for you. I'm standing about 2 foot away from the target and it was getting dark so I had a flash-light in my hand to shine on the target so he could see it. I would be standing there and would hear ziiiiiiip and an arrow would hit the target. About this time a real estate guy walked up and asked if I was Roger, ziiiiiiip, and I said, "no he was busy and ziiiiiiip he would be free in a minute," ziiiiiiip The guy said, "what is that sound?" ziiiiiiip and I said, "Roger is shooting at this target beside you see," ziiiiiiiip. I never seen a guy move so fast, he said, "I'll see him tomorrow," ziiiiiiip. Roger was done shooting and said, "What did that guy want?" I said, "he wants to sell your house, but he was a little nervous about flying arrows." Roger said, "If I would have known that I would have shot his pants leg. Just another regular day!

There was another Indian Chief who had two boys, this was in modern times. The two boys complained that the local Sailing club would not let them join the club because they were Red men, the old Chief took the sailing club to court and beat them, and they had to let the two boys into the club. Chief was always bragging about his "Two Red Sons in the sail set."

Boy! These Indian Chiefs and their boys, this one tribe had a smarter than average boy so they all chipped in to send him to college. He graduated as an Electrical Engineer. And when he came home they had a big party for him, all the trimmings. He told the Chief, "I don't know how I will ever repay the tribe." The Chief said, "I know one thing you can do for us, we really need a light in our bathroom. We have trouble in there at night." The man said, "That is a simple thing to do," and he run wires and put a light in the bathroom. Get this. He became the first Indian to wire a head for a reservation.

When I was younger, two of us would go over the football field and stand at about the opposite 20 yard line facing each other and shoot arrows on an arc toward each other. We both shot at the same time. The game went like this. When the arrow would come toward you, you would move your bow and make the arrow pass between the bow and the bowstring. One time we hit each other's arrow in the air. Hey, we didn't have a football!

One time Roger and I were going out bow hunting and was walking back to the woods. Just as we got into the edge of the woods, here is a huge cat, appeared to be wild, course to us guys any cat away from it's house is wild. Roger pulls up and put an arrow in the cat, it just hissed at us and pulled the arrow out with its mouth. By then Roger had his knife out and threw it and stuck the cat in the throat. That was that. We got our knife throwing from Dad, he would be sitting at the table eating and my Uncle Ed would come in and throw his hat at the door and Dad would pin it here with a knife. Our front door looked like a screen door from all the knife marks. Talk about a guy that hated cats. Dad came home one day and 4 cats were on our dinning table. Dad grabbed each one and threw it out the door, then he went over and opened the door and threw them the rest of the way out, there were no survivors.

I think about the Indians, here they are, the women put up the teepee, gather wood for the fire, skin the animals, cook them, tan the hides for clothes they would sew, plus tend the kids, while the man sits by the fire, smokes his pipe, hunts and fishes when the mood strikes him and he pays no taxes, and the white man thinks he can improve on this?

Chapter 22

1980

I had been working at the State Home for 14 years and was a Supervisor there, this is before I accepted the Lord, but like I said He spoke to me one day at work, "The least of my brethren." I was later to find out what that meant. I never worked many Sundays, as I was always off some where to a motorcycle event. Hill climbing, Motocross or Eduro. I had a BSA 441 Motorcycle, had special forks, it had a 32 tooth sprocket and I changed it to a 69 tooth sprocket. The sprocket was almost as big as the rim. Had the engine punched out from 441cc to 500cc, and that baby would haul. Lee came down to the house one day and I had the BSA out in front of the house checking it out. Bear in mind that this bike would wheelie in 4th gear. Lee goes over and sits on it and says, "Care if I take a ride on this bike?" I says "No just be careful, that thing has a mind of it's own." He was wearing Levis, boots and a white T-shirt. He got it started and revved up the engine. I knew what was going to happen, remember he is sitting on the bike on the sidewalk; he popped the clutch and away he goes, on the hind wheel! He went about 50-60 feet before he could get it shut down, when he got the front wheel back on the ground he came slowly put-putting back to where he started. You could not tell where the t-shirt and skin started, he was white, and he said, "That's enough riding for today." Now Randy on the other hand jumped on the bike and wrung it out. It was so funny to watch, Randy was small and the bike big and it went where he said, but

173

remember he was a dirt track Champion. I got off the track here. I was working at the State Home (this is where the mentally retarded lived) they were cutting back and looking for any excuse to get rid of employees. The fact that I had missed so many Sundays was against me. They cut me back from a Supervisor to and Attendant. That I could not handle and soon had enough. I walked out and got a hold of the Union, but they were sucking up to management to keep their jobs and said they could not help. I got a lawyer and sued the State, and of course I won and they give me a large settlement. There was this Chopper I had been eyeballing, and when I got the money I bought it. It was 9 foot long, had long extended forks, (21inch over) and was a hard tail, (didn't have a rear suspension). It rode hard but the rear tire would really bite into the road on take off. And it was cool man! I forgot to mention the draft; drafting is what they do in Nascar race. One car rides close behind the leader, the leader breaks the air and the car behind is almost dragged along. I knew this and wondered if it would work with a motorcycle behind a semi truck, it does! With my Harley, I used to ride behind a semi, about 2-3 foot behind, and I found if the semi had the rear doors open I could kick the bike into neutral and it would drag me along. The Chopper was too low to do this, besides who wants to go a measly 70 miles per hour. I was always getting into trouble with drag racing on the street, car or bike. Somebody revved their exhaust at me I was going, there could be a hundred cop cars sitting there and they didn't matter, we were going. Or just plain speed on the road, it was always a go. I would ride the Chopper to work sometimes, lived 9 miles from work. I always had to promise myself no funny stuff this time, never helped, but I knew the end was coming. This one time I headed to work and there was this large sweeper curve almost to town. Here's the problem. When you ride with extended forks the front wheel will walk across the road on a large curve. Here I am sitting at a stop sign waiting to pull into the traffic. Ahead of me was a pickup truck, and then a motorcycle (stock bike) and then I could go. I pulls out and got up beside the bike, he looked over at the Chopper and sticks his nose in the air. OK! guess he needs to know how a real bike goes. I cranked her on and away I go right into the sweeper. I dove deep in the curve, there was no one coming in the other lane, the Chopper starts walking across the curve right into a bridge, how I missed it I don't know. Sold the Chopper the next day. And the dirt bike with it.

While I was working at the State Home I got into a deal. All of the kids had a number after their name. This was a safety thing to make sure the right medication, treatments at the doctors, etc. I have always had a good memory for numbers and of course I knew all the kids names. (Always made me mad as we could not call them kids, had to call them patients.) So when it came time for their X-rays I was the one who was at the hospital telling the technician which kid was which and their numbers. And I would hold them still while they were shooting the x-ray. We had 208 kids to x-ray. In comes a female doctor and said to me, "You need to have a lead apron on or you won't have the ability to father any more kids!" I said, "That's Ok I have enough kids anyway." Then she says, "But the ability to perform will be lost also." I said give me two aprons, one for the front and one for the back just to be sure!"

These kids all had a skill. One kid would unravel his T-shirt and socks and roll them into balls about 2-3 inch diameter. They looked perfectly round. I took a few home and measured then with a micrometer, they were just a few thousands out a round. Another kid would unravel his T-shirt and would stick his hand out the window and fly the string?? Sometimes he would put a cigarette paper on the end. We found them 40 yards from where he flew them. One time I was an extra Supervisor and asked the building Supervisor if I could do some bus trips and projects with some of the better kids He said, "Go for it." One of the bus trips is described in the next paragraph. Another thing I did was to get some kites and let the kids fly them. The guy who flew the string could not get a kite in the air?? There was also this one kid who could make keys from large paper clips. One day we were showing a new attendant how he could do it. I mean this kid could unlock any door! So after he showed the new guy they sent the kid back to his area. One of the other Supervisors's stuck the paper clip key in his shirt pocket. The next day when he came to work he was telling us that he had locked the garage and his keys to the house were still in the car. No way to get them and his wife would not be home for 4 hours. He resigned himself to the long wait and set on his front steps. He reached in shirt pocket for something and there was that paper clip key, You guessed it, it unlocked his front door.

When we had to have kids at the hospital we would call, what they call, the Safety department and they would drive the kids wherever they needed to go. Couple kids they would bring in a car, lots of kids here come a bus. This one Safety guy was a real pain. Once I had three kids to go to hospital for tests. I bring out two of them and ask the driver, (name was Smith) "would you keep an eye on these two while I go and get the other one?" he snarls at me, "its my job to drive, your job to watch kids!" I said, "Fine, they will be ok anyway." About a month later I was to take 40 kids on a bus trip, who's the driver? You guessed it, Smitty. So away we go, had a good trip. When we get back to the building Smith backs the bus up to the building. The food service gal's car is sitting there and Smith doesn't see it. I was standing where I could see the whole deal. First he tears off her front fender, then the driver's door, then the rear door and started the rear fender. He yells out, "Did I hit something?" I never said a word. Smith gets out and sees what he did, gets back on the bus and says to me, "Why didn't you tell me I was going to hit the car?" I said, "Remember about a month ago you told me it was my job to watch the kids and your job to drive? I was watching the kids!

1986, this was the year Dad died. He had smoked all his life and ended up with lung cancer. He also had drank all his life and also had liver cancer. I tried to prepare myself for his passing, it didn't work. I was the tower of strength for the rest of the kids as I was the oldest. When I got home that night, just as I pulled into our drive, I lost it. Lois was with me and she was a great comfort. I still miss Dad very much. It's a real chore to sing, "Silver Haired Daddy". I did spend a lot of time with him and so glad I did. When I first got into the Church, after he died, I beat myself up for not accepting the Lord earlier. I could have led Dad to the Lord? I know he believed in God, I have his Baptism papers. But then again, a lot of people believe in God, But Jesus said, "I am the Way, the Truth, and the Life, no man (woman) comes to the Father but by me." However the word also says there is now no condemnation, so I trust in that. As Paul said, "Forgetting all the past." I had heard that when someone dies their spirit was over their body for a bit. This comes from near death experiences. So when Dad went, I looked above his bed. I thought I might see a light or a glow. The next day when I run trap line it was a though he was with me, to the point I even talked to him. They say time heals all wounds, thats about it, just a saying. Or as the shoe cobbler said, "Time wounds all heels." I would have to say that the sense of humor the Lord has given me got me thru a lot. One of the big things, I used to smoke a pipe and when I seen what smoking did to Dad, I quit. Wasn't even a problem to quit. I think all people who smoke should try spending a while with those dying of lung cancer. When I first got in to the Ministry I had to watch myself, I was so against smoking. And like the amateur lawyer I looked for the verse covering those things not specific covered. Like smoking. Found the fine print in 1st Corinthians 3; 17. " If any man defile the temple of God, him shall God destroy. For the temple of God is holy, which temple ye are. While this paragraph has been hard to write I hope it has brought Peace to some.

Chapter 23

A Stranger

At a yard sale my in-laws were having, I was over talking to my Wife. I got ready to leave and this was when I still had the Chopper. This Mexican said "Hello" to me and I just grunted at him and away I went. Not even suspecting that our paths would cross in a mighty strange way. I have to tell you about how I was on that chopper. Around the sissy bar, (a back rest for the passenger) was a chrome chain, 3/8 and 6 foot long, it had several uses. Padlock it around the wheel so no one could steal the bike, if a car or truck got too close or smart mouth it could be wrapped around the windshield. Had a guy tell me one time, "You are going to swing it at the wrong person and be in a world of hurt" I said, "Now we are coming to why I had a pistol in my boot." Back to yard sale, it was in the fall of 1988. The first part of Feb of 1989, 3 women showed up to my door. I would usually slam the door on them as I knew they were from the church. I knew one of them in earlier years, so I let them in. We had coffee and talked, they talked mostly about God, the one I knew said, "Sing us a song," I got the guitar and sang a few songs. Then the one I knew asked if I would come to the Church and video a guy they had coming to the Church and wanted to video tape for the shut-ins, (people who could not get out of their houses). I said, "I guess I could." wasn't very enthused about it. He was going to be there Friday, Saturday and Sunday. Now I had known a few religious people and could not say much good about them. They said one thing and done another. But this guy, his name was Steve Coia, and he confirmed what I had known for many years, God is good. The stories I knew of the Bible bore this out. In 1962 I had an experience with God. I was losing my 1st Wife and went to see a preacher I met, he led me thru the prayer of salvation and I would go see him now and then. One time I went to his house and he had painted the steps to his porch and the porch. There was no sign and I walked across them. He came out like a demon and hollered at me. I left and never seen him again. Then I run from God until 1989, when I went to videotape Steve, done Friday night, OH! Guess who the Pastor was? The Mexican that had said "hello" to me at the yard sale. His name was Angel Rojas. Saturday night I was taping and had trouble seeing thru the viewfinder, eyes kept tearing up. I had on eye glasses ¼ inch thick, and my legs were trembling, course that's to be expected, with all the beating they had taken racing motorcycles. I knew in my heart it was more than that, but I fought it, then I surrendered and went to the Alter and accepted the Lord. I knew this was why the Lord had preserved me all these years. I knew right then I had a calling. Think of this. I had totaled 2 Cars and 2 Motorcycles, No Broken bones, now you can break up cars and survive but when you start breaking up motorcycles you are all most positive going to die, and I still have never had a broken bone! I had also trimmed trees for 35 years with ropes. We never used a high ranger as the big money jobs were on hillsides like a the lakes and places where there was not room to get one in. All the times I rode bikes over 120 miles an hour, a bird could have done me in at that speed. And the Church, it was a Pentecostal Full Gospel Church. I had found a home Church. The night I gave my life to the Lord I told the Pastor so long, He said, "Where you going?" I said, "On the road, there's a lot of people who need what I have." Well he says, "Don't pack your bags quite yet, while that's an admiral calling you need to learn the word and study first."

Painting Porches, I remember a story of a guy who was down and out and was looking for any kind of work. Went up to this house and knocked on the door, a man came to door and said, "What can I do for you?" the guy says, "I really need some work to get a meal and a room for the night." The man says, "Tell you what

I'll do, I will give you $50.00 if you paint my porch, everything is in the garage including the gray paint." Guy says, "Thank you so much." And away he went. About 3 hours later he knocks on the door and says, "I'm done!" the man gives him $50.00 and as the guy is walking away he says, "That's not a Porsche you have, it's a Lambraggreia!"

I began to go to Church and also study. My brother Roger told me much later that he was afraid for me, as he knew that anything I done, I done all the way. I also started to study to be a Minister, and also to learn about the speaking in tongues. I found out this was the Baptism of the Holy Ghost, and was very anxious to receive it.

After I was in the Church a month (now I am a night owl as I always worked the 3rd shift and I still am), one morning at 5: 30 the Lord woke me up and said to me, "Today you are out of bondage!" Un Hun! What does that mean? I could not go back to sleep, so I got up and got a cup of coffee and my paper and started reading. I forgot something, my glasses, remember I said they were ¼ inch thick, and now here I am reading with out them, never wore them again. About the Lord speaking to me, people say yah, right. I am here to tell you he does, only a lot of people don't listen or seek Him. So you will see where the Lord spoke to me many times. I called the Pastor later that morning and his Wife Carole answered, I said, "I am reading my paper." She says, "So!" I said, "the Lord healed my eyes and I am reading with out my glasses," she said, "Praise the Lord".

Around this time I had done many jobs around the Church, like fixing things, driving the Church van, cleaning, and I was an usher when the need arose. We had a bunch of kids who were a little rowdy now and then. The county fair came to town and some of us went over there. Angel and I had our picture taken at a booth, the photographer had a lot of getups you could wear. He took those old style sepia (brown & white) pictures like the old west. He had Angel and I dress like old time cowboys. We put on our mean and sour faces, the picture was great, we sure looked the part. We showed the picture around Church and the kids looked at my mean expression and after that I only had to speak to them once.

Shortly after this I had to renew my driver's license and could not wait to show them that I no longer wore glasses. I took the test and now for the eye test, of course I passed with no trouble. The woman behind the desk looked at my expired license and said, "You wear glasses?" I said, "No, I don't wear them anymore." I got already to witness to her about the Lord healing my eyes and the Lord said, "Do not witness to this person." So I got my license and left. By now I knew the Lord's voice and that He talks to people if they pay heed to His voice. I said, " Lord what was that all about?" He said to me, "She had the power to undo what I did." Then it hit me, she did not know the Lord, and with a stroke of her pen she would have put on my license that I wore glasses and I would have to have them on if the police stopped me. That's the law. And the Lord would not void the law for me when in His word He says obey the laws of the land.

One time I ask Angel why babies died, they could not have committed any sin, and He gave the perfect answer, "Because there is sin in the world." I said, "No wonder you get the big money!" Angel said, "Hear him Lord he's praying." I have since found out those children who have not reached the age accountability go to Heaven.

I also started helping around the Church as I can fix anything. Angel asked me if we could put a steeple on top of the bell tower. I said, "I will check it out tomorrow." I showed up with a 24 foot ladder and a 12 foot ladder, the Church roof was just short of 3 stories high and then the bell tower was another 10 foot. I leaned the big ladder against the side of the Church and started up with the other ladder in my hand. Angel said, "What are you doing?" I said, "I have to go up the big ladder then carry the small ladder across the peak to the bell tower and go up it and check to see if the bell will support the steeple." And away I go, Angel just stood there shaking his head. I checked out the bell tower and seen there was plenty of support for the steeple and came back down. I told Angel it could be done, I said, "How tall a steeple do you have?" he says, "I don't have one, I just wanted to know if it could be done." I said, "Well I have a friend who owes me a favor and I will have him build one." The next week I called Angel and said, "I have the steeple, it's 12 foot tall and I will put it up Saturday morning," he said, "Great I will meet you there!" I got to the Church Sat morning before Angel got there and was sitting on the tailgate of my truck, steeple sticking out the back. It was a nice warm sunny day. As I sit there thinking how wonderful life with Jesus was, the devil spoke to me and said," WHEN YOU GO UP ON THE ROOF TODAY I AM GOING TO THROW YOU OFF!" WOW! Did that sit me back on my heels, not many things in this world frighten me, but until you have heard this voice, I sat there wondering what to do. Then I remembered I am a child of the most high Lord, Jesus Christ and I have the power to command the devil to be gone, and that's what I did and I even reminded him the Jesus Christ is Lord of all! Went up there 2-3 times to put the steeple up.

Later in the same year I was saved I went on a trip to Israel with Angel, Carole and Pat. I had some of the greatest things happen while I was over there. I had got a new video camera before we left and when I bought it I asked the sales guy if he had a Skylight Filter for the Camera. He didn't even know about them. A skylight filter goes on the front of the camera lens and here is what it does. Did you ever take a picture with the big billowy clouds in the sky and when you got the pictures back they were gone? A sky light filter keeps them in the picture and it does not require an exposure change as do most filters. I went to a high end photo shop and asked them if they had a sky light filter for the camera they said, "No, its takes a 53mm filter and they don't make that size and I don't even have an adapter that you could put it on with, and besides it will mess up the electric eye on the camera." So here I go to Israel without the filter. We ended up in Cairo, Egypt and when I was filming the pyramids I swung the camera across them and when I stopped the camera I looked at the ground. Guess what was laying there? The 53mm skylight filter. I picked it up off the ground and it was so clean I put it on the camera, fit perfect. That's good for a filter they don't make and won't fit my camera! Carole was standing a little ways from me and I said, " Look at this! The filter I needed lying on the ground." Her faith is such that she said, " The Lord knew you needed it and put it there for you, now lets go over this way." This is a woman who not only knows about miracles, but She depends on them. But bear this in mind, over there the only thing you could buy was film, nothing else. In fact several of the people tried to buy my video camera. Later on we were at Pontius Pilate's house where they kept Jesus in the hole over night. What this hole looks like is a flower vase, the kind with the bulb at the bottom and then a slender long neck. They lowered him down and he stayed there. Today they had cut a stairway down to it so you go down and see where he was held. When they first tried to cut the stairway they run in to an image of the Lord in the wall, so they moved the stairway over. I was standing there filming the image and I felt Angel put his hand on my shoulder, when I looked over he was on the stairs. I stopped the camera and looked behind me, I was the only one visible there, it had to have been the Lord! This did not surprise me as He has had his hand on me all my life. But it was still a great feeling. When we went to the garden where Jesus was put into the tomb I was overwhelmed by the feeling and could not move. Angel finally had to come and get me. During the trip we went to the upper room where the last supper had been, I started speaking in tongues (Acts 2:4) and went into another world. Here comes Angel again and got me to quiet down to a roar. I make no excuses for my love for my Lord and Savior. We also went to the Red Sea. Before we went to Israel I asked Pat if she ever seen the Red Sea. She said no and I handed her a paper with a C on it written in red, Red C. (Red Sea), Oh, you get it! After we got back home, one of the buses we had been on was bombed. It was strange because you would see kids about 12-16 years old standing around on the streets with automatic rifles. I done a couple of funnies while we were over there. I went into this shop to buy an Arabian outfit. It was a long narrow shop and there was about 6 girls working there. Pretty girls I might add. I tried to explain what I wanted and all of a sudden here come 4 more girls out of the back and they all gathered around me. I was getting frustrated, about that time here comes Angel He speaks Arabian and starts laughing. The girls thought I was looking for a wife to take back to the states. They all wanted to go. The other thing I did was we had an Arabian guide, a girl about 4½ feet tall. We are walking down a street to get on a ship, she was walking ahead of me and I handed Angel the camera and got about 3 steps ahead of her. Angel filmed us and said into the cameras mike, " Here is Bob with a girl he met over here and she is walking 3 steps behind him as women are supposed to do". Boy did that go over big with the ladies at the church. Today they walk 10 steps behind the men so if a land mine goes off it misses them.

I heard a story about a guy who went to the Pastor of this one Church and asked if he could ring the bell on Sunday. The Pastor looked at him and was thinking, I wonder if you could too. Pastor says to the guy, "You don't have any arms." The guy says, " Lets go up to the bell and I will show you." Up they go and when they got up to the bell the guy rears back and hit the bell with his head, he rears back to hit again and misses and fell out of the bell tower and hit the ground, as he lay there someone asks, "Who is that guy?" Someone else says, "I don't know but that face sure rings a bell." About a month later another guy shows up to the same Church and ask the Pastor if he could ring the bell, and this guy has no arms either, Pastor says, "No way, a guy with no arms got killed trying to ring the bell, " The guy says, "I know that, he was my brother and I know what he did wrong and it won't happen to me." So up they go to the bell tower and the guy rears back to hit the bell with his head and misses and falls to the ground, a crowd gathers and one person says, "Who is that?" another person says, "I don't know, but he sure is a dead ringer to his brother."

I got the Baptism of the Holy Ghost and started speaking in different tongues, reference to this is in Acts 2:1-8, Oh, Oh, here we go with the Bible lessons. You will see a lot of this from now on. Anyhow, speaking in tongues is really something, but a greater thing is when some one speaks in tongues and you know what they said. For tongues to be effective they must be interpreted, the Bible says, pray that you may interpret. I remember one night after listening to a sermon on the power you have as a born again Christian. You can say to the mountain, be thou removed and it will move. On the way home I looked out in a field and saw a tree standing there, and I think to myself, "If I say to that tree be thou removed, it will move!" scared me, never heard of that much power, much less have it. Getting the gift of speaking in tongues was so great to me that when I got home that night I went out into the yard and starting praying in tongues to make sure I hadn't lost the gift on the way home. I guess I should mention that there are two kinds of tongues, one for the edifying the Church and one for your prayer language. I have always thought of speaking in tongues this way, the devil don't know what you are saying to the Lord and therefore can't use it against you. I will guarantee you that the devil will come at you every chance he can. I believe that this is the reason for a lot of marriages failing. The devil hates it when a man and wife are one in the Lord. It's like the woman who said, "That old devil hasn't bothered me in quite a while." The Minister said, "Oh! Oh! We better pray for you right now!"

I will tell you a greater thing is to be used of the Lord, think about it, we are really are nothing. The Bible says we are but a vapor, here then gone, but God loves us so much that if we are willing he will use us. I think back on a time later in my Ministry when I went to the pulpit to preach and was unable to speak. Then the Lord directed me to take a message to this one man. For reasons unknown to me when I give someone a message from the Lord I speak in the old thee and thou. And here is what I said to guy as I remember it. My job is giving the message and be done with it, but I am asking the Lord to remember the words that you might be blessed also. "My Son, thou have been faithful in the small things and I will add the more to thee, and you will be a blessing to many. Thus saith the Lord." This man helped the Pastor with things around the Church and was always there when he needed him, but in the services he mostly sat on the pew, after this message I moved away and when I came back this man now runs the video camera, takes up the offering, and I see where he wrote a sermonette for the bulletin, this usually reserved for the Ministers and studying Ministers. I will have more on these things the Lord has used me to deliver.

I love to preach, and it is a very great honor to do so, and I have a good time doing it, like this I throw in when I am preaching, "You know God has a sense of humor, he has servants like me," everybody laughs, I say, "Don't laugh he has servants like you too!" As I said when I started this book, I know a ton of stories, I tell Angel a story and he never repeats it right, when he tells one and no one laughs he says, "That's one of Bob's jokes.

He is like the guy who was a distributor for cleaning products, he stops at this apartment house for older people and asks to see the manager, the desk clerk says, "Go down the hall to the end and there is the coffee shop and everybody is down there on Tuesday morning for coffee and such, the manager will be just inside the door," he goes down and finds the manager and he says, "Set down and have a cup of coffee." The disturber sits down, a guy steps up to the mike and says, "23." and everybody breaks out laughing, another guy steps up to mike and says, "35." and the people split their sides laughing, the disturber says, "What's going on with this?" the manager says, "Well these people have heard these stories so many times instead of telling the whole story they just say it's number." The distributor says "I would like to try that." the manager says, "Go ahead, " the distributor steps up to the mike and says, "78." and nobody laughs, the distributor sits back down and said, "What went wrong?" the manager says, "Well some people can tell them and some can't".

I was telling Angel about this guy named "Max" had terrible headaches, went to the doctor, had a lot of tests done and still couldn't find the trouble. Told Max he should go see a shrink. Max goes to the shrink and he talks to Max about 3 hours, and finally said, "Max you need to get out and meet people." Max says, "I know everybody." (Now this was about 25 yrs ago) Shrink says well meet some important people, like movie stars." Max says, "Funny you should mention movie stars, I'm going to play golf with Bob Hope and Bing Crosby this weekend." Shrink says, "Of course you are, I'll be there to see that." Max said, "OK, here's where we will be playing." And give him a map. Next Saturday there's Max playing golf with Bob Hope and Bing Crosby. Following Monday here's Max back to the shrink still having headaches. Shrink says, "Did you ever think of meeting important people overseas?" Max says, "Funny you should mention that, I'm going to have tea with Winston Churchill." shrink says, " Sure you are!" Max says, " Come over and I will introduce you to him." Shrink says, "I'll go you one better than that, I'll bet you $ 50.00 you don't see him!" Max says, "OK lose your money if you want to." Over seas they go and sure enough Max had tea with Churchill. Shrink has an idea, with all these people Max knows, he hasn't had time for religion, Says, "Max do you know the pope? " Max says that's my next stop." Shrink says, "Nobody gets near the pope, I'll make the bet double or nothing!" Max says, "OK, lose more money." Next thing, here stands the shrink in the square looking up at the balcony and out walks Max with the pope, the shrink can't believe it. Some guy standing next to the shrink, says, "Hey, who's that with Max?"

A short time after that Angel gives me a big coffee mug and printed on the side is MAX.

After I been in the Church for a while, Angel seen one of the CO's that knew I had accepted the Lord, the CO told Angel, "When Bob accepted the Lord it was a great day in my life. He's been a thorn in my side for 11 years!"

Angel was remodeling the Church and I was helping him. He put his office in the back and needed a switch to turn the lights on from either side of the door. I had done a little electric work, but the switch had me puzzled, Angel said, "Lets go get a cup of coffee and take a break." This I was to find out was his universal answer for any building problem. As I walked by the piano, the Lord said, "Sit down!" I did and had a pen and paper and into my mind the Lord showed me the wiring for the switch. I said, "Thank you Lord." Went back to the switch and wired it up, worked just like it was supposed to. I said, " Now lets go get the coffee." Before you call me a crazy old man, try working for the Lord and listen when He speaks. I was a young man at the time. The same thing happened when we put the bathroom in, we needed a hole straight up for the vent. I told Angel the odds of it going where we wanted it were bad, however when you work for the Lord suddenly things change in your favor. It went straight.

Angel decided he wanted chandeliers in the Church and we run all over to a store chain that only had a couple at each store. (About 400 miles) So now we have all of them and they need to be put together. After services one Sunday I decide to put them together. If I recall, there were 180 pieces to each one. Angel wanted to help. I let him for a few minutes then told him to go eat lunch and I would put them together. And I did, during the week I had to hang and wire them, the ceiling in the Church was very high and I would have to put a sheet of plywood across the pews, take the biggest ladder I had and put it on the plywood, go up with one in hand and wire them. Angel had to go out of town and asked Evrette to hold the ladder for me, now these were heavy so up the ladder I go put a hook in the overhead beam went back down and got the fixture, was up there working and I hear this strange sound, looked down and there was Evertte asleep against the ladder. Good thing the Lord watches over me. It was very touching. Angel wanted a large chandelier in the center. A guy who had lost his Son in a car accident wanted to pay for it and have it be in honor of his Son. I took two of them and built one large one, heavyeee! But at least Angel was there to hold the ladder for this one. Remember what the word says," To whom much is given, much is required." And as I said before the Lord has always blessed the work of my hands. And in Romans 12:1 there is something about your reasonable service. I have always believed that to mean anything you can do for God, DO IT!

Anyway, I keep studying and I ask Angel when I can go on the road, he says, "The Lord will tell you, when its time or even if that's what he wants you to do." I keep working with Angel and one day he says, "Do you want to go to Detroit and work with me, I have some work to do for the Arabians, and you can make some money." Away we go, and while we are there the Lord calls me to a fast, if you read the Bible Jesus told his disciples to fast and pray. I believe the reason is that food has some acid in it and dulls your brain. Think about it when you have that big turkey dinner and then go sit in your easy chair, bang you are asleep, speaking of easy chairs I just found out some dishearting news, moving the reclining lever on the easy chair is not considered exercise. When it came time to eat with the Arabians I said," I can't" They got all over Angel as they thought he told me not to, Angels says, "No not me," pointed up and said, "Allah told him." They were satisfied with that, I'm working away and the Lord calls me to go somewhere. I told Angel "I have to go!" now Angel never questions the what the Lord wants and said, "OK," I headed down the street not knowing where I was going, Detroit is not a town to just take a walk in, I seen a small park between the East and West road and I knew that was the spot, there was a tree there I knelt and I began to speak in tongues, almost like pleading, and I knew I was interceding for someone or something. Went on about 45 minutes and I knew I had got the victory, when I stood up there were Arabians all around me and they stood there smiling. I always wondered if I was speaking Arabian. Went back to where we working and got back at it. Angel didn't even have to ask, he knew. When we finished the job we were sitting in this truck and the guy was figuring up what he owed us. I thought to myself if someone told me that one day I would sitting in a truck in Detroit with an Arabian and Mexican, figuring what my pay was, I would have told them they were crazy. By the by, Arabians believe that if a man works for them, you have to pay them before the sweat on their brow dries.

I told Angel the story of the two guys who were very best friends and had got into a fight and the one friend had killed someone by accident, but the jury found him guilty and sentenced him to the electric chair. When his friend came to see him the last time, he didn't know how to say goodbye, so he just said, "More power to you!" I know Angel laughed about that for a week.

One time Angel asked me if I wanted to go to the VA as he had to see the Doctor, when we were in the room and the doctor checked Angel, he got real excited and told Angel to lay down and not to move, the doctor said his blood pressure was so high he was afraid Angel would have a heart attack, when it was finally lower Angel had to go for some other tests, the doctor told me to push Angel in a wheelchair, we finally got thru and started back home. When we got back to Coldwater I told the people at Church that I had to push Angel around, and I said, "Of course that's the thing I do best."

Angel asked me if I wanted to go with him to see a guy who was in the Vets hospital, Hank, with gangrene through out his whole body. I said, "Sure I would go with him." When we got to the hospital we had to go up a couple of flights to get to the room where he was. We talked to him a while and then before we left we prayed with him. On the way home Angel and I agreed it was the last time we would see him here on earth. This was on a Monday night, the following Sunday we when to Church and who comes walking through the door, Hank. Angel and I both looked at each other. The guy when up on the platform and told Angel he wanted to give a testimony. He said, when we left he went into a sleep and said he seen a huge book bound in Gold, it was Gods book of life, a voice said, "Your name is in here but your time is not yet." A chill went down my spine, we had left him for dead and God raised him up. Taught me a lesson, don't put any limits on God. I always think about this when I pray for someone in really bad shape. But I will tell you one thing I don't do, and that's to pray for someone to stay here when its their time to go. I believe you can keep someone here if you pray that way. I always pray Lord, have your will in this matter. I would hate to think I kept someone in a bad state here.

I went into the church one day and here is Reba behind the pulpit. I said, "Are you practicing your sermon?" she said, "No! I don't practice what I preach!" There was no way I was going to touch that line.

Here is something that changed my life. At the Church I would video tape the service for the people how were unable to be there or were shut-ins, This one night I was at the platform taping and this person comes and kneels at the alter and the Lord spoke to me and told me to go tell that person that he loved them. Whoa! back there a minute, I was sure it was just me, and then I made this decision that I would rather be wrong than disobedient, I went down and told this Woman Minister, "I said the Lord told me to tell you, He loves you." She said "ohh! Thank you I needed to hear that."

I know what you are thinking, women Ministers. No way! But like I tell everyone who has this attitude, if the men are not going to step up then don't fault the women when they do. And they are not to be in charge, that's what the Bible says, and also the word says, "Touch not my anointed, nor do my prophets any harm" I guarantee you will answer for this. And big time too! It was important enough for the Lord to put in the Bible twice 1st Chronicles 16:22 and Psalm 105:15

I am going to beat this drum a little harder, read Judges 4:4 and you will see that a woman was in charge of Israel! Deborah, she was a prophetess, and she judged Israel at that time. To point she even told Barak to get an army of ten thousand and go and fight, Judges 4:7 Sisera the captain of Jabins army I will deliver him into thine hand! (God said this thru Deborah) Barak was unsure of himself and said unto her, " If thou wilt go with me, then I will go: but if thou wilt not go with me, then I will not go." And she said, "I will surely go with thee notwithstanding the journey that thou takest shall not be for thine honor for the Lord shall sell Sisera into the hand of a woman." She is talking about herself. She was the judge of all Israel!

Deborah was the weaker vessel, yet hath the stronger faith. Note that she calls the march to war just a journey! Now that's faith!

Here's another woman, Esther, read about her in Esther. Read the whole chapter, you will really see some courage, but to my point, Esther 9:29, Esther wrote with all authority! When the Bible says all authority that what it means! How about this. Carole, Angel's wife, does she have authority over me? Of course! Both in the fact that she is a Minister of the Lord and the Wife of my Pastor and shares his calling. My own thinking is that if you do not believe that God forgives sin, then you have a good reason to not want women Ministers! Here's why, in the Garden God says, "If you eat from this tree you will surely die!" the Lord cannot lie, so to save his people He sent His only begotten Son, that whosoever believes on Him should not die but have everlasting life.

My thoughts are that when we see Him he is going to say, I wish you had worshipped me with the same conviction you had about what you thought people were doing wrong. How many more souls would have been saved and how much better the world would have been.

But back to my decision, it has borne itself out as long as I can remember. I made another decision also when I read in Isaiah 6:8 when the Lord said "Whom shall I send, and who will go for us?" Then said I, "Here am I, send me." And I said the same thing. Around this time I was pretty comfortable with the word and anxious, to get to work. I had been out to the Nursing Home, done Home visits, I remember one visit I made to two blind people, when it started to get dark, and they did not turn any lights on, why should they. Kind of funny. I was still going to Muzzle loading meets and this one Sunday night they the tent meeting at the Fair Grounds. It was August 23, 1992. I would guess 150+ people were there and this Preacher, his name was Ray Bloomfield, stopped Preaching and came over in front of me and started giving me this message from the Lord:

And I will also put wings to thy feet, wings to your feet.
And thou shall not be cemented into one place
But thou shall also go in the way of My choosing.
For I shall lead from one place and then another.

And those who will not hear, pay them no heed, but move on, for saith the

Lord there are those who are ready, ready to be saved.

Thou shall go with faith in thy heart.

Thou shall go in the simplicity of the gospel.

And minister my miracles and in My Name.

And there shall be no more fear, no, none at all.

Neither shall thou be hindered by the past.

Neither shall thy tie thyself to unprofitable vessels.

Living the least and saith the Lord, with a filling of fresh oil for there is

Much yet for thee to do.

This still tingles all the way down my spine when I read it.

I guess you know what came next. I was headed on the road. And where did I go, where else but the Muzzle Loading meets. Now this is a new and touchy area, very few Ministers been out here. They are held Friday, Saturday and Sunday, for the most part, so for the whole summer the muzzle loading people were not in Church, so the Church came to them. One thing about Buck skinners and Mountain men, they told the truth, and so for all my years of going to the meets and dealing with these people when I started the Ministry, They said, "All my years of knowing the "Wolverine", (my Indian name) he has always spoke with a straight tongue." And so I had a head start when I went out. Speaking of these people being as good as their word, I have seen $20,000 gun deals go on the shake of a hand, Like here take the gun and send me the money. Some of the things that went on in that Ministry is so great that only the Lord could have done them. Now since these people did not go to Church they also did not have communion, and it was a great way to remember how many people were at each service.

I was single at the time and went alone, one day I was given a sign that there was going to be a woman in my life, went like this. I was out to my brother Randy's house I was trapping some wood-chucks that were in his garden, as I walked back to the Garden he yelled at me, "I got something for you, I will leave it in your truck." I just waved my arm so he would know I heard him. When I get back to the truck there is a women's guitar, a woman was coming into my life! I feel about 10 foot high as I drive back to where I was staying. I got another miracle, I heard the sound of music in my head, it was a Johnny Cash sound, no words, what's Johnny doing in my life at this time. I shrugged it off. That night after I was asleep the Lord woke me and said, "Are you ready for the song I tried to give you earlier today, I said, " Here am I" now this is 2:00 in the AM, I got pencil and paper and started to write, the name of it was "If Jesus came today." 5 versus, God is so good, He knew how well I liked Johnny's music and that was the beat to the song, got a lot of strange looks when I would do the lead-in to the song, Johnny Cash in Church? But when they heard the message the song had. They are blessed.

OH! Back to the woman, I have learned when you need something and are going to pray about it, pray for someone else too. After I had prayed about it, I got up and done something, this is a theory of mine also, don't sit and wait for your answer to prayer, do something. Don't just wait for your ship to come in, Row toward it. I had seen an ad for Christian singles, so I wrote to them, 23 letters, here how this works. You send a letter to some one you see in the book, they all have a number, the letter is then forwarded by the Christian Singles so neither party knows the address of the other person you wish to contact. I sure got some nice replies like I can't go on the road with you but the woman who does will sure be lucky to. But nothing serious, then I got a letter from Grand Rapids, and the woman had even given me her phone number. I called her and she said, "How did you get my phone number?" I said, "It was in the letter you sent me." She said, "I mailed that letter last night and you have it before noon the next day! We talked on the phone a lot and decided to meet halfway between Grand Rapids and Coldwater, which was Kalamazoo, we were married two weeks later, and this year will be 16 years. Her name is Cora. But I have always called her Sis. She is a real blessing. She also has a true servants heart.

We were at a place called, East Jordan, This where I met a guy named Doug, in an earlier visit here. In front of my tent I had the American and the Church flag. He came up to me and introduced himself, he was a retired Marine Chaplin, and said, "I have had a dream of a Ministry at these meets for a long time, but the Lord never opened a door to it for me." He also had a small Church; He said, "If you ever need anything call on me." I had a 15 x 21 foot tent, the kind they had in early America, I would hold Church under the big Oak tree unless it rained and then I would hold services in the tent, This one morning as I came out of the tent the Lord stopped me and said, "Tell my people I am still doing healing!" now as a Minister, I wondered who did not know that, But as I said before I would rather be wrong than disobedient, so off I went to do the message the Lord had given me for that day, Now here is how we done, Sis would walk thru the camp with a rope with a lot of loops in it I made for her and she had a train whistle, the wooden kind, and the kids would grab the rope and she would take them to where I was, this rope tripled our Sunday school. She called it her Gospel Train. We would sing and praise the Lord, and then she would take the kids to a place and have Sunday school for them. I would then preach the message, and she would come back and we would have communion and I would close the service. Then I remembered the words of the Lord and I told the people the Lord had told me He was still in the healing business, and if anyone wanted prayer for healing to come forward and I would pray for them. Here comes an assistant Pastor, (I found this out later) and he was pushing a guy in a wheelchair and his Daughter was with them, the guy had an aluminum walker laying on his lap and when they came up to where I was, she opened it and stood it by the wheelchair. I called Doug and his Deacon up to where I was. As I said, I come from a Pentecostal Church but out here I had to be nondenominational. But one of the things I always asked is if they knew who the Lord Jesus Christ was, I asked him and he said, " I accepted the Lord many years ago." I said, "We have a problem here, my Bible says that the devil has to get his hands off God's property, which you are, when a man of God tells him to, Do you believe this?" now he talked real brokenly has it appeared he had a double stroke, He said, "Yes I do!" now I want you to know that I am not into long prayers as if it's too long you start getting into your own self. I put oil on his head, had the others put their hands on him, and I said "devil in the name of Jesus get your hands off this man who is Gods property, and be gone, never to bother him again! Amen, and I walked away. We had 67 people at the service and as

I walked away they all started clapping. I turned to see the man getting out of the wheelchair, he had the walker and took a couple faltering steps, now I had dead eye contact with the man and I seen his shoulders slump and I knew he had surrendered to the Lord, the Lord healed him right on the spot! He folded up the walker, stuck it under his arm and walked, toward me and was praising the Lord in the clearest tongue you ever heard! The hair on the back of my neck stood straight up. I competed against this man for the next two years in the shooting matches. I was telling out family doctor about this and he said, " What I would give to see that." He knew the impossibly of the situation.

The season for the Muzzle Loading meets was giving way to winter Doug ask me if I would like to be a Chaplin with some of the groups, I told him that I take my leading from the Lord and if that is what the Lord wanted I would do it. I told him I would pray about it, never got a word from the Lord.

As I said I had to be nondenominational, but many times Pentecostal people would come up to me after the service and say, "You are Pentecostal aren't you? I guess it's hard to hide. We never stand still in a service. I may sound a little prejudice, but I find so many different ways fail as to what the word says. I am going to stick my neck out and say this, the religion that bows down to any man, is in error. God says, "I am a jealous God and I will share my Glory with no man or graven image." Deuteronomy, 5; 9. Course this is also true of any worldly thing, I see signs on trucks, "I love my Truck." I guess the one that's really gets to me is the sign that says "Fear This". The word says the Fear of the Lord is the beginning of wisdom. Proverbs 9; 10. Another one I like is when I see men and how advanced they are in outer space, operations on people through electronics and such, I think of the passage where God says, " Men's wisdom is God's foolishness" 1st Corinthians 3; 19. Well I guess that's enough Bible study for this paragraph.

I wondered why the Lord was doing so many healings with me when I first got into the Church. He healed my eyes, healed my side one day when I had an attack of some kind, protected me on the roof of the Church, I think I still have the most healings of anyone in the Church. Then the bell went off, I could not carry Faith into the Ministry on the road unless I had it.

One day I was moving a freezer, I was walking it across the floor of the garage and it slipped and came down on the instep of my right foot, I always wore western boots. I pulled the boot off and then took my sock off and there was an abrasion on the top on my foot. I had to be in Church in an hour, I just figured I would ask the Lord to heal it when I got to the Church. I set up the camera and my foot hurt so I got a stool to set on. After the message they had a prayer line and I remembered a man that I had to stand in for and I went down to the prayer line and had the Ministers pray for the guy and I walked away, about 5 steps I thought to myself, " I forgot to have them pray for my foot." Then I stepped down on the foot and it did not hurt. No, I went over to the pew, set down and took off my boot an sock and the foot was completely healed, no mark of any kind on it. This is one of the reasons I always say if you need something pray for someone else.

I was at home and got a phone call from a woman, she ask if I would marry them at the next Muzzle loading meet at the Nationals. She had a strange request, could I marry them without the paper work, no license, blood test, she reasoned that the Bible had no reference of any paper work. I said, "I am afraid there is paper work in the Bible. Moses told men that if they wanted to divorce their wife they were to give her a writ of divorce, and a writ is paper." All was quiet for a couple of minutes, so I said, "Are you ashamed of the man you about to marry?" in a real meek voice she said, "No", I said, " That I and my Wife usually counsel with people that I am going marry, and if she wanted to get things in order for when I got there I would marry them." She said, "OK!" and hung up. I thought I had heard the last of that. No, here they come hand in hand to my booth. We talked at length with them and it was set for Saturday night. It was raining Saturday night as I went over to the place they were to be married. It was a hall belonging to the National Muzzle Loading Assoc. Having been a photographer and done a lot of weddings I asked the couple if they wanted pictures taken during the wedding or would they rather wait until after, they decided to wait until after. I told the friends their request and asked that please observe this event for what it was a solemn joining of two people into one. I was afraid they would be noisy, by the looks of them. The Holy Ghost was there and after the service several people ask me what that bright light was. What a chance to witness.

When I headed back to booth I could not believe how rain had fallen, to get to the booth I had to wade water above my knees. I knew the event would be canceled. Now for the 12 years that I done the ministry we had never taken up an offering. We did get a few handshakes with money in them. But depended on the Lord to pay our way. In a dream he showed me how to build a "Gun Builders Bench" and we sold these plus early American toys, and Sis always had big dill pickles, popcorn and lemonade she sold. I had 11 of the builder's benches with me and it usually took a week to sell them all, when I got back to the booth Sis had sold all of them. She said, "Guys waded thru the water to get them before they left to go home." Well, this is how the Lord works.

After Cora and I were married I moved to Grand Rapids as the business Sis had was better than I had in Coldwater. The neighbors had 4 kids and the one, I'll call her Sue, was 12-14 yrs old and called us Grandma and Grandpa, one day she said to Sis, "Grandma can I go with you to the National Shoot and will Grandpa baptize me? All the kids in school are getting baptized but they are doing it as a fad, I want to be baptized because that's what the Lord said to do." Sis said, "I don't see why not, but I will ask Grandpa to be sure." I agreed it would be an experience for her. The first Sunday at the shoot we had church and I told the people we have a girl who wants to be baptized and all that would like to, come down by the river and sing and praise the Lord before, we had 86 people that service. A bunch of them walked down to the river with us. This is a small river and with flea markets at each end I don't have to tell you what the river looked like, I think you could have walked across it on the trash. This guy comes up to me and said, "I am a studying Minister, and can I help?" I said," Be glad to have your help." We got down to the river and it was as bad or worse than I remembered, it didn't even want to stick a finger in that mess, In my mind I said, "Lord I need your help with this one." About that time the Minister yelled at me and said," Come here and look at this." I went to where he was and this pool of water looked clean enough to drink. Sometimes the Lord answers right away. Now this river was about 30 feet below the roadway and the road ran beside it and there was a bridge across it, when I looked up there were cars parked everywhere watching the baptism. So we sang and praised the Lord and then we baptized Sue. And I dismissed everybody. Many people came to my booth and asked me how I got that spot in the river so clean and clear. Boy, was that a good witness to the Lord.

One time I preached about never giving up. I told the people to be just like George Washington, Abraham Lincoln, and Ivan Jimson, never give up. I waited a little bit until some one said, "Who is Ivan Jimson?" I said Oh! You don't know him, cause he gave up.

I told about one time I was at the national shoot and this guy was having a bad time. Looked like he was having a stroke. I told him, "I am a Minister can I pray for you?" he said, "Yes" and I prayed for him. About this time here came the paramedic's, there was one of those take charge women and she said, " Get a cloth and soak it with cold water," I said, " I have handkerchief that is clean will that work?" She said, " Clean or dirty, just get it soaked." Away I went and soaked it and she put it on the back of the guy's neck, I told her I had prayed for the man, she said, " You done more for him than we can." then they hauled him away. You know why they call those people paramedics? Because there are always two of them, (pair a medics) she had underestimated the power of prayer. He was back at the shoot 3 hours later.

I mentioned early about tomahawk throwing, you had to stand a certain distance from the target and throw the tomahawk and knife and hit a playing card, it was always so funny when the guys I was competing would say, "Remember Reverend no help from above!"

When Sis and I first went on the road we had a Baker Lean-to, very comfortable but we could not hold church in it if it rained. The last time we stayed in it was at Three Rivers Michigan. A guy came by and ask if he could look inside the Baker, I said, "Sure." Afterward he said, "Do you want to sell it." I said I did, He asked would I take $ 50.00 down and $ 50.00 a month. I said, "I don't know come back a little later." I took Sis by the hand and asked the Lord what we should do, He said sell it, so we told the guy after the shoot it was his. Remember where the prophecy said going with the least, we had lost our cleaning business and was at the shoot with $7.00 to our name. I told Sis that if we sold the Baker we would have to go in the truck camper until the Lord got us the tent we needed. Now it turned out that I had to hold Church in the rain, the Buck skinners said, "Preacher, if you want to hold Church in the rain we will be there, and I did, and they were. I still carry the Bible with wavy pages, and proud of it. About this time a guy came up to me and said, "Heard you are selling your Baker, what you going to get now?" I said, "I need a 15 X 21 foot marquee (this is the kind of tent George Washington had) we had already looked at them and they were $1600, without the poles." He said, "Do you know who I am?" I said, "No.", he said, "I am Two Bears nephew." Now Two Bears was a very good friend of mine and I had some of his beadwork on my gun case. His house had been broken into and all his guns stolen. I had just finished a long rifle and I gave it to him with all the stuff to shoot it. 2 weeks after I gave it to him he hit the $200,000 dollar lottery. Anyway the guy said, " I am a distributor for the tent you want, how does half price sound to you? I know what you are going to use it for." I said to him give me a little time and I will let you know. I took Sis by the hand and said, "Lord what say thee to this?" the Lord said, " Order it and I will pay for it!" now I don't know if you have ever stepped out on the word of the Lord, but it is a huge step. I went over to guy and asked if he had to have any money down, as I was a little short at the moment. He just laughed and said, " The word of the Wolverine (my Indian name) is as good as gold in the hand, not to mention of a Minister of the Lord. It will be here in two weeks." The next week we went back to East Jordan for the shoot with the truck camper and was gone 3 days, when we got home of course as usual had a pile of mail. Right on top was a letter from our house mortgage. I said to Sis, "Oh No! Did you forget the house payment?" She said, " NO! Open it up and see what it is," I did and there was a check for $ 300.00 refund as we had paid too much into the escrow, then the next letter was from the IRS. I said, "Oh No! We didn't pay enough in and they are to audit us!" Sis said, "Will you quit that! Open it up and see what it is before you get so upset!" I opened it up and there was $ 260.00 refund they had shorted us. I finally just opened the mail in silence, when I was done there was $ 830.00, the price of the tent and gas money to go get it. People call this coincidence. I call it the fulfillment of the word to me from the Lord. Oh almost forgot the guy that bought the baker lean-to called me 2 weeks after he took it home and said he would not be making the payments of $50.00 a month. He had a windfall and was sending me the total amount owed.

There was a black powder meet down in Fulton County. I had been there once before and it was OK, after I married Sis we got an invite to go down there, Fulton County was about in the middle of Indiana. Had a good time there and after I was loading the stuff up, I see this little girl talking to Sis, thinking it was someone who needed prayer I went over there, turns out the girl was singing to Sis, the Father Abraham song. I had never heard or seen what goes with the song. I offered the girl a quarter to sing it again. She did, "Father Abraham had many sons, many sons had Father Abraham, I am one of them and so are you, so lets just praise the Lord. Right hand, then Father Abraham again as above, then Left hand, then Father Abraham again, then Right foot, Father Abraham again then Left foot, and at the end of the song she fell on the ground. I said, "OK!" never did figure it out. I guess it was a song for kids to praise the Lord.

Sis had an experience with a child and I have asked her to give her version of that incident;

While teaching Sunday school at the National Shoot in Friendship, Indiana children in early American costumes surrounded me. One little girl, whom I will never forget, was dressed as a young Native American in a dark brown buckskin dress, her hair in long brown braids with a freckled face. We were sitting near a log cabin, some of the children on stumps and some children on a split rail fence. I was talking to the kids about sometimes having to be alone while they were going to sleep at night or when they were sent to their room as a punishment. But I reminded them that we are never alone and that Jesus is always with us no matter where we are. We can tell Him all of our problems and He hears and answers our prayers. The unforgettable little girl spoke up in excitement and said, "I know that! I always hated onions and my Mom puts onions in everything.

I prayed and asked Jesus to help me like onions and the next day she put onions in chili and I liked them and now I like onions no matter what she puts them in!" I was so impressed that when she prayed she didn't asked that her Mother stop cooking with onions but that the Lord would change HER. What a lesson that is for us to be willing to have God change us and not that He change the other person or our circumstances. AND, what a faith builder for her to realize that God is faithful to hear and answer our prayers.

Great story. After a while in Grand Rapids, I was standing in the front yard and the Lord spoke to me and said, " Get out Grand Rapids, there is devastation coming to Grand Rapids," and in a vision I saw what looked like an earthquake had hit bridges out, wrecks everywhere, bands of outlaws robbing every house. I went into the house and told Sis and we prayed about this, in faith we put the house up for sale and got $ 5,000 more than any house had sold for on that street. I knew Sis hated to sell the house. While the house was being sold I told Sis I thought we were to move north, we were drawn to the Howard City area. Its about 40 miles north of Grand Rapids, we went there about 6-8 times, we had lunch about a mile from where we moved, I asked the Lord for ten acres, house, building for a shop, that's exactly what we found. The bad part was it was 6 miles from Croton Dam where they catch the Salmon, hard to take. Sis said to me, " You ever catch any Salmon? I have always wanted to can some." I told her, "I went snagging once and didn't get any." I said, "We would go over to the dam when we get settled." We went over and I walked among the fisherman asking what they were catching Salmon on, they all just smiled, I found out later they were snagging and snagging had been against the law for a while. I went over a few times, what you had to do was park on one side, walk up the hill, cross the bridge, down the hill and this is where the good fishing was, in pools below the dam. I went a few times, and this one night I was standing out in the water and here come a bunch of drunken guys, one with them seemed sober and he was the one that was going to fish. The other guys on the shore kept hollering at him, he said back to them, "I lent you my fishing tackle and you brought it back all broke up, this reel won't even work!" I said, " I have another reel in my truck you can use," I walked over to truck and got it, walked back and handed it to him, he was really grateful and said so. All this did to the drunks was to stir them up, and they said they were going kick the tar out of the guy in the water, there was 6 of them and they reminded the guy in the water of that, Well Sir, I was a biker for a lot of years and if two guys want to go at it fine, but for others to jump on one guy, was a No! No! in my book! I had found out the guys name was Fred, after I had heard enough I said, "To the guys on the bank, Fred's not alone here, either one of us is as good as any 3 of you and if you would care to have us prove it say so!" Man it got quiet, they said, " Fred we are going to leave you here, get home the best way you know how!" I said, " Fred's got a ride home you boys just move along so Fred and I can fish in peace." I had made a friend, I told Fred that I was a minister, he said, "Really and you told those guys where to go?" I said, " Right is right, I used to be a biker and that kind of stuff did not set well with me." I said, "I'm not perfect, just born again!" It was funny after that guys would swear and Fred would say, "Hey you guys there happens to be a Minister standing here." I was later to find out what a tough guy Fred was. People said he would fight at the drop of a hat and drop the hat. Anyway, we got done fishing and we headed to the truck, we both had a bunch of fish. We took mine to my house so I could tell Sis I was going to take Fred home. When I took him in to meet her we then could smell the booze on him. But we both liked the guy. We head out to Fred's house and on the way there the headlights began to dim, turns out Fred is a mechanic and he said, "Your alternator is going bad." By the time we got to Fred's house we could hardly see. Fred said, " I am a mechanic and I can fix it for you." So Fred takes me home in his car and Fred's car needed a muffler, Sis thought it was the guys at the dam looking for Fred and I, she was very relieved to see it was us. I asked him how much the alternator would be, he said he wasn't sure, so we gave him a blank check and he left. I turned to Sis and said, "You see what I just did? I left my truck at this guy's house and sent him home with a blank check. I don't even know where he lives. But the Lord is my rear guard and the next day here he comes with the truck all fixed. He had brought his father-in-law to take him back home, to say we were relieved! They ate a bite with us and we paid Fred for fixing the truck. I was to see a lot of Fred the next month. I found out he was selling Salmon, I can't judge, that used to be me. I talked to Fred a lot about the Lord, one time when his Father-in-law was with him he said I made a difference in Fred's life. About a month and a half after I first met Fred I got a phone call, the caller said, "He just dropped dead!" I thought the caller was someone telling me Fred's Father-in law had died as Fred told me he had a bad heart. I said, "Who dropped dead?" the caller said, "FRED! We took him to the hospital with a bad headache and they could find nothing wrong so we came home and Fred walked out to get the mail and fell dead in the yard. He had an a broken blood vessel in his head." Oh Lord, I hope Fred knew you! At the funeral I was talking to a guy and he said, " I owe Fred more than I can ever repay. My kids were driving a pickup, lost control and rolled over back on its wheels and caught afire. They could not get the doors opened, here comes Fred wades thru the fire and with super human strength tore the doors open. Got the kids out and burnt his hands pretty bad. I didn't realize how much Fred meant to me. Goodbye Fred.

Back to the place we moved to, I had asked the Lord for 10 acres, a house and a barn for my shop. That's just what he give us, the pole barn was a 100 yards from the house, huge pine trees all the way. I was standing up by the pole barn and was enjoying the day, the Lord, I looked towards the house and there was a clearing about 40 feet wide all the way to the house, as I looked I seen a vision of trailers with people fleeing from the mess that was coming. I told Sis I guess we better get ready, people will be coming here when things go bad. I started raising bees, for the honey, we started buying seeds, wood burning stoves, Sis started canning a lot of food. We were working at a Christian school, Sis was the Supervisor of the custodial, and I was the Maintenance Engineer. My what a nice sounding title for a janitor. They had lunches for the kids and whatever was left over was thrown away. Not on my watch! We started taking it to Families who needed it. We ended up with 14 Families we were taking food to. We also put in a quart of honey from the hives, Sis had canned 119 pints of salmon, and we put a couple of pints in with the food. I got so tired of doing this, I told Sis I wanted to quit. We had the Christian station on the radio and just then the Minister said,

"Weary not in well doing." I said, " Ok I will deliver the food." The Lord blessed the beehives. One year I got 1200 pounds of honey from 7 hives. We sold very little of the honey. The honey I had was what they call raw honey, it had not been heated, they heat the honey to keep it from crystallizing on the store shelf, problem with that is you take all the good stuff out. I had people come to my door and asked if I had raw honey, said the doctor told them to get it for their family with asthma, helped them breathe. All the people we took food to are back on their feet doing fine. Praise the Lord.

After we had moved to Howard City, I was far enough north to use a center fire rifle for deer, and thought I would try the Weatherby 22-250, I had always used 55-grain bullets in the gun. I decided to try some 60-grain bullets as I thought it would be nice to have a little heavier bullet. They shot good at 100 yards, and since I had a scope that would figure the drop of the bullet that's all the sighting in I had to do. Went out opening morning and where I was going to hunt was on a rise where I could see 300 yards. No more than sit down and out walks 4 deer, I put the scope on them and it showed they were at 180 yards, I made the adjustments, and fired, the bullet hit 6 foot behind the deer I shot at. Now I am unhappy, I pride myself on accuracy and this didn't get it, what had I overlooked? I checked everything and could find no reason for the flyer (shot going off target) and then I called Hornady, they are the makers of the bullets and they have a hotline for things such as this. I told them the problem, the gun, bullet and powder charge I was using. The guy said, "Here's the problem, the Weatherby is rifled a turn of 1 in 11, (bullet turns once every 11 inches of barrel) and this 60-grain bullet was designed for M-16 which is 1in 9, (bullet turns once every 9-inches of barrel). Your barrel is not fast enough for the 60-grain." Well I'm a guy that's wants to use what I want to use. Started looking at guns that would take about any bullet there was, 30-06 seem to fit the bill. Since I don't have any guns I don't shoot I sold the Weatherby and bought a Remington 30-06, bolt action. Another barnburner, I messed around with it and got some good results. I was looking at a gun book that had guns for sale and all the stuff that went with them. And here's a listing for sabots for the 30-06, a sabot is a plastic sleeve that would hold a smaller bullet than the caliber of your gun, these happen to be for a .224 bullet, same bullet that I shot in the 22-250. So I ordered 200 of them. I still had a bunch of .224 bullets around. Now the 30-06 with a standard hunting load, 150-grain bullet would go 2800 FPS (feet per second) with these sabots and a .224, 55-grain bullet they would go 5600 fps, that over a mile a second. To give you an idea of this speed, look at a clock with a second hand, when it ticks one second the bullet had gone over a mile. Hornady came out with a bullet that was a hollow point with a pointed nylon cone in the nose. Here's the problem. The hollow point is the most accurate bullet but the hole in the front of it is drag, so with the cone in the front it was more aerodynamic and picked up some more fps. The bullet is called a V-max, and does this bullet explode when it hits. Guys use these for varmints, woodchuck prairie dogs, crows and etc. These are so explosive that if you hit a twig or stalk of grass they explode. Which of course, makes them the safest bullet around, other bullets ricochet all over the place. A friend of mine shot crows at 300 yards with these bullets, said all you see is a puff of black feathers. I forgot to mention the scope was Tasco 4 to 16 power with a range finder, had a set of bi-pod legs on the gun for a steady rest. Quite a toy. This is the gun that shot all 4 Caribou when Randy and I went to Quebec. What happened was, I had my 2 Caribou and the guide was with Randy down at a lake, I was sitting on the hill waiting for them. I hear this snowmobile coming at full bore, it was Randy, said, "Have you got more shells with you, My gun won't fire." I said, "I do but they won't fit your gun as they are fire formed to only fit my gun, here take my gun and shells." So that's how my gun shot all 4 Caribou.

One morning I woke up with a start, sit up in bed; this is not like me I wake up slowly as a rule. Sis said, "You are awake!" I said, "I just had a bad dream, some one blew up our garage and there was broken cement and rerod all over the place, what a mess to clean up." We didn't even have a garage. About this time her daughter called us on the phone and said, "Turn on your TV!" we did, guess what? 911 just happened. You can draw your own conclusions about this. I figure that the Lord showed this to me so one day when something happens that I would have a hard time believing I will look back at this incident.

I had so much stuff when we moved to Howard City there was not room for it so I covered it with tarps, had piles all over the place. We had a yard sale and for being out in the country a lot of people came. This one lady, found out later her name was Donna, she and Sis ended up being best friends. Any way, she came to the sale then went home and got her husband as I had a lot of guy's stuff. His name was Maylan and we got to be good friends, he was quite cantankerous like I used to be. But we got along well. He was very distressed when he found out we were moving to Arizona. After we moved back to Michigan we went north to baby-sit some girls while their Mother went on a trip. This was about 40 miles from where Maylan and Donna lived. I brought a couple of guns to show Maylan and to ask him if he knew anyone who wanted to buy them. Saturday I ask Sis to call Maylan and see when I could catch up to him. While she was on the phone, Donna had answered, I seen Sis face turn funny, and she told me Maylan had died of a heart attack just hours before Sis called. I was shocked, now Maylan and I were not that close, I thought. Anyway, we went to the funeral home to see him one last time. Now as with everybody I talked to Maylan about the Lord. Maylan went to this Church and did a lot of work for them. But I never felt like he was ready to meet the Lord. So when we walked into the funeral home I expected to feel and see stuff I did not want to. I have the gift of discerning spirits and when I walked up to the casket all I felt was peace. About that time Maylan's Pastor told me Maylan had given his life to the Lord a week before he died. Praise God. Sis and I headed back to Coldwater, I told her I didn't know how I felt about Maylan dying, I cried most of the way home. Now like I said, Donna was Cora's best friend and she had told Donna we would come up for the funeral if we could. I forgot to tell you that at the funeral home Maylan was in a casket that he had built. They wanted to put the casket on those black wheelie things. Donna said no way, the casket would be put on the saw horses Maylan had built the casket on. They did too! here he is, a plaid hunting shirt, at the end of the casket was his 300 mag rifle and on the floor was the last bear he had shot made into a rug. We made arrangements to get puppies hair cut the day of the funeral, he would be there and not at the funeral. We got to the Church and there was the same setup as the funeral home had. Maylan had been a fire fighter and the fire department was there. Maylan's fire boots were by the casket too. When we got ready to go to the cemetery we came out of the Church and the hearse was gone. I looked down the road and could not see it. Maylan's son was driving Maylan's truck. We go to the cemetery and here come Maylan's truck, they had hauled Maylan in the bed of the truck. So here we are at the graveside and a pager from the fire department beeped and said, "Last page for Maylan for fire duty." That one got to everybody. After all was done I went up and laid my hand on his casket and said, "Goodbye Maylan."

Another thing I had happen was that one day Cupid did not want to go for walk and do his business. We lived off a blacktop road, you turn into the drive and go straight about 60 yards and you would come to the pole barn where I had my shop, turn left and the road went around to the house, when you came into our drive and hung a left instead of going to the shop you went to the house, about 80 yards, it was a huge circle drive. If I was going to walk Cupid to the mail box which was at the entrance to our drive, I would tell him in the we were going to the mail box, (turn right) or if I had to go to the barn I would say go to barn. (Turn left) I would put his leash on in the house and would walk down the center of the drive so I would not influence him and he always turned the way I had told him in the house, He's a smarty. Anyway he would not go out the door, this went on for 3 days, He done his business in the house, and he never did this. The third day I was headed up to the mailbox by myself and when I got to the end of the drive my eyes about popped out of my head, I hurried back to the house and grabbed the 35mm camera and a 4 foot yard stick. I laid it by the tracks there and shot pictures, when I got them developed I took them over to Steve, he had mounted my Caribou head, I said, "Steve are these Cougar tracks?" the paw print was 4 ½ inches across, the step between the front foot and the back foot was 37 ½ inch stride. Steve said, " Not only are Cougar tracks, it's a big one, I would guess a lot over 200 pounds." No wonder Cupid would not go out. From that point on I carried the 357-mag pistol. Before we moved we had a yard sale, and one guy asked why I was carrying the 357, I told him about the cougar, he just looked at me for a minute then said, "I seen him on the other road, I would not tell anyone about him as they would think I was seeing things, the Cougar crossed the road in front of me and when he went across his nose was on the edge of the road and his tail was on the center line, he is huge."

You will see that I talked to people about the Lord every chance I got. There is in Ezekiel, chapter 3:16-17, about how God has set you as a watchman, and if you don't tell people about the Lord and they go to hell, their blood is on your hands, but if you tell them and they don't heed your words and end up in hell, there blood is not on your hands. When I preach about this I call it the self-defense chapter. I think about people you are around and never say anything to them about the Lord, and one day when we all stand in front of God at the judgment and we look around and don't see someone, we think where are they, the voice of the Lord will come to you and say, You never told them!" how will you feel?

I got hurt at the school we were working at, the custodian did not come in so I was picking up the trash, went up to this one and grabbed the 55 gallon plastic bag out of the container and someone had put a bunch of books in it (weighed about 60 pounds) and when I tried to lift it my fingers on my right hand cracked and really hurt. Went to 3 doctors, all said they knew my hand was hurt but there was nothing they could do for it, said it was nerve damage and would either heal itself or I would have trouble the rest of my life. I started getting work-men's comp check, after three months they quit sending the checks, then the school fires me. I'm still having trouble. Anyway now I can't work and we had just put up a new house 4 years earlier on the ten acres. They wanted both Sis and I at the school and so they let us both go. We ended up losing the house, land and barn. I wondered about the people who were going to come when things went bad. Sis said the Lord was just trying me to see if I would have all those people there, as I am a very private person. Sis has a son in Arizona that had a coffee shop and said if she was not doing anything to come out and run the coffee shop. So here we go, was out there 9 months and he had to go bankrupt and lost the coffee shop. I always felt bad that we lost the place in Howard City, what if things did go bad and the people had no place to go, But I guess if the Lord would have needed us to stay there He would have made a way. We moved back to Michigan and here we are,

When we were going to move to Arizona I thought about building another chopper, got some books where I could order parts I needed, took my tools with us, and I had a gas and electric welder that I took with me. We can justify about anything and make it seem right. I knew that would be the place for a scooter (motorcycle) as you could ride all year long. Got out there and got the shop set up, I also have a bunch of wood working tools, but got set up and was looking around for and engine and frame. Then one day the Lord said to me, "Haven't you tempted me enough?" I didn't want a bike anyway.

When we got back to Coldwater, one of the first things I had to do was replace the well pump at the Church, it was really needed and I went to Church that Sunday in work clothes and while the service was on I replaced the pump. Hey! The Ox was in the ditch. As I said before God blesses the work of my hands, and gives me the knowledge to do things. And as I said before, " To whom much is given, much is required." There is also in Romans 12: 1 a word or two about your reasonable service. But anyhow got it done about the time the service had ended and Sis and Angel came out to see how I was doing. Sis said they had communion and I said, "I hated to miss that, so Angel gave me communion where I was working. I prayed Lord let there be no strife among men.

At the Church we had on Perkins street, a couple of times I seen a glowing blue light in the balcony, not bright it was just there. Course I knew what the Lord said, " Where two or three are gathered together in my name I am there." I saw more miracles at that Church. The Anointing of the Holy Ghost is all over the Church. People write to the Church from all over the world and ask to be put on the prayer board. The Church has about 1000-1200 answered prayers a year.

Here's a smile, Angel and I were working at the Church one time and we heard sounds like someone talking and couldn't understand what they were saying. The Arabians had a mask next to the Church. I looked out the door and there were some of them talking in their native language, I came back into the Church and told Angel it was some guys from Arabia speaking in tongues.

Chapter 24

Ebay

Cora's Son, Dan gave us a computer and we used it to keep in touch with the people we met at the Muzzle Loading meets during the off-season. In 2002 I started doing Ebay, I also taught myself for the most part. I found a job I really liked. I bought a few things, mostly Shakespeare Fishing stuff. Then I noticed that a lot of things being sold I had laying around, and then I started seeing a lot of things I seen at yard sales. I started buying at yard sales and flea market and putting them on Ebay for sale, this is an auction type sales. I started making a little money. Took a lot of trial and error. But pretty soon I was doing real good. Things I wanted to buy no longer came out of my paycheck, but from Ebay sales. In 2003 we were going to work, it was the middle March, Sis was driving and we saw a basement sale sign, there was still snow on the ground. Sis says, " I suppose you have to go to that sale?" I said, " I suppose I do." The guy who was having the sale had lost his job and said he had to raise money. First thing I see is a Fred Bear Bow, 4 patent numbers on it, I said, "what do you have to have for that?" He said, "$9.00." I bought it; Later on Ebay I got $ 87.00 for it. Then I see he has a wooden lure box with a modern plastic lure with it. I said, "how much?" he said $5.00. I bought it and that was about all that was there I could sell. I took the lure box home and looked it over, there used to be a sliding wood lid, it was gone. I took the box to my shop and built a new lid for it, I antiqued it, looked like the original.

I put it on Ebay for $ 9.99, in less than 18 hrs I got an e-mail from a guy who said he would give me $ 250.00 for it if I would take it off auction, This is how it works, if take an item off auction and Ebay finds out you sold it off line you can't sell on their site anymore. And also the guys that were looking at it will not come back to your auctions again. And then I figure if it's worth $ 250.00 it will still be worth that tomorrow. I tells the guy, "Sounds like you will win it anyway, just bid on it." Now Ebay charges 35 Cents to list the box with one picture. And then they take 7% of the final price it sells for. So it runs along the next week and I'm putting my new items on. Looks at what I owe Ebay, $42.00, puts on another item and I owe Ebay $ 72.00, Whoa Nellie! I must have sold something, I look at my sold items and collapsed in my chair, the Box and lure sold for $765.00. But get this the guy who bought it told me he was so happy to get that box at that low price. I later found out that the old lure makers made a box for their lures, when the modern tackle boxes came along the boxes would not fit in the tackle boxes, so they threw them away. And now they are collector items.

After I got hurt at the school Ebay kept us going for a while, but I was spending the money I was making and not buying any new items. But I had a ton of stuff and kept selling until it was gone. I had about $ 20,000.00 in wood working tools, a ton of fishing stuff. Most of it is gone.

Here's a funny I started going to flea markets to get Ebay items, I had a cart about 18 inches square, about 3 foot high, had two wheels the handle came about a foot high above the basket, I had bungee straps hooked on it in case I bought stuff like bows, fishing rods, etc I could wrap them in the corners and they wouldn't be all over the place. I came up to the one vender, had something I wanted to see closer, I let go of my cart and walked a couple steps closer, it was nothing I wanted, I backed up and grabbed my cart and started to walk away, about 3-4 steps I felt some eyes on me, turned around and looked, I had grabbed the wrong cart and their sat a little dog in the cart looking at me, I started laughing and took him back. Some of the venders I knew I was telling them about the incident and from then on they would ask me if I was doing any dog napping today.

These flea markets are great, I have always been one to barter, and many times the best time to deal is when they are getting ready to go home, they know that a $5.00 bill is much easier to carry then the item they want $10.00 for. So many times I arrange my time this way or go back at closing. I sold a lot of bows and arrows, I had to refletch the arrows, and get strings for the bows. One time I walk up to this guy that has a box of bow strings, new in the package, 118 I think, now these sell for $12.00-$16.00 each. He had $8.00-$10.00 ea, I said to him, "How much you want for the strings?" he said, "The price is on each one." I said, "No I mean the whole box." He thought a minute and then said, " What will you give." I'm thinking I would go $1.00 ea and so I said, " I'll give you $50.00 for the whole box." He said, "I can't do that!" and I done my favorite trick I started to walk away, he said, "Wait a minute, can't you do better than that?" no dealer in his right mind would let a customer walk away without trying to get their money somehow. I said, "The problem is, a lot of them are way to long for what I need, I guess I could sort out the sizes I need, I would give you .50 cents ea for them." See what is happening, the dealer is seeing a 50-dollar bill floating away. He hesitated and I start walking away again. I knew he was thinking how long it would take him to sell them with mostly compound bows being used, these were strings for long bows, he calls me back and said, "I'll take the $ 50.00." Don't ever be afraid to walk away, you can always come back later. I done the same thing another time, guy had an airnailer, good name on it, said he had only used to roof a garage, exactly what I wanted it for. He had $180.00 on it, I knew these sold for $230.00-$250.00, I said, "You are about $100.00 higher than I want to give, being a used tool with no warranty." I said, "Thanks" and walked away. About an hour later I walked by him again, came in behind him to see if he still had it. He did and I walked by and never even looked his way. He hollered at me, "You still want that nailer?' Who's hollering at me? Oh! It's that guy, I walked over to him like I didn't want to be bothered, he said, "If you want it for $80.00 you can have it." See! After I had left he could see the nailer setting on a shelf at home. And he would still be wanting that other tool he wanted.

When CB's first came out I got one and you have to have a handle (name) to use when people holler at you. The one that I chose was, "Michigan Trade rat". I was always swapping something. This was before cell phones. I was traveling south on the freeway and I hear these truck drivers talking to each other. One says, "Hey parking lot (car hauler) were you going with those two beavers (girls)?" then I hear another yell at him, "Hey parking lot where you going with those two beavers (girls)?" and when I finally see the guy with the car carrier he is stopped and the police are there, afterward I heard on the CB the two beavers (girls) were in the top car over the cab of the truck, they got in while the trucker was eating lunch. Can you imagine the rush when you would be sitting in a car on top of a car carrier and see the overpass coming at you? Never a dull moment.

The thing to remember that until CB's came along, there was no way for truckers to talk to each other, now they could chatter their whole route. And of course this means warning too, like, "Hey there's a Smokey in the grass, (there's a cop sitting hidden ahead) or there's a Smokey handing out green stamps. (Giving a motorist a ticket.) Even when the weigh station was open or closed. And especially when you broke down you could tell who ever where you are and the problem. My son drives a thermos bottle, (Tanker truck.) and he tells me they have a GPS, (global positioning system) in the truck so they know where you are all the time, and elapsed time when you have to take a rest. how fast you are going, on and on. Ahhhh this modern age.

Then there's the guy driving the truck and in it he had a small CB radio, barely got out, didn't have the dollars for a powerful radio. Guys would rib him with, "Roll your window so I can hear you better!" or "Do you have a volume control button?" I mean this gets old quick. Guess what? He hit the $100,000.00 lottery; first thing he does is take his truck the CB shop and says, "I want the biggest, best radio you have! " The man says are you kidding, that will cost you $2,000.00 plus installation!" trucker says, "Put it in by tomorrow and there's an extra $100.00 in it for you." The man says, "Yes Sir!" the trucker picks up the truck and on the road he goes. Looks down at the radio and all it has is three buttons, two black and one red, first black button says on it "Low" second black button says, "Med" and the red button has nothing on it. Well, he says to himself lets see how good this is, he is driving down Route 20 in Ohio, pushes the "Low" and says. "Breaker, Breaker Anybody got a copy on this mobile?" (Anyone hear me?) Another Trucker comes back to him, (answer's) "I got you loud and clear, what's your 20?" (What is your location) trucker with the new radio says, "I'm on route 20." The trucker who answered says, your right next to me, I'm also on route 20 in California." New radio says, "I'm on route 20 in Ohio, and says, Bye, Bye. He thinking to himself, this radio is Ok. Then he pushes the Med button and says, "Anybody got a copy on this mobile?" Guy says, "Go ahead Mate, I copy you." New radio says, "What's your 20?" the guy says, "Australia here!" new Radio says, Bye, Bye, he's thinking, Wow this is some radio, wonder what the red button is? Pushes the red button and the radio starts shaking and smoking! Radio guy says, Oh, Lord!" And a voice says, YESSSSSS,

Chapter 25

Words of Wisdom

It came to me that some of the sayings we hear are not really words to live by, but then again:

Like I heard about a guy who was training a Brown Bear and it killed him, He forgot this saying: You can take an animal out of the wild, But you can't take the wild out of the animal.

How about this: Never argue with a fool, people watching don't who is who.

And; If Mama ain't happy, nobody's happy.

Here are two for people in charge; if you are the Boss you won't have to tell anyone. Or; you can lead a thousand, but you can't push one.

Husbands when you get dressed to go somewhere, never forget to leave a button unbuttoned or a part of your collar turned up so the Wife can fix you and then say, "I don't know how you will ever get along without me!"

If you go to someone's door to sell something no matter what age woman answers the door always ask to see her Mother.

All that glitter's is not Gold, might be broken glass.

Don't judge a man until you have walked a mile in his shoes.

Even a fish would not get caught if he just kept his mouth shut.

They say gunpowder and whiskey don't mix, I guess that's true, taste's bad and the gunpowder won't fire.

Never could figure out why they say "Good Morning" when it stats with getting up?

The guy said, " Cheer up things could be worse!" so I cheered up, and sure enough things got worse!

We learn from others mistakes, But sometimes we have to be the others.

Time flies when you are having fun. Or as the frogs in the pond say; Time sure is fun when you are having flies.

Chapter 26

Today

Today is February 25, 2008, back in Coldwater, Michigan. Just got back from ice fishing at Randall Lake. No fish but got to talk to three guys at the lake about the Lord. Snowing heavy again. Went to Messenger Lake earlier in the week, but no luck there either. Had 17 inches of the hardest ice I ever seen. Sure am hungry for a mess of crappies. I only eat them in the winter, as they are mushy in the summer.

The devil has been trying to kill me this past week, But I called on the Lord day and night, and when I went to Church tonight and the anointing was upon the Pastor's wife as she was praying for people, the Lord spoke to me and said, " You have passed the trial and the more shall be added unto you." So I don't know what I will be doing for the Lord now. Always a little scary. The Lord has always blessed the work of my hands, and He gave me many gifts, the reason its scary is the word says, "To whom much is given, much is required." Like I said earlier.

I have to tell you here that throughout this book you have seen many times where the Lord said to me, people say the Lord does not speak to people anymore, that was the Old Testament, Funny my Bible says that God is the same yesterday, today and tomorrow, and guess where the Ten Commandments are? But this I have to say, You have to make yourself available and be willing to listen, I am convinced that He does not trust his word to just anyone. But to those who Love Him and are obedient to Him and His word. 2nd Timothy, Study to show thyself approved unto God a workman that needeth not be ashamed, rightly diving the word of truth. It works for me and blesses people. Speaking of the Old Testament, there was a woman I knew told me that the 23rd Psalm was the funeral verse.

There was once a very rich man who just could not stand to think of going to Heaven and leaving all of wealth behind. He begged the Lord to let him to let him take some of it with him to Heaven. The Lord told him he would have no need of his wealth in Heaven. The man just wouldn't give up and kept pleading and begging until the Lord finally said, "All right, but only one suitcase full of anything you choose". The man gave it much thought and finally decided to turn his possessions into Gold bouillon (bricks) and put all he could in a big suitcase. He died soon after and when he reached the Pearly Gate Saint Peter told him he wasn't allowed to bring the suitcase into Heaven. The man explained that he had made a deal with God, so Saint Peter said he would look inside. He did and then looked at the man and asked, " You brought pavement?"

I was telling the people at the Church in Coldwater, the Church of the Holy Spirit, about a couple of Churches we went to Grand Rapids, one you could call the Lord from the Church and talk to Him for $100.00, another Church was $50.00, I said I was glad to be back in the Church of the Holy Spirit where it cost nothing to call the Lord, as it was not long distance from this church.

I seen a great sign the other night in Church two women came out with prophesy. Why is that so great, the Bible says in the end times women would prophesy, and your old men will dream dreams, The disciples asked the Lord, "Master how will we know the end times?" and He told them, " How is it you can look at the sky and say tomorrow will be sunny, and yet you cannot see the signs of the end?" Yes, I know people have been saying for ages it surely must be time for the Lord to return, but all the pieces are falling into place. Things men can no longer fix. Look at your newspaper, global warming, violence, on and on.

Stopped over to the church last fall to help the guys with two small buildings they were putting up, 12 x 16 I think, they had the sides and ends built and all we had to do was stand them up and nail them together, we laid them down where they went and the one end we laid on a yellow jackets nest, when we went to pick it up it had a bunch of them on it, the first guy got stung on the rear and run away. I said, " Here let me pick it up, they won't bother me." I stood it up and they went back to their nest. Thinking back on what I said it would sound like I was invincible, truth was I raised honeybees for a long time and had learned to control the pheromones that my body gives off. People who are afraid of something give off this smell (pheromones) that excites bees or dogs into attacking.

One time I was getting ready to tend the bees and had put on my suit I wore and walked up to the hives and there is a turkey eating my bees, I yelled at her to get out and she came at me, looked around and she had 9 little turkeys and they were also eating bees. I finally got them on their way. When I would take the honey out of the comb I would cut the caps off and then put the frame into a machine, hand crank type called an extractor, it would throw the honey out by centriful force and it would drain out the bottom and into 5-gal buckets with spigot on the bottom and a nylon screen across the top to filter out dead bees, wax and any other junk. Then I would fill the containers from the spigot. The frames that had the honey in would still have a lot of honey in them that I could not get out. So I would feed them to the bees, they would have to be 100-yards from the hives as all kinds of bees, yellow jackets, wasps bumble bees, on and on would come to eat from the frames and I didn't want to show them where my bees were making the honey. They would invade and rob the hives and kill the bees in the process. Anyway when I would put the frames out to be cleaned I would stand in the mist of all these bees, when they are feeding and collecting they won't sting you. That is if you had your pheromones under control. I had Sis take a picture of me standing in the middle of them.

For Valentines in 2004 I told Sis she could have a puppy for a Valentines day present, She always wanted a dog. But I said don't get a mongrel. She got to looking around and found a guy who sold Shih Tzu puppies, so we went over and looked at them. The one little male pup came up to her and wanted her to pick him up. He was a cutie, she decided he was the one and we made arrangements to buy him. Why not he chose her, He was not ready to leave his Momma yet so she would have to wait a week. The puppy had a brother for sale and when we got home we called my Son Ron as they had been looking for a pup also. Ron's wife Judy said buy him and bring him down. So we bought both of them, the one that came up to Sis was the one we were going to keep. They had a ton of paper work for each of them. While we were doing the paper work we see that the pup was born on our Wedding Anniversary so She named him Cupid. He turned out to be the joy of our lives, I would be setting at the computer and I would feel eyes looking at me, I would look down and there he was, when I looked at him he would say "Out." Wanted me to take him out, the other word he would say was Ma ma when we were going on the freeway, he knew what rest stops looked like and he would start saying Ma, Ma, he wanted her to stop so he could smell where other dogs had been, and do his other business. While we were in Az I was walking him down the street and two 80-pound Rottweilers attacked us. One grabbed him in the middle and other had him by the back leg, I was beating them with a 3 cell mag light and could not get them to let go, I stuck my hand in the ones mouth and pried him off my pup, (I did not know that if you want to get a dog to open his mouth just reach in and pinch down on his tongue) when I did he bit me and now I have nerve damage on the other hand. The dippy girl that owned them stood there yelling, "Don't ruin my life! Don't ruin my life!" They had been told if the dogs hurt somebody they would be liable. We took pup to vet and they said they didn't think he would not make it though the night. But he did, Poor little guy gets scared every time a dog gets around him. They don't know how lucky they were that I was not the man I used to be. That little guy is just like our kid. Now when I walk him I carry a 5-foot pole with a metal hook on the end. I was attacked when I was 8-years old, a pack of dogs dragged me off my bike, later years when I would deliver papers I would carry a squirt gun full of battery acid, that did the trick.

The other pup we took to my son Ron and his wife Judy, they named him Zeke, after we left Ron's Cupid began to cry for his brother, Sis was driving and I put Cupid on Sis's shoulder's and he rode there all the way home. These kinds of dogs are supposed to be able to recognize 200 words, Cupid has got about 50 down pat and he knew when we were going to see Ron and Judy we would tell him he was going to see either Zeke or Brother and he knew what we meant. Moms in the nursing home and She and Cupid love each other. We tell Cupid we are going to see Grama and he cries all the way there and knows when we pull in the Nursing home drive, He even knows the way to her room. All the people at the nursing home really like him. They ask my Mother, "Is your son coming out today and is he going to bring the cute little dog?" Can you imagine that a lick on your hand by a puppy would be the highlight of your day! Funny thing, the same day Cupid and I got attacked by the mutts; Zeke got hit by a car and killed.

While we were in Arizona I had this dream, I was on the Mount of Olives and I had a baby in each arm, the one in my right arm had a hat like a baseball cap, and on his face was something, and I knew the one in my left arm was a girl, all of a sudden they were not my arms and I was standing in front of a big iron ring and in my hands was an iron rod, the Lord said, "Strike!" I did and I felt power go thru my body, then I had the two babies in my arms again, the one with the cap had something on his face, as I said before, the Lord spoke again and said, " the stuff on his face is from his stomach." I have to tell you the sound of the Lords voice is the sweetest sound I have ever heard. That was the dream and the Lord put in my heart and the understanding of it. It was for the neighbors across the street, the man was going for cancer tests and the woman was going for an operation. I knew I had to tell them, I went over and I said, "I have a Word from the Lord for you that came to me in a dream." I told them the above and then said, the two babies that I held were you two, the one with the cap was the man and he was going to be sick and throw up, but will soon be okay, the other was the woman, you too will go through some thing and will soon be okay, but I said here is the great part the Lord put this word in my heart, "Those whom I have put in my Son's hand can not be taken from Him!" She went through her operation fine, and the guy did not have cancer. Praise the name of the Lord on high.

March 9th I preached at the Church to night, the message the Lord gave me was in Acts 16:16-34, it was about when Paul and Silas were thrown in prison and the Lord sent an earthquake and all it did was open all the prison doors and make the chains fall off all the prisoners. I thought of this; " Who but the Lord could shake the ripe fruit tree, and only the leaves fall off!" when the guard seen that all the prison doors were opened he thought they had escaped and was about to fall on his sword and kill himself. Paul said, " We are all here do thyself no harm." Then the jailer fell down in front of them and asked, " Sirs, what must I do to be saved?" Paul said, "Only believe on the Lord and you and thy house shall be saved." And the whole message was that your kids will be saved, Proverbs 22:6 says, Train a child up in the way he should go and he will not depart from it. I have seen so many Christian people's kids wander off, but they come back. I was thinking later how people make their kids or try to make them responsible drivers so they won't get hurt, but they don't show them the way to the Lord and escape eternal hell! forever is a long time, where will you spend it ?

Guess what, Angel wants to put a steeple on the new Church; Of course I said we can do that. At least this Church is only half as high as the other one. Should be some smiles. One of the problems I see is that aluminum has gone out sight price wise, but here is the great thing, guess who is in charge? The Lord will provide.

March 16, 08, Sunday night, had a great day at the Church. The Lord gave me a message for the people, I don't usually remember them as when I give them I am in the spirit and just give them, and as I have said before, I don't remember them as its my job to give them and go on my way. But this message stuck in my heart,

To my people I say, come to the Throne of Grace in boldness, boldly as thy faith, boldly as thy love is for me. Is it not written? Have I not said: he who denies me before men, him will I deny before my Father who is in heaven. In a truth I tell thee, boldly encourage one another, that I may be lifted up to men.

Strong message.

Today is March 23, and I turned 71 today, at the Church they have you stand up front and everyone sings Happy Birthday to you. In the bulletin they had my name and 23, I told the Pastor someone thought I was 23 years old.

March 25, I went into my office and the Lord told me to sit down, He began to give me a message for the people, I will be preaching it soon, The above message as I said was stuck in my heart, I found out why it was stuck in my heart, it is part of the sermon. And a sermon I don't like to think about as it targets my weakness. My mouth, the Bible says man cannot not tame the tongue. Funny thing its been on my heart for a while to sing Hank Williams, "Stones that you throw" its about tongue and gossip. Course Christians don't gossip, they share. If I am still writing after the sermon I will comment on it.

Went in to the prayer line to pray for someone to publish this book and the next day Sis showed me a book a Christian publisher had printed for her friends, looks like they are the ones I need. I filled out their application and wrote them a letter. I have never written a book before and don't have any idea how to proceed. The name of the company is' Xulon Press, Xulon is Greek for Revelation 22:19, where it says: anyone who removes any of these words (Bible) his name would be removed the Lambs book of life. They print nothing negative about the Lord.

The paragraph prior to the one above I mention that it was laid on my heart to sing " Stones that you throw", Sunday Morning after Church Angel asked me if I wanted to give the message to the people, I had already asked both Him and Carol if it was alright to sing the Hank Williams song, They said it was fine. I guess they trust me enough to know that I would not shame the Lord or even them. I sang the song, the message was "Tongue", and I said at the start that I was going to step on some toes, mine, said, "I may as well, everybody else does, just kidding." But I told them that I was there to do as directed in James 5; 16, Confess your faults one to another, and I have a problem with my mouth, especially when I am driving, that morning I was almost in a head on crash as some person make an illegal pass right in to my lane, Someone told them the person was idiot, I heard someone say it, looked around and it was me. A small girl got up from her seat to go to the bathroom and I said, " When adults don't say the prayer of faith these children will, and things will start happening in a big way." I said, " magicians hate to have children for and audience as they see right through their tricks, I like magic as long as the devil is not in it," Then I said, "Did anyone ever see a person levitate?" I then went in front of the podium and I went about 3 inches above the floor, then I showed them it was a trick and how I done it. Turn ¾ angle to the persons you are showing this to, your back will be ¾ toward them, the side that is toward them, raise the foot that is toward them up slowly, and then at the same time raise the other foot by standing on the ball of your foot, they will not be able to see the toe you are standing on as it will be shadowed, looks good. Then I told about the message that I gave to the people before and said it again from memory, we have to be careful that we are not ashamed of the Lord, I said, " When you pray in a restaurant, do you look around to see if anyone is watching you or that you are holding hands with others, or do you just pray with no thought of who is watching. Like the message says, " If you are ashamed of me I will be ashamed of you before my Father in Heaven. I felt like I was not reaching the people, but I did like I always do, exactly as the Lord told me to do, when I had the prayer line people said that my message was just for them. Thank you Lord!

I like to watch the History channel on TV, but so many times they say if Jesus really lived, or if Noah and the flood really were real. I just turn the channel. But a couple of nights ago I got what I knew was going to have to be. They said evidence found that there is no doubt that Jesus was real and they had the proof. OK, lets take a look at this program. They were so intent on proving that He was real that they were not looking in the right direction. I could have saved them a lot of time; all they had to do was ask me. I do see now where they might be right about some of the future floods, famine and earthquakes.

I read the King James version of the Bible as I know the story of it, goes something like this; The Bible at the time of King James was written in Greek, he got all these scholars together and told them he wanted the Bible translated into English. He had about 60 scholars and put them in pairs, he put each pair in the dungeon in a separate room with no way of talking one pair to the other, and told them he wanted them to translate the Greek to English. Any pair that did not agree with the rest would have their head chopped off; quite an incentive, and I might add an accurate translation. People say to me, " It's so hard to understand the King James Version!" and I say, "That's because you are reading it alone, never read the Bible alone, ask the Holy Ghost to help you understand it." The Bible bears this out: James 1; 5 if any man lacks wisdom let him ask God, and He will freely give it. I have to add that all the answers are in the Bible.

I was talking to a Jewish man at the coffee shop in Arizona and I was telling him how I interpret the Bible and He said to me, "I have never met a man who understanding is as yours." I said, "I hope that's good" But here is my thoughts, in 2nd Timothy 2; 15 the word says Study to show thyself approved unto God a workman that needeth not to be ashamed, rightly dividing the word of truth. Rightly diving at first meant to me speaking that which is the Jews and that which is Gentiles, then after much study and prayer I came to this conclusion, and it pointed to the fact that the Gentiles had no part of the Bible, until the New Testament, when in Ephesians 3:6 That the Gentiles should be fellow-heirs, and of the same body, and partakers of His promise in Christ by the gospel. Until that time Gentiles had no part of the Bible, but now are joint heirs of the whole Bible. It appears that the honor that belongs to the chosen people the Jews is still intact. And I tell you that the Jews are not ignorant of the fact that the Gentiles would be heirs with them to Christ, for it was spoken in Isaiah 42:1 It is believed, that God was speaking of the Lord Jesus Christ when He said, "Behold My Servant, whom I uphold: Mine elect, in whom My soul delighteth: I have put My Spirit upon Him: He shall bring forth judgment to the Gentiles. For in Matthew 3:17 And lo a voice from heaven, saying, This My beloved Son, in whom I am well pleased. But it goes without saying that the Jews were the chosen people, I believe that those with out respect to both the Jews and Israel will answer before God. And now rightly dividing the word is telling all people what the Word says as the Spirit has given me understanding.

I sent chapter 8, to my Lawyer; I knew he would get a kick out of it. He sent me the nicest letter, it said: Dear Bob, I really enjoyed your story, "My Day in Court" from chapter 8, of your book. A lot of times lawyers lose sight of the fact that we have to tell a really simple story to convenience the jury of our positions. I think you did it beautifully. I look forward to more your stories and reading your book. And signed his name. I guess you know that letter is a treasure to me.

From here forward I am going to write what the Lord is doing through me now, for a blessing for anyone who reads this and to show what I said in the preface that you can have more power than you ever thought. Until the Lord tells me the book is Done!

April 6, 2008 Angel had an emergency at the hospital, called me and asks me if I had a word for the people and could I preach it tonight. I said I did and that I would go to my prayer closet and commune with the Lord about the message. I always have some messages ready in case I am called on to preach. I think I had 6 messages ready, the Lord said to me we are not going to use those, here is a new one and I wrote the scriptures he told me. We have a time at the Church where we invite the Holy Ghost in, and usually someone has a message, to night the Holy Ghost gave me a message for someone who would lay their burden down at the Lord's feet and then pick it up again and it was grieving the Lord, I could feel the pain of the Lord as this person was doing this, guess what, it fell right into my message. Several times I told the person to leave the burden with the Lord and that would be the end of it. My message was about the devil getting in peoples business with forgiveness from the Lord. I looked in the Matthew Henry and found a saying that is so true, the devil likes to fish in troubled waters. And this right on the money you have a small problem, here comes the devil and blows it into something huge. After the message I had people come up for prayer and of all that did none said they had a problem with leaving their burden at the feet of the Lord. Then after the closing prayer a person came up to me and said that is me you are talking about.

My plan at the present is to keep the book going with messages like above. If the Lord tells me to quit I will, but now I feel like I need to keep writing. I know the messages like the one above Blesses people. And of course I keep going over the whole book and putting in stuff as I remember it.

April 13, we usually have Church in the morning and then again at night, the city had to turn off the electric power to upgrade something? So today we had a pot luck and then had Church at 2:00, during the singing and the praising of the Lord, He spoke to me with a message for some one who was at a cross roads and had to make a decision, and He reminded me that He said, "Many will come in my name, believe them not." I spoke this aloud so the person would get the Word from the Lord. Guess what? The Word I spoke was not only for some person, but also in the Pastor's message for the people. The Bible says that where My Word is spoken there will be signs and wonders following.

April 15, Cora came home from work and said that the two women she worked with was giving her a bad time and saying things about her. The one Cora had been working with and really enjoyed working with her, the woman said, "I made those pies for dessert and I told you not to put them out with out putting the whipped cream on them!" I told Sis when she told me this that I would have liked to have a video camera so she could see what a child she was. Cora said, "My first instinct is to go tell the boss, but I thought better of it and just let the Lord handle it. One of the women said they were not happy with the work Sis was doing. She used to be the cook/manager before Sis got the job and wanted to run things the old way. The 16th I went to Church and got there early for prayer meeting before Church services, when we prayed I said, "Some people at Cora's work place are saying some things that are untrue, we need to pray those people they are messing with one of God's kids and they could be in big trouble," so we prayed for them, not for Sis, she knows the Lord will fight for her. The 17th when Sis went to work the boss called her into her office and wanted to talk to her, the boss gave her a cup that says, "We appreciate You." And Cora said, "I thought you were unhappy with my work." And the boss said, "What do you mean? and Sis said another worker said so. The boss said, " Unhappy with your work, if I was would I give you this cup and a $ 1.00 per hour raise?" He who sets on the Throne controls all! And the last word on this deal is that the two women are both out. One took another job there and the other one just quit.

I raked out the leaves from around the bushes on the side of the house, I look down and there's a early American Indian hide scraper, around 150 years old, most people would see that there was a rock that was broke, but if you look close you will see where someone had knapped it on the edge. Of all the things these hide scrapers fit your hand perfectly, the heel of your hand fits the depression in the stone and it s quite comfortable to hold. You wonder how someone had the time to sit and make this, back then there was nothing but time. Not like today, everybody rushing and running.

Last Sunday at Church we had Missionary Sunday and as I was once on the road myself I am partial to their work. They passed the offering plate around and when I looked into my billfold all I had was a 10, I pondered for a minute, still had a week before check was coming. All of a sudden the Lord said, "Give it I will supply!" so as always I listened to the Lord. On the way home I had just turned the corner and was going to speed up and I looked and there in the middle of the road lays a roll of dollar bills. Is anything to hard for the Lord?

April 27, Had a Spirit filled night tonight, the Lord gave me a message for the people. Let me stop a minute and explain what the Lord giving me a message is. We sing and praise the Lord and the Holy Spirit comes unto us, many people have the baptism of the Holy Spirit and speak in unknown tongues, and then they interpret what the Spirit has said to them. OK? If the message is for a certain person the Lord will show you who it is and you will go to them and give the message, if you don't know who the message is for you just speak it out, sometimes the message is for more than one person. So the message the Lord gave me was,

"That obstacle that you had in front of you, I removed and I tell you in a truth that I am also your rear guard. Thus saith the Lord."

One of the usher's was out of town and so I picked up the offering and took it to the office, I brought the offering plates back to the platform and went to set down, Angel said to me, "Bob don't set down, the Lord told me to have you pray for the people now." We usually have the prayer line at the end of the message. Different to night, at our Church we go by the leading of the Lord. And what a prayer line, I felt answers to prayer with every word I spoke. I am nothing on my own; it is the working of Jesus through me. "He said anything you ask in my name I will do," One guy I was praying for (Joe) and I had ended the prayer and one of the Ministers came up and said she had seen a dark cloud over Joe's head, I laid my hands on his head and commanded what ever that was over his head to be gone in the name of Jesus and to be replaced by angels, we both felt it go, WOW! One lady who I prayed for had her chain broken and is free to do the work of the Lord, which is always what she wanted to do. There were a lot of people that just wanted prayer for Gods work in their life. After Church we went out for coffee and Angel got a message that one of his flock was in the hospital and away he went, I had already ordered so after I finished eating I went up to the hospital and visited with the man. I stayed until 2 am and then got home and ready for bed, 3 am when I got to bed, I just could not sleep so I got back up at 4 am and started writing, finally quit at 8 am and went to bed.

April 30, about a week ago the Lord gave me a sermon for the people, I told Angel, "I'm ready." He said, "Ok." So later he said, "You ready for Wednesday?" I said, " That I am." Now this sermon the Lord gave me seemed incomplete but I did not add to it like I would of in days past. I just figured I would do as He had said, after all it was about obedience. Wednesday afternoon I was sitting at the computer and the Lord gave me the rest of the sermon, what a high I got on. I was walking on air. Went in early for prayer meeting before Church and the Lord brought this one young girl to mind and we prayed for her as she is going into the Air Force. That night when Angel called me to preach I went up on the platform and got my guitar and I sang, Learning to Lean, then I put the guitar down and was walking to my Bible and the Lord stopped me, turned me around and I went down to where this young girl was and the Lord gave me a message for her, He said, "I know that thou are a willing servant, I judge by the heart and I will go before you and open doors that you may witness and I will fill your mouth with what you should say, thus saith the Lord." The anointing was all over me for the message. And what I thought would offend some came across just the opposite and what the people needed to hear. The Lord is so good!

May 3, Ladies had a Mother-Daughter Dinner at the Church today, I had told Judy the other night I didn't know if I could make it or not, she said, "If you do you better have a blonde wig and a short skirt on. Sis took Mom, they rode the bus. I took the stuff Sis had made out to the Church. I told Sis before we left the house that I have all that photography equipment lying at the house and I may as well go and take some pictures of the Mothers and Daughters. So I did, as usual the Lord blessed the work of my willing hands and the pictures came out real nice. I took them to the 1-hour developer and the clerk asks me the general questions, double or single prints? 1 hour? Last name, I told her, she said, "How do you spell it?" I said, just like it sounds, so and so, Oh! She says, 'Just like it sounds!" I said, "Yes, that's what had you confused." Then she says, " First name?" Now she got into my area, I said without any hesitation, "13013," she said, "What?" then she wrote it down and then seen that by connecting the 1s and the 3s you would have BOB! She says, "You are a smart eleck!" and she was laughing while she said it. Who has more fun than people? I saw Angel at the store and he said, "Carol is around here somewhere and he called her and she told him where she was and I went there and gave her the pictures. Then I saw some others that were there and give them their pictures. I will take the rest to Church tomorrow. All worked out pretty well. And I wasn't doing anything anyway. Just glad I could help. I suppose I will be invited next year, the good Lord willing and the creek don't rise.

By the way, down south they call a creek a crick. Know what a crick is? It's a noise a Japanese camera makes.

May 4, Sunday morning I took the pictures to Church from the Mother-Daughter dinner, they were all happy with them and I was happy that I could serve in this small way. When the service started there was Dave, a guy I used to work with at the state home, great guy and a good friend. Angel had guided him to Lord and now he was working with the Gideon's keeping the word in front of people in hotels and motels and anywhere else it's needed. Another man witnessed to Dave's love of his fellow man, the guy was out ice fishing and the fish were biting like crazy, he had his limit and was going home and when he got to his car he had left his lights on and his battery was dead, he went back on the ice and yelled, "Does anyone have jumper cables?" My battery is dead, of all the people here come Dave. Dave said after the testimony that he doesn't fish much any more. Sis said, "You fish for men!" and Dave said, "Yes, I catch them and the Lord cleans them.

Sunday night we had singers, the Covenants, while I was at the Mother-Daughter dinner and taking pictures I glanced at the flier for these singers and the Lord spoke to me and said, "These people have a need beyond monetary!" that's all He said. I told Angel and after Sis and I sang a song and were returning to our seats Angel told the people what the Lord had said to me. And I later told the lead singer what the Lord had said and that we would be praying for them.

Lord lead me to take home the video of the last sermon I done at the Church, we shoot videos of the Church services so the shut-ins can see the services. Anyway I brought the video home and laid it on the VCR and forgot about it then the Lord gave me my next sermon, I wrote it down and began to see something I had missed, went and looked at the video and all the pieces fit together, the last three sermons and the one I just got are about listening and talking to the Lord. It's really quite simple, shut up and listen. I have to mention again the conclusion I have come to, food has a lot of acid in it, and this must be why the Lord told the disciples to fast and pray, not pray and fast. To this end that I never eat before I go to the Lord's house. I find that I am more open to His words. May even hear a little better.

Looking back in writing this book when I was writing about what I was before I accepted the Lord, I found myself slipping back to that time and back to the way I was. Sis even said, "I will be glad when that book is done, the way you are acting!" I know now it was a trick of the devil, but like I said before I am the Lords and the devil has to flee at the mention of the name of "Jesus."

I am getting a feeling that the end of this book is near, several signs, and I take my signs from the Lord. It has been a real learning experience. And I hope you can take something from this book and be blessed. And if you have never accepted the Lord Jesus Christ here's how, Say this prayer:

Lord Jesus I know I am a sinner, I ask You to forgive me of my sins and make me a new person, You said that my sins would be removed as far as the east is to the west. Lord I will serve you to the best of my ability all my life, Write my name in the Lamb's book of life that I may have eternal life. I thank you Lord Jesus for forgiving me.

Amen

Romans 10, 9 10, 13; For whosoever shall call upon the name of the Lord shall be saved.

As I watch for the coming of the Lord, I think of Revelation 22:20 He which testifieth these things saith, SURELY I COME QUICKLY. Amen. Even so. Come, Lord Jesus.

Appendix

All scriptures are from the King James, Special Study Edition;
Word Resources Group
P O Box 395
Humble, TX 77347

Black Powder Loads suggestions;

I Lb can of Black Powder is 7000 Grains.

This is the formula Bob Wolf gave me in 1967:

Ball Diameter to 3rd Power X 1506.2 = Ball Grain Weight.

Ball Grain Weight = Grains of Powder = 1600 Feet Per Second.
    3

Here are some of the Popular ball sizes with Powder Charges for 1600 Feet Per Second;

25 Caliber,	.285	Ball Grain Weight,	35 Grain	= 12 Grains Powder	
36 "	.340	" " "	59 "	= 20 "	"
45 "	.437	" " "	126 "	= 42 "	"Loose Bore,
45 "	.440	" " "	128 "	= 43 "	"Tight Bore,
54 "	.490	" " "	177 "	= 59 "	"
54 "	.535	" " "	231 "	= 77 "	"
58 "	.562	" " "	267 "	= 89 "	"

Please bear in mind that these are only a starting point and as each gun is different, and also remember that a Flintlock will lose some gas or power as there is an opening, (Vent) Cap locks are all but sealed. And PLEASE, ABOVE ALL BALL MUST BE SEATED ON THE POWER CHARGE! Air between the ball and charge is very dangerous. As I said before mark your loading rod so you can see the Ball is Seated. Put your knife blade against the loading rod and turn rod and it will leave a small line for your loading mark. As you shoot your gun will build up some Black Powder residue and the mark will be a tad high. Don't bounce your loading rod against the ball after it is seated, this will deform the ball. Again these are tips for SAFE and accurate shooting. I did not sell a gun until it would shoot 5 shots in one hole at 25 Yards.

Printed in the United States
122700LV00004B/127-300/P

9 781606 474198